The Interfaith Imperative

The Interfaith Imperative

Religion, Dialogue, and Reality

ROSS THOMPSON

CASCADE *Books* · Eugene, Oregon

THE INTERFAITH IMPERATIVE
Religion, Dialogue, and Reality

Cascade Books
An Imprint of Wipf and Stock Publishers
199 W. 8th Ave., Suite 3
Eugene, OR 97401

www.wipfandstock.com

PAPERBACK ISBN: 978-1-62564-142-7
HARDCOVER ISBN: 978-1-4982-8832-3
EBOOK ISBN: 978-1-4982-4191-5

Cataloguing-in-Publication data:

Names: Thompson, Ross, 1953–.

Title: The interfaith imperative : religion, dialogue, and reality / Ross Thompson.

Description: Eugene, OR: Cascade Books, 2016 | Includes bibliographical references and index.

Identifiers: ISBN 978-1-62564-142-7 (paperback) | ISBN 978-1-4982-8832-3 (hardcover) | ISBN 978-1-4982-4191-5 (ebook)

Subjects: LCSH: Religious pluralism—Christianity | Dialogue—Religious aspects | Christianity and other religions | Religions—Relations

Classification: BL85 T525 2017 (print) | BL85 (ebook)

Manufactured in the U.S.A.   JANUARY 24, 2017

For Emily.

With us too briefly,
you learnt for yourself
faith that transcends boundaries.

Table of Contents

List of Tables

Introduction:
Beyond Toleration—The Interfaith
Imperative

PERHAPS THE MOST CRUCIAL question faced by nations and societies today is whether being multicultural and multi-religious forces us to be secular. In other words, can we do justice to all the great religions without occupying a "neutral" standpoint that lies above and beyond them all? And, for fear of undue and intolerant influence being wielded by one of the religions, do we have to exclude religion as such from any real influence on our educational systems and other policies? Globally we seem torn between local, exclusive forms of religion that can cause immense spiritual and physical damage to people, and a bland common ethic, too thin to base a life on, which threatens to secularize us all.

In terms of Christianity, theology and church life both mirror this increasing dichotomy. Some theologies withdraw from public accountability to live by their own internally verified criteria for truth. Others attempt a thoroughgoing immersion in contemporary culture through dialogue with secularism and other faiths, but often exhibit a loss of nerve regarding what is distinctive about Christian claims. Interfaith dialogue has tended either to be seen as too difficult to be attempted, or to be emasculated and over-irenic: regarded as culturally important but marginal to the reality with which theology seeks to engage.

Can we find a way to dialogue constructively in our distinctiveness? This book argues that we can, and that paradoxically it is through dialogue between faiths that what is distinctively *true* in them emerges. It aims to show that theology has been, in the broadest sense, an interfaith enterprise from the first, and that dialogue with other traditions is what sustains claims of theological language to relate to realities beyond itself.

There are thus two interwoven themes that run throughout this book. One concerns the primacy of dialogue: interfaith dialogue, but also intra-faith dialogue and the many kinds of dialogue that are the lifeblood of theology. The other concerns the development—taking on board all that postmodernism has thrown at us regarding relativism or the "constructed" nature of belief systems—of a new realism, a confidence that theology engages us with realities beyond and within us.

I use "theology," here and throughout, in a broad sense to mean the reflective development of religions in terms of doctrine. Clearly in this sense we can speak of Buddhist theology, even if Buddhism is taken as an atheistic religion. That said, my focal concern in this book is with what I shall term Christian theologies. Despite my strong affinity with Buddhism, I am only familiar enough with Christian theologies to ask of them the questions this book is asking. It may be the case that Christianity is inherently dialogical and called to dialogue with other faiths in a manner in which others are not. Or it may be that all religions are so called in their own terms, because as I also argue, without dialogue there can be no engagement with reality. But each religion must address these issues in its own way.

Writing this book has, in a fashion, brought me back to Christianity as my home ground, the context in which I most naturally think and feel. Whether this represents a retreat from the "Buddhist Christianity" I have recently professed,[1] only others can judge. My Buddhist Christianity is asymmetrical in that the Buddhist in me has not had the long experience of learning, converse, practice, and inculturation that the Christian has, but is relatively naive. This book has been written from the point of view of the Christian in me looking at (among many other things) Buddhism. The Buddhist in me who looks at Christianity also exists, but is not experienced, learned, or articulate enough in Buddhism to write the equivalent book from the Buddhist point of view. If it is possible to write that book, I hope someone will one day write it. And the fact that the founders of both religions expounded their teaching in dialogue with others gives me hope that it is a possibility.

ARGUMENT AND STRUCTURE OF THE BOOK

The book falls into two roughly equal halves. Part 1 argues from a variety of grounds that dialogue is the basis of our grasp of reality, and the practice of interfaith dialogue needs to reflect that. Chapter 1 argues that the relativism associated with postmodernism has been inimical to realistic interfaith dialogue, because it means that all positions collapse into a kind of exclusivism. But the threefold paradigm—exclusivism, inclusivism, and pluralism

1. Thompson, *Buddhist Christianity*, *Wounded Wisdom*, and *Creation, Co-Arising*
. . .

regarding other faiths—is something we need to move beyond. Chapter 2 is mainly philosophical in content, arguing that a positive, epistemological constructivism needs to be distinguished from other kinds of relativism. It proposes dialogue in its many varied forms as the practice that enables us to establish a critical realism that is free from the dogmas of modernity. Chapters 3 and 4 are argued from the point of view of Christian theology. Chapter 3 works from the doctrines of creation and Trinity towards an understanding of God as the "view from everywhere," while chapter 4 analyzes the development of theology to establish—in the face of some pertinent possible criticisms—that dialogue is central to the Christian understanding of reality. Hence in Part I two independent kinds of reason are advanced for a dialogical understanding of reality, one philosophical and independent of faith, the other specifically Christian. Those who find the first kind of reason too general may be persuaded by the second, while those who are not convinced by Christianity may still accept the first. (Chapter 2 may therefore be omitted by theologically minded readers who find philosophy difficult, though the philosophical discussion presupposes little technical knowledge of the subject.) Finally, chapter 5 applies our dialogical understanding of knowledge to the questions of interfaith dialogue raised in chapter 1, developing a challenging fourfold approach to dialogue on the understanding that authentic dialogue is an engagement together in the search for truth.

Part 2 considers three types of postmodern theology, arguing that the dialogical approach developed in Part 1 is capable of bringing these to work together and to overcome their present limitations. Chapter 6 affirms the importance of narrative in theology, but argues, against postliberal and narrative theologies, that the Bible is more than a story, and tells its story in a manner that invites metaphysical questions. Chapter 7 likewise affirms liberation theology, but argues that what counts as liberation cannot be decided in advance either within or outside a religious system, but has to be established through dialogue. Moreover, doing justice to others inherently involves openness in dialogue with them. Chapter 8 considers the arguments against the "ontotheological" God, both in atheist theology and in the notion of "God above being." It argues that ontotheology is only "sinful" when it neglects the personal, dialogical dimension of God, who engages with the world not as one being to another but as his action and beloved creation. Chapter 9 argues for theology as an intricate interplay of analogy and metaphor, story, metaphysics, and deconstruction. The conclusion relates the story of Jesus' transfiguration to illustrate how these processes, and the kinds of theology discussed, can combine to give rise to a transfiguring "view from everywhere," fully intersubjective, dialogical, and real.

Aesthetically the book follows a kind of sonata form, which mirrors the principle established in the book itself, that theology proceeds by dialogue and consequent mutual transformation of initial viewpoints or "themes." The first theme is the philosophical argument for dialogue-based realism introduced in chapter 2 as a resolution of the relativist quandaries of chapter 1. The second is the biblical story of creation, presented in chapter 3, which expands into a Trinitarian, dialogue-based theology. These two themes transpose, interweave, inform, and transform each other as various models of theology are considered. Finally, in chapter 9 and the conclusion, they find a resolution in the suggestion of a transformed theology, by way of the template offered by the second biblical story, that of the transfiguration of Jesus.

It remains to state the two main aims of this book: the rejuvenation of interreligious dialogue, and the affirmation that (though of course it does not always do so) religion can relate us to reality. The latter picks up concerns I have had since my teenage years, and in written form, since the writing of my Ph.D. thesis *Objectivity and Religious Symbol* in the late 1970s. The former also relates to teenage concerns arising from the contest at that time between Buddhist and Christian faiths, but these are issues that have only come to the fore for me in written form since *Buddhist Christianity* in 2010. This is the first book I have written (and perhaps the first book written) that explicitly unites these two concerns, and relates them to each other.

AIM 1: DIALOGUE RENEWED

What, it may be asked, is a religion, and what is the fundamental analogy on which the notion of "interreligious dialogue" is based? On the whole I use terms like "religion" and "interreligious" in preference to "faith" and "interfaith" because this book is concerned with a dialogue that takes place not simply at the level of ideas and beliefs, but between whole bodies of belief and practice, as chapter 2 in particular will explain. But am I suggesting that religions are discrete "people" that can talk to one another? Are religions like nations, or perhaps supernations, and interreligious dialogue like diplomacy, in which authorized representatives talk to one another and arrange deals, treaties, and concessions? Or are they like stalls in a marketplace, competing to sell their wares to the public, but sometimes buying and selling ideas from one another? Are religions like fortified castles, joined by precarious drawbridges that can be lifted up at any time? Are they suburbs of a great city, ill defined as to boundaries, constantly interchanging traffic and people, some of whom live near a center, others on the borders, while nobody can identify the center of the city itself? Clearly the personal, political, economic, military, and geographic analogies—though we resort to them more often than we like to think, and I do think the suburb analogy has mileage—all have severe shortcomings.

Wilfred Cantwell Smith[2] plausibly argues that the very idea of *a* religion is the invention of modernity and its desire to amalgamate complex realities into discrete systems that it could compare and contrast. In addition, the colonialism and evangelism of that period created a need to formalize the religious beliefs against which one's own (most often Christian) faith was arguing; and the local believers responded by formalizing systematic positions they needed to defend. In our own time this process of consolidation is proceeding apace, most often in opposition to the forces of secularization and globalization that threaten to create a public domain and educational system that is free from religion. In previous times people were aware of having religion, or faith, in the form of regular practices of devotion following traditional patterns, accompanied by related beliefs about the world, and an awareness of these having been handed down by forbears, often from original founder figures like Jesus, Mohammed, or Buddha. Those different founders would confer differing senses of religious identity, of course, though—except in the case of Mohammed, Smith points out—it seems unlikely that those founders themselves had any wish to create a world religion.

If this is the case then dialogue created the religions. This was often a hostile, negative dialogue borne on the one hand of the attempt to study, colonize, or convert, and on the other, of the defense against those attempts. In another way the practices of devotion in the religions often took the form of dialogue—addressing and being addressed by God or the Ultimate. This being the case, dialogue can be seen as the lifeblood of the religions themselves, and interfaith dialogue is simply an extension of what happens when people differing in tradition talk to one another about their beliefs and practices. It is not really something that takes place between entities called religions, but something that happens between religious people whenever there is religious difference between them, whether or not this amounts to their being of different religious "identities." That is why this book moves so readily between interfaith, intra-faith, and other kinds of dialogue, including dialogue with God.

It goes without saying, therefore, that I am not concerned through dialogue to resolve all religious difference and help to create one mega-religion. The end of difference would be the end of dialogue, and in terms of this

2. Smith, *Meaning and End of Religion.*

book that would be the end of religious discovery and development. The different religions will not be like the schools of early, pre-Socratic philosophy, which gradually learned to adopt a scientific methodology that would be capable of testing all theories and deciding which is true, in a manner which all scientists of whatever culture would accept. What I hope will happen is more like what has happened in the history of philosophy. Here some arguments have gained widespread acceptance, often changing the basis on which all future argument will be conducted. But most of the big issues remain as contested as they were in the time of Plato and Aristotle. There are still idealists, materialists and dualists, empiricists and rationalists, relativists and absolutists, determinists and believers in freewill, and those who think mathematics discovers truth and those who think it merely clarifies definitions. Yet the boundaries between these positions remain fluid and exist in different combinations. And philosophers do not establish republics and take up arms to fight for their ideas against those who believe differently.

In the same way in the future I believe there will still be Christians and Buddhists and so forth. There will still be those rich mixes of architecture and art and ritual and culture and idea and ethical practice that we call religions. But while there will always those who hold tenaciously to one particular package of these, others will explore different combinations, and no doubt new religions will evolve. No doubt too new ways of placing the religions in lived space through art and architecture and liturgy will emerge. And in the process of dialogue there will be discoveries and advances that change the basis on which future dialogue will take place. We have already seen some; there is a broad consensus that slavery is wrong, and that authentic belief involves some kind of fight for justice. There are still some (notably the kind of Islam represented by ISIS) who would still contest the slavery issue, but rightly their "religion" is not taken to be truly Islamic either by many fellow Muslims or by others. But dialogue will not settle the big issues in religion any more than in philosophy, because there is more than one way to understand the world and live well in it, and to do justice to the Ultimate and to one's fellow beings in a manner that makes logical and psychological sense. Nevertheless the relationship will, I hope, change fundamentally. From seeing one another—as in the pre-modern and modern periods—as inhabitants of rival systems, through seeing one another—as often in postmodernism (see chapter 1)—as inhabitants of incommensurable systems, who can admire one another but cannot understand one another, we will move to a period of greater exchange where we affirm both difference and convergence as the two interdependent aspects of dialogue, both of which can involve discovery.

AIM 2: REALISTIC RELIGION RESTORED

That, then is one of the book's two interrelated aims. The other is that the religions might once again be taken seriously as parts of the dialogues in which we make discoveries and humanity grows in vision. In the United Kingdom at least, public and media attention to religion varies from a positive belief that religious traditions have an ethical and/or aesthetic contribution to make, through an interest in established religion as adorning great public occasions, through concern not to offend unusual minorities, to downright fear and hostility that our democratic foundations or the secular basis of science may be undermined. The religions broadly adapt to these expectations, "speaking out" on ethical issues, gracing public occasions, adopting more extreme and sectarian beliefs in deliberate defiance of prevailing culture, or becoming ideologically militant and sometimes violent.

But if the argument of this book is true, we cannot do justice to reality or to people without embracing something of a religious view. The secular standpoint has transformed our lives for the better in terms of science, medicine, and technology, and offers us a rich vision of the world that can evoke an almost religious sense of mystery. But it does not teach us the beauty and quality of our ordinary day-to-day lives. It has left us (as chapter 7 will make clear), if we are rich, as consumers not knowing what to consume next, strangers to ourselves; and if we are poor, redundant, strangers to the mainstream of society. We need the day-to-day graciousness and festive solidarity that religious faith can provide, if we are to have a full grasp of reality. So the other part of this book's aim is a restoration of religion, in dialogue with the secular, at the heart of the human search for meaning and truth.

But the aims are interdependent, of course. If religions remain competitors for the human soul, secularity will be entitled not to take them seriously. There is a great danger that thinking and feeling people, in revulsion against the arrogant excesses perpetrated in the name of religion, will turn away from religion as such, even though religion cannot turn away from them. It is as dialogue sharers, co-participants in the search for meaning and truth, that the religions earn the right to be co-participants with this other partner, which calls itself non-religious and secular, but is in fact another religion, another valid dialogue partner, no more and no less.

There is a lot in the world that increasingly militates against achieving both of these aims. If this book can shift the balance a little in the direction of dialogical, realistic religion, it will have been worthwhile.

PART 1

Religious Dialogue and Reality

CHAPTER 1

Postmodernism:
The End of Dialogue?

THIS BOOK ARGUES THAT dialogue with other faiths is integral to the development of theology. The theological view we take on other faiths and the possibilities and risks involved in dialogue with them is therefore a crucial matter for this book. How we understand the other faiths theologically will be something that has huge impact on how we understand our own theology. This chapter therefore explores different theological understandings of other faiths. We shall encounter views that suggest that dialogue with other faiths is dangerous for the integrity of theology, and others that affirm dialogue in a vaguely benign way but render it fundamentally unnecessary for the development of theology. Neither of these positions will prove satisfactory from this book's point of view.

A while ago Alan Race[1] introduced the typology that has dominated debate about interfaith dialogue and approaches to "other faiths" ever since, classifying approaches as exclusivist, inclusivist, or pluralist. This chapter will explore what these terms might mean, and how Race's typology has dominated our understanding of interfaith relations, before criticizing the typology as rendering interfaith dialogue either inimical or redundant. Alternative approaches will then be considered, which suggest a far more important *theological* role for dialogue.

The threefold paradigm, as described in the next section, was originally advanced as a way of opening people up to interfaith dialogue. The implication is generally that the move from exclusivism through inclusivism to pluralism represents an advance. Hick[2] compares it with the scientific advance from the earth-centered through the sun-centered to the relativistic

1. Race, *Christians and Pluralism.*
2. Hick, *God and the Universe of Faiths.*

3

nowhere-centered universe. At each stage the estimation of faiths other than your own improves.

However, the threefold paradigm has lately been challenged with arguments that suggest that both inclusivism and pluralism involve a hidden exclusivism. The argument is that in a postmodern perspective there is no standpoint from which we could see the equal validity of all faiths; we have to see things from one faith perspective or another, or else a no-faith perspective that itself requires a kind of faith. The general effect of this postmodern turn has been—as we shall see—to place severe limitations on the possible fruitfulness of interfaith dialogue. One prominent theologian has therefore urged that postmodernism spells "the end of dialogue." For "the moment of contemporary recognition of other cultures and religions . . . is itself . . . none other than the moment of total obliteration of other cultures by Western norms and categories."[3]

Of course, in this postmodern perspective interfaith dialogue may remain important in sociopolitical terms, as a means of generating better relations between faith communities that otherwise seem destined to become increasingly intransigent towards one another. But it can no longer hope to create greater mutual *understanding*, since understanding and knowledge are now deemed to be found only *within* and *not between* particular faiths. No longer is the possibility envisaged, as it was under inclusivism and pluralism, that interfaith dialogue might discover truths that need to be taken on board in the mainstream theological and religious traditions.

The chapter will argue that this postmodern move represents a collapse, not into old-style exclusivism, but into a new, but now very familiar, exclusive kind of pluralism. In its own terms each faith is exclusively true for its followers, but because no terms are allowed to be meaningful across faiths, each faith has to be regarded as equally so. Typically in postmodernism, all faiths are equally tolerated, and for the purposes of any faith, including the secular, faithless faith, all other faiths can be equally ignored.

For the purposes of this book, this is a disastrous turn of events. This chapter takes the first crucial step in the argument that the turn is not inevitable. The turn towards what I shall call exclusivist pluralism may be seen as the partial development of a move whose completion leads somewhere quite different, to a place where dialogue, far from disappearing offstage, begins to be the central actor.

---

3. Milbank, *End of Dialogue*, 175.

THE THREEFOLD PARADIGM FOR INTER-FAITH APPROACHES

There is no need to reiterate the intricacies of the threefold paradigm, but an outline will be helpful at this point. The paradigm has been applied to two main questions: "Where does truth lie?" and "Where do humans find salvation?" The questions are not identical, of course, but they are related; nobody of any faith would believe that salvation and truth are incompatible, or that salvation inevitably involves delusion or deceit, or that knowing the truth leads us away from salvation. Our concern in this book is with the question of truth, so we will focus on how the threefold paradigm applies to that, leaving the question of salvation in the background. Though the paradigm can be used by any faith—there are doubtless exclusive, inclusive, and pluralist Muslims, Jews, Buddhists, etc.—on the whole it has been developed in debate about how Christians should understand other faiths, which is how it is presented next, in a summary that follows closely one outlined elsewhere.[4]

Exclusivism. On this understanding, truth and salvation lie exclusively in the Christian faith. Other faiths do not lead to salvation but, if anything, away from it, and where they conflict with Christianity they are false. The mainstream approach of the Catholic Church from the time of Augustine, and declared as official teaching from the thirteenth century, was *extra ecclesiam nulla salus*—there is no salvation outside the (Catholic) Church. And the Protestant tradition with its emphasis on salvation by faith alone gave, if anything, even less scope for the notion that the good works of non-Christians could be a means of salvation.[5] In the twentieth century Karl Barth's radical view that "religion is unbelief"[6] had the effect of negating the value of non-Christian religions, along with Christianity itself when considered as a religion. So it has to be conceded that exclusivism has been the mainstream, consensus view for most of Christian history.

Inclusivism. On this view, truth and salvation lie in Christ but not exclusively in Christianity. Other faiths contain truths and the practice of goodness, but Christianity has in Christ the full explicit revelation of what is implicit elsewhere. Clement of Alexandria believed that God's Word was scattered like a seed throughout pagan culture, while Origen believed salvation in Christ was universal. Such beliefs formed a constant undertow to exclusivism, allowing the church as it spread to "inculturate" its own

---

4. Thompson, *Christian Spirituality*, 203–7.
5. See Netland, *Dissonant Voices*.
6. Barth, *Church Dogmatics*, I/2, 299–300.

worship and teaching into the forms of local philosophy and spirituality. In the twentieth century, Karl Rahner developed a rationale for this approach. Those who follow their own religions devoutly and faithfully are, in Rahner's well-known phrase, "anonymous Christians."

> Anonymous Christianity means that a person lives in the grace of God and attains salvation outside of explicitly constituted Christianity—Let us say, a Buddhist monk—who, because he follows his conscience, attains salvation and lives in the grace of God; of him I must say that he is an anonymous Christian; if not, I would have to presuppose that there is a genuine path to salvation that really attains that goal, but that simply has nothing to do with Jesus Christ. But I cannot do that. And so, if I hold if everyone depends upon Jesus Christ for salvation, and if at the same time I hold that many live in the world who have not expressly recognized Jesus Christ, then there remains in my opinion nothing else but to take up this postulate of an anonymous Christianity. [7]

Each religion, then, is a way to salvation because in some way, if covertly, it points to Christ.

Pluralism. According to this view there is only one God or Ultimate Reality, and all authentic religions lead to the truth of God and salvation in God. Thus, it has often been asserted that the mystical essence or goal of all religions is the same. The Presbyterian, latterly Quaker, theologian John Hick and the Roman Catholic Paul Knitter are major proponents of this view, which is often described as relativist—inaccurately so, since this view proposes a very strong view of an objective Ultimate Reality transcending the descriptions of the different religions.

"Pluralism" however is sometimes used to describe the different, more postmodern and genuinely relativist or constructivist view that religions are incommensurable. On this understanding, advocated by Mark Heim[8] among many others, all religions lead to their own goals, which cannot be identified as the same. The goals cannot be identified with any Ultimate Reality because, for example, what a Christian understands by salvation is defined by the Christian revelation and may not be the same as what a Jew or a Muslim understands by it. There is moreover no precise equivalent term to salvation in Buddhism or Hinduism, for example, and no guarantee that Hindu terms like *moksha*, liberation, or Buddhist ones like nirvana, mean the same as "salvation." Indeed, on the face of it there are many

---

7. Rahner, *Karl Rahner in Dialogue*, 35.

8. Heim, *Salvations*.

differences. Elsewhere I have used "universalism" to refer to the many-ways one-goal understanding of Hick and Knitter, and "pluralism" for the view that religions are incommensurably different. In this book I prefer, to avoid confusion by calling the former view "universalist pluralism" and the latter "exclusivist pluralism"—a term whose paradox I shall explain later.

D'COSTA AND THE COLLAPSE INTO EXCLUSIVISM

Roman Catholic theologian Gavin D'Costa argues that the threefold paradigm presents misleading alternatives, because inclusivism and pluralism alike *inevitably* collapse into a kind of exclusivism.[9] They all result in a position that excludes any truth the other offers unless it conforms to a schema known to be true in advance. The only stance allowed in dialogue is agreement, such that we never really learn anything challenging or new.

This is more obviously true for inclusivism than for pluralism. Exclusivism affirms a single faith account—my own—which is known to be true, and asserts that where other faith accounts conflict with this account they are false. Exclusivists might take as their motto the early Q saying ascribed to Jesus, "Whoever is not with me is against me" (Matt 12:30; Luke 11:23). Inclusivism likewise affirms a single faith account that is known to be true, and asserts that insofar as other faiths contain truth they cannot be in conflict with this account. The inclusivist might therefore take a motto from Mark, "Whoever is not against us is for us" (9:40, cf. Luke 9:50). However, these positions, and their mottos, are logically compatible, and differ only in emphasis. Both make Christian faith the touchstone of truth, and assert that where other faiths say the same they are true and where they conflict they are false. It is just that the agenda of the exclusivist is to emphasize the latter and wherever possible to argue for Christian difference and the falsity of other faiths, while that of the inclusivist is to emphasize the former and wherever possible to argue for the compatibility of other faiths with Christianity. Neither position countenances the idea that another faith might have something to add to the Christian faith: a truth Christianity has not recognized as such. For both positions, Christianity contains all the truth we need to know to be saved; it is just that for the inclusivists a great deal of the content of other faiths also contains this truth, albeit in a hidden or "anonymous" form, whereas for the exclusivist very little of it does, and there is much that is actually inimical to salvation.

D'Costa's crucial move is to argue the more contentious position that pluralism—by which he means what I have termed universalist

9. D'Costa, *Meeting of the Religions.*

pluralism—also collapses into exclusivism. Pluralist accounts all involve a metanarrative that determines what counts as saving truth within any faith. D'Costa argues this with detailed reference to five pluralist authors: the Christians John Hick and Paul Knitter, more briefly the Jewish Dan Cohn-Sherbock, the Hindu Radhakhrishnan, and the Tibetan Buddhist, the Dalai Lama.

In the case of the first three writers, the grand metanarrative is supplied by what D'Costa calls "modernity's hidden God," and John Milbank—whom D'Costa generally cites with critical approval—terms "secular reason." All the authors considered, he believes, draw on a tradition stemming from Immanuel Kant and his proposals for what must count as rational for all humanity in all times and places.

> Hick finds that all the great traditions teach "love, compassion, self-sacrificing, concern for the good of others, generous kindness and forgiveness." [But] he has to sever these values from their tradition-specific narrative contexts. He writes tellingly that the above ideal "is not an alien ideal imposed by supernatural authority but one arising out of our human nature," and which happens to concur with the "modern liberal moral outlook." . . . The basic criterion for judging salvific religions is, therefore, a commonly accepted set of values which are rooted in human nature and modern liberalism, not in any authority within differing religious constructions of "what is."[10]

Those religious accounts of "what is"—such as the Christian account of the incarnation and the Mahayana Buddhist account of the three bodies of the Buddha—are precisely what have to be ruled out, or at least treated as roundabout mythological ways of encouraging the good ethical instincts that are common to us all. Hick's account forms a procrustean bed to which all faiths must be tailored; what cannot be so tailored must be amputated as not making any kind of sense.

D'Costa treats Knitter and Cohn-Sherbock in similar fashion as offering a liberal account that is deemed to be the universal essence of authentic religion; in Knitter's case it is based not on liberal values but a more liberationist focus on justice, human liberation, and ecological balance. So though these authors are not exclusivists of the Christian or any other traditional faith, they are exclusivists of the modern liberal faith in human nature, experience, and reason. They exclude a great deal that is important to the practitioners of faith in the interests of conforming all faiths to a universalist schema of their own.

10. Ibid., 29.

I shall not pursue D'Costa's arguments to the same effect regarding Cohn-Sherbock, but turn to the two figures he considers who are not Christian and not obviously modernist. Firstly, the Hindu Radhakrishnan proposes a universal account of liberation that at first sight seems much more accommodating than the classical, more exclusive forms of Hinduism. This account—of how the soul, *atman*, finally realizes its non-dual identity with Brahma, who is the one true *Atman* of the world beyond the delusions of separation—has become so familiar that many now identify it with Hinduism as such, finding in Hinduism the same "perennial" mystical philosophy that is found in the West in Plotinus and other neo-Platonists, and the medieval mystical writers such as Meister Eckhart. But D'Costa detects here[11] an ultimate exclusivism based on the truth of the Advaita Vedanta school of Hinduism—a truth established, however, not on the basis of Hindu scripture, in the manner of the original proponents, but on general Western style philosophical argument. So in Radhakrishnan we find an exclusivism that is in part exclusively Hindu, but in part based on Western modernism in the manner of John Hick. And certainly those aspects of traditional faiths that are decisively dualistic or otherwise unable to be accommodated to the Advaita non-dual scheme are decisively rejected.

Finally, the Dalai Lama is well known for his generous accommodation of other faiths. He writes, for example

> The development of love and compassion is basic, and I usually say that this is a main message of religion. . . . The important thing is that in your daily life you practice the essential things, and on that level there is hardly any difference between Buddhism, Christianity, or any other religion. All religions emphasize betterment, improving human beings, a sense of brotherhood and sisterhood, love—these things are common. Thus, if you consider the essence of religion, there is not much difference.[12]

However, D'Costa points out that the ultimate basis of this tolerance for the Dalai Lama is rooted in his own specifically Buddhist distinction between conventional and ultimate truth.[13] Each of us needs to find the conventional truth appropriate to our stage of development, and at many stages other faiths will serve to induce the love and other values that will further our future development. Therefore, it might even be counterproductive in trying to convert a Christian to Buddhism, for in the process

11. Ibid., 67.

12. Gyatzo, *Kindness*, 13 (cited in D'Costa, *Meeting*, 76).

13. D'Costa, *Meeting*, 78ff., 81.

he might lose the "skilful means" that work for him and adopt patterns that are for him alien and unhelpful. However, for the Dalai Lama we can become a Bodhisattva dedicated to the liberation of all beings, only at a stage of development prepared for and defined within the context of his own Gelugpa tradition. This is a specific form of Madhyamaka Buddhism, which affirms the full-emptiness (*sunyata*) of all existence. Our karmic state may dictate that we spend many lives on lower pathways like Christianity, but at this higher stage more dualistic or god-oriented forms of faith will hold us back. The Dalai Lama's tolerance is therefore based on his own exclusivist scheme in which, though all religious ways may benefit people at appropriate stages, only a form of Buddhist faith can lead to the ultimate liberation. And though he has himself affirmed that he has learnt much from the example and teaching of Christians about love and compassion, ultimately his account of reality—like that of Hick, Knitter, and Radhakrishnan—is complete, having nothing fundamental to learn from other perspectives.

To sum up, these authors' pluralism collapses into exclusivism. The particular details of each faith are excluded in the interests of a single, often thin and highly general account of ultimate reality and salvation. The liberal, gentlemanly ethic of Hick, the eco-liberation dynamic of Knitter, and the perennial philosophy or Radhakrishnan, valuable as they may be, all alike prove too thin and abstract to capture this compelling richness; though D'Costa concedes that the Dalai Lama's Tibetan Buddhist-based inclusivity, based as it is on the richness of his own particular tradition, might succeed in avoiding this criticism.[14]

THE RELATIVIST COLLAPSE INTO "EXCLUSIVIST" PLURALISM?

At this point we need to ask to what extent D'Costa is right to describe these authors as exclusivist. In the case of the modernist exclusivists—Hick, Knitter, and Cohn-Sherbock—it seems to me to depend on how far modernity is regarded as an absolute test or procrustean bed. This depends on whether for them the modernity that tests all claims by experience and reason is seen as *an* indispensable means of discovering truth or as *the* means to which all others must conform; the ultimate test as to whether they can be true or even meaningful.

D'Costa himself certainly uses reason and experience as means to discover truth. Indeed, he would be contradicting his own Roman Catholic tradition if he did not believe there were some truths proclaimed by his

14. Ibid., 91.

faith (like the existence of God, and natural law ethics) that were amenable to universal reason. The question is how far the authors he criticizes go beyond the use of reason and experience in this way towards absolutizing their claims, making them not just essential dialogue partners with the more particular and faith-based claims of the religions, but the judge and jury to whom they must give account. D'Costa is right to argue that insofar as they take this step, their pluralism collapses into an exclusivism for which modernity holds all the keys to knowledge, and people of faith can be regarded as non-deluded insofar as they are anonymous modernists. However, chapter 4 will distinguish this kind of view—which represents an ideological Liberalism, an intolerant form of tolerance—from a more generally liberal approach that allows for dialogue within the framework of an undogmatic use of rational argument.

Moreover, the opposite kind of collapse—of exclusivism into pluralism—is also possible. A faith that cannot *partially* explain itself to those of other faiths and none and dialogue with them by means of arguments constructed by basic rules acceptable to all—that is, a faith that spurns the exercise traditionally known as apologetics—cannot persuade those others of its truth, and cannot justify its own claims to affirm truths about the reality they share. (More on this in chapter 4.)

Hence, a wholly exclusivist faith is bound to collapse into the new kind of pluralism, which I call, paradoxically, exclusivist pluralism: the relativist or constructivist view that in one form or another is more widespread than it deserves to be. This is because once one renounces appeal to criteria of judgment that are external to faith—whether rational criteria or others that all reasonable people acknowledge—then it follows logically that the only criteria left are those internal to the faith in question. Religions become what philosopher Thomas Kuhn termed "incommensurable" (of which more in chapter 2): lacking any common standard for comparison. Each faith will be true, and probably exclusively true, on its own terms. Hence the relativism: truth is no longer something we can assess in absolute terms, but only relative to the framework of a particular religion or worldview. But by the very move by which the faith grants to itself the sole criteria for judging its own validity, it follows that other faiths will need to be judged by their own criteria, by which they will be found true. Effectively my faith is exclusively true for me and yours for you. Inclusivism is ruled out, as faiths cannot lay claim to the anonymous souls of those of other faiths by universalizing their own claims. What remains is what is commonly known as pluralism, which paradoxically combines exclusiveness (*only* my faith is true in its terms, or "true for us") with pluralism (other faiths may well, for all I can possibly know, be true by their own terms, "true for them.")

The postmodern turn overturns all "views from nowhere,"[15] despairing of the possibility of judging faith traditions from any point outside of them. We shall see how this move has the effect of as it were collapsing exclusivism and pluralism into each other, squeezing out any possibility of inclusivism. Each faith is seen as exclusively but relativistically true, true in its own terms. A kind of "exclusivism from the inside" holds because other faiths cannot assail it, lacking as they do the understanding and practice whereby one's own faith is understood and found true. But a kind of "pluralism from the outside" holds because conversely it is inappropriate to judge other faiths in the terms of one's own faith.

Hence, as Milbank argued, incommensurability spells "the end of dialogue" (1990). That is to say, the end of dialogue with any epistemological bite: dialogue as something that might offer me something beyond what I already believe to be true on my own terms, something that might call into question my own criteria for truth and set things in a new perspective. Dialogue might remain as a polite exercise of seeing what in the other's faith might be accepted as true in the terms of mine, or as trying to understand what the other might mean in my own terms. Another way of putting this—explored further in chapter 6—is that dialogue remains on the level of the conscious mind, and what we already affirm and know, and does not engage the unconscious or address what each faith might be denying or repressing, or tacitly embodying (for good or ill) in its religious practice without realizing it. The dialogue then falls far short of what Moyaert terms "hermeneutical openness."[16]

BEYOND THE PARADIGM: A NEW HUMILITY

The threefold paradigm still has its champions, and is still widely used in teaching and research in interfaith relations, but on closer analysis the paradigm collapses. On the one hand, pluralism (of the universalist kind) and inclusivism involve a kind of exclusive paradigm, while on the other, exclusivism and inclusivism cannot sustain their claims against an overarching pluralism of a very different, relativistic kind that rejects all universal metanarratives. Within this confused situation can any future be rescued for interfaith dialogue beyond the paradigm?

Certainly recent writing on interfaith dialogue tends to withdraw from general theorizing in favor of a much more focused approach. Increasingly in postmodern times we have come to see faiths in rich terms, consisting

15. Nagel, *View from Nowhere.*
16. Moyaert, *Recent Developments.*

not just of arguments and descriptions of the ultimate, but also of myths, stories, rituals, art, and practices of prayer, worship, and meditation. What draws us to a faith and keeps us belonging, or converts us, has to do with this rich mix, which includes but transcends the verbal. The haunting chant, the spacious architecture and geometric beauty of the mosques, the prostrations and prayer, the puritan ethic and the absence of the religiosity associated with idols and devotion, are all of a piece with the Islamic message of the transcendent Oneness of God and the definitive declaration of his word in the lilting Arabic of the Qur'an. The icons and incense, the more solid and passionate chant, the long and intricate liturgy, the rich vestments of the hierarchy, and the contrasting traditions of silent prayer, are likewise of a piece with the Trinitarian theology of Orthodoxy and its emphasis on the God who became human that humans might become divine. The staggering richness of a Buddhist temple, with the multiple Buddhas and nagas and the stupas repeatedly puncturing the skyline, the quiet offering of gifts to the monks and the receiving of guidance in return, the austere, restful chant and the stillness of meditation that somehow reaches out and embraces all the complexity in a spacious lack of business and striving, once more, are of a piece with the Buddhist eightfold way to nirvana. It is what unites these religions within themselves and makes them distinct from each other that seems to hold the truth that invites or compels us to adhere to them.

For these reasons Marianne Moyaert argues that the old "soteriological openness" based on a broad understanding of the different faiths as ways of salvation needs to give way to a "hermeneutical openness" much more sensitive to particular texts and traditions and what another faith can bring to their interpretation. She points out that none of the three approaches has much to offer to real interfaith dialogue. Exclusivism very obviously makes such dialogue pointless, necessarily replacing it with a mutual attempt at conversion in which the other partner is seen as fundamentally misguided, and not on the way to salvation. Inclusivism fares little better; it does not help Christian dialogue with Buddhists to tell them that they are anonymous Christians, and that the underlying salvific reality of their religion is a disguised Christianity; or vice versa. Thus, Moyaert quotes Paul Knitter:

> In claiming to open myself to the "truth" of Buddhism, I am really only opening myself to . . . what is already implicitly contained in Christian revelation. In my deeper feelings and convictions that Jesus is God's last word, I cannot hear, because I cannot recognise, any other Words that might say something different and new.[17]

17. Knitter, *Catholics and Other Religions*, 330, cited in Moyaert, *Recent Developments*, 33.

Superficially pluralism may seem to fare better, but arguably in this case each participant is being treated as an anonymous Hickian, or Knitterian, or anonymously adhering to whatever ultimate perspective on religious truth and salvation is being assumed.

> Even when the topic of common ground does not obtrude into the discussion directly, the assumption of common ground inhibits real dialogue. This is because real dialogue involves listening to genuinely strange ideas, whereas the assumption of common ground limits the strangeness of what can be heard. The listener who is convinced of common ground will not be able to hear the full novelty of what is said.[18]

Moyaert points out the similarity in these comments, suggesting that the "common ground" provided by pluralism can be no less an inhibitor of true dialogue than the assumption that one religion has the full truth. In either case the urge to reconcile the other to one's own salvation story mitigates against accepting, let alone being challenged by, the otherness of the other.

Moyaert argues that hermeneutical openness is what is replacing the old soteriological opennesss, as we move away from grand schemes of salvation in which other faiths must either be included or excluded. It involves an openness to the particularity of the other, combined with an affirmation of the particularity of my own stance, and a suspicion of generalities. Hence the often-used name for the resulting position, which Moyaert regards as a fourth alternative to the threefold paradigm: particularism.

The question for us is: does particularism in this sense represent a real alternative to exclusivist pluralism in our sense? If it does not, it cannot offer hermeneutical openness in the sense Moyaert describes, or dialogue with real epistemological bite. But that is precisely what Moyaert argues that particularism can now offer. For her, what we call exclusivist pluralism is only one among the alternatives now on offer. There are others that are better news for dialogue.

The alternative she focuses on is Comparative Theology, but another very focused mode of interfaith dialogue is that represented by Scriptural Reasoning. These will be discussed and compared in the next section, while in the one that follows I touch on a third alternative to dialogue offered by D'Costa, before offering my own suggestion, which will be developed throughout this book.

---

18. Cobb, *Dialogue without Common Ground*, 148, cited in ibid., 33–34.

ALTERNATIVE RESPONSES: SCRIPTURAL
REASONING AND COMPARATIVE THEOLOGY

Scriptural Reasoning arose in the mid 1990s when scholars of the Jewish, Muslim, and Christian faiths got together to study each others' scriptures with the same close attention, but without the theological presuppositions, they would normally bring to their own. It is well described in recent articles by David Ford and Mike Higton.[19] It is essentially a kind of interfaith dialogue in which the discussion does not range over doctrines and beliefs, and indeed "the wisdom of experienced practitioners of Scriptural Reasoning is that the attempt to frame the discussion of those texts in [theologically thematic] terms . . . kills the conversation."[20] Rather, discussion focuses intensively on a particular text, without preconceiving the direction discussion may take. Scriptural reasoning has tended to involve exchanges between the three Abrahamic faiths, and this is obviously helped by the fact that many of the texts, or the stories behind them, are shared, as well as by the degree of emphasis all three faiths place on scriptural exegesis. But there would seem to be no immutable reason to restrict the discipline to these faiths.

Comparative Theology differs on four counts. It is not dialogical, or rather the dialogue is internal to one scholar. It has (so far) tended to use Hindu and to some extent Buddhist texts alongside the Christian ones. It is not restricted to the sacred scriptures of these traditions but can include other parts of the traditions. And most important, its aim is explicitly theological. Higton writes

> In Comparative Theology, the primary site for wrestling with doctrinal questions is in the internal dialogue of the comparative theologian's own rumination, albeit fed by the experience of live interfaith dialogue. By contrast, Scriptural Reasoning is a practice in which the primary form of engagement is in live conversation, albeit fed by the internal deliberation of the individuals involved.[21]

For all these differences, Comparative Theology shares with Scriptural Reasoning an avoidance of the abstract and a focus on the particular. It works from a close comparison between particular writings, writing theology out of acceptance of and reflection on a difference of perspectives that cannot be resolved by grand theory. Thus, Clooney reads Aquinas' *Summa Theologiae* in the contrasting light of Hindu Vedanta thought, and this he

19. Ford, *Interreligious Reading*, 1ff., 93ff., and 120ff.
20. Ibid., 125.
21. Ibid., 121.

believes offers new insight into Aquinas' own vision of God,[22] while Fredericks views Jesus' Parable of the Prodigal Son alongside the story of Krishna and the milkmaids, and approaches New Testament thought on the resurrection through the lens of Zen Buddhism.[23] Comparative Theology

> ordinarily starts with the intuition of an intriguing resemblance that prompts us to place two realities—texts, images, practices, doctrines, persons—near one another, so that they may be seen over and again, side by side. In this necessarily arbitrary and intuitive practice we understand each differently because the other is near.[24]

This kind of "interillumination" provides part of the raw material for theological reflection and development. In due course (cf. "Dialogue between Two Objects" in chapter 2, and "Metaphorical Interillumination" in chapter 9, below) we will need to examine and test the power of such interillumination in relation not only to texts, but to images, practices, and persons, shifting the focus, in the particularist way, away from an exclusive focus on texts and doctrines.

Does this make Comparative Theology a kind of interfaith construct, rather than a Christian, theology? Clooney insists—rather ambivalently—that it remains, for him, Christian. It is

> distinguished by its sources and ways of proceeding, by its foundation in more than one tradition (although the comparativist always remains rooted in one tradition), and by reflection which builds on that foundation, rather than simply on themes or by methods already articulated prior to comparative practice.[25]

One might ask what the difference is between a foundation and a root, that might save the first half of this statement from contradiction. But the second part of the statement fares better, introducing a vital distinction between building on the foundation of both faiths in the comparison, and utilizing methods established in advance of the dialogue. It is only in the latter case, where a fixed methodology is applied to the comparison rather than arising from the comparative process, that the latter could be accused of the kind of "modernist exclusivism" criticized by D'Costa.

---

22. Clooney, *Theology after Vedanta*.

23. Fredericks, *Buddhists and Christians*.

24. Clooney, *Comparative Theology*, 11.

25. Clooney, "Current Theology," 522, cited in Moyaert, "Recent Developments," 39.

Despite welcoming Comparative Theology, however, D'Costa indeed questions its Christian credentials. He asks two questions.[26] Firstly, what is the Christian theological basis for embarking on this new discipline, that is, what in Christianity might make us believe that its theology might develop thorough the comparative process Clooney describes? And secondly, how are the results of Comparative Theology to be assessed for their theological truth? In the absence of a theological motivation and assessment, in what sense can the enterprise be termed theological? In other words, we might ask whether the hermeneutical openness Moyaert describes in relation to Comparative Theology remains just hermeneutical, just an exercise in extracting possible meanings in other faiths and new meanings for our own, rather than achieving epistemological openness, that is, generating through the interaction of faiths new truths, new discoveries and developments that could be termed theological.

Though so far as I know D'Costa does not discuss Scriptural Reasoning, his questions might be applied *a fortiori* to that discipline, given its reluctance to discuss theological themes deriving from Christianity at all. Higton would disagree. For him, theology is essentially a disciplined dialogue with Christian scripture, and

> Doctrine is . . . a set of acknowledged constraints upon the reading of scripture—a set of rules for reading that have emerged from the practice of such reading and that shape its continuation. . . . Christian doctrine disciplines holy reading for the sake of that holy living which is knowledge of God.[27]

The initially strange notion that doctrine is "a set of rules for reading" scripture is one to which this book will return when we consider postliberal and narrative theologies in chapter 6. But insofar as engagement with readers from other faiths in Scriptural Reasoning has the power to sharpen and deepen Christians' reading of their scriptural texts, it has a good Christian motivation. And though Scriptural Reason itself lacks theological content, its results may reasonably be fed back into and assessed by Christian theology with its well-honed disciplines and restraints.

D'COSTA'S SPIRIT-BASED INCLUSIVISM

D'Costa's Roman Catholic understanding of theology differs from Higton's in giving the church a more proactive role in relation to scripture than is

26. Cf. Moyaert, *Recent Developments*, 40–41.
27. Higton, *Scriptural Reasoning*, 128–29.

suggested in Higton's assessment of Scriptural Reasoning. Hence his own alternative to the threefold paradigm is rather different. The first part of his argument, as noted, suggests that exclusivism is the only alternative, into which all other views collapse. But despite his immersion in his own Catholic tradition and his reliance on Papal and Vatican declarations, his argument is more subtle, namely that Christianity itself can offer, *on the basis of its own resources and goals*, grounds for openness to truth in other faiths. A transformative engagement with other faiths can be something from which Christians can learn new truth on the basis of their own faith commitment.

This is because of the nature of the Trinity, and in particular the Holy Spirit. First D'Costa makes the important point that "the traditional teaching *extra ecclesiam nulla salus* (no salvation outside the Church) was never formulated or applied to non-Christian religions,"[28] and the Catholic Church has never explicitly denied salvation to those of other faiths. Secondly, though the Catholic Church has repeatedly and consistently denied that those other faiths and their founders, rather than Christ, can be the means of salvation, recent Vatican documents repeatedly affirm the presence of the Holy Spirit in other faiths. One might then question how, if the Holy Spirit—the worker of salvation—is present in those faiths, can salvation not be accomplished in them? The answer is that it is, but not by means of those faiths or the efforts of their adherents, but through Christ, because according to *Redemptoris Missio*

> the universal activity of the Spirit is not to be separated from his particular activity within the Body of Christ, which is the Church. Indeed it is always the Spirit who is at work, both when he gives life to the Church and impels her to proclaim Christ, and when he implants and develops his gifts in all individuals and peoples, guiding the Church to discover these gifts, to foster them and receive them through dialogue.[29]

At this point it might seem that D'Costa is only offering a new form of inclusivism, in which the Spirit is a kind of anonymous Christ working in all religions to bring the redemption the church already knows fully in Christ. But crucially, *Redemptoris Missio* affirms that the church can *discover* the Spirit's gifts, and *receive* them through dialogue with other faiths. As D'Costa goes on to show through a careful exegesis of the later chapters of the Gospel of John, the church does not yet know or understand this fullness, and therefore may discover and receive it from those outside the

---

28. D'Costa, *Meeting of the Religions*, 101.
29. *Redemptoris Missio*, 20, cited in D'Costa, *Meeting*, 115.

Christian fold.[30] On the one hand, the Spirit will "lead you into all truth" (John 16:13)—so the church has yet to know all there is to know. On the other hand, "he will take what is mine and declare it to you" (v. 14)—what is revealed is not some new revelation, additional to Christ, but some new understanding of a Christ who is already there in his fullness. The church has much to learn from other faiths, where the Spirit is at work, sometimes with more clarity than in the church itself, so that the other faith may bring the church to repentance. But what it learns more fully in this way is the Christ, whom it already knows in part and in whom all salvation dwells for everyone.

If D'Costa is right, both in his exegesis of John and his understanding of official Roman Catholic teaching, then indeed interfaith dialogue is not just a polite extra but an essential enterprise from which the church and its theology needs to learn. In that sense much of what this book argues is affirmed. D'Costa has carefully identified a radical fault that is shared by exclusivism, ordinary inclusivism, and pluralism alike: namely, they leave the faiths with nothing essential to learn from one another, since according to all of these views, each faith knows everything it really needs to know. But for D'Costa's Spirit-based understanding, Christianity at least—though it has, in Christ, all that is needed to bring us to salvation—has much to learn from other faiths in terms of the fullness of truth that is in Christ.

TOWARDS MUTUAL INCLUSIVISM

D'Costa's argument thus prescribes openness to the other regarding the content of dialogue. However, there remains an exclusivity in the goal. A person of another faith might not be entirely happy; he might not feel treated as an equal, or motivated to continue, if the goal of the dialogue is seen only in terms of enhancing Christian understanding of Christ. For the open inclusivism advocated by D'Costa to work, it needs to be possible for the other to participate as a way of deepening her own faith and understanding, in parallel with the Christian. The inclusiveness needs not only to be open, but mutual. So for a Buddhist, for example, to join fruitfully in interfaith dialogue with a Christian, there would need to be *Buddhist* reasons to participate; there would need to be that in Buddhism which affirms that, although the final goal of nirvana is defined for him by the life and teaching of the Buddha (in just the same way as that the goal of the Christian is defined by Christ), there are reasons in Buddhism itself for believing that the Buddhist practitioner does not yet understand the fullness of what nirvana means,

30. Ibid., 118ff.

and reasons in Buddhism for believing that she might have things to learn, in terms of both theory and practice, from a Christian.

I use the Buddhist example because it is fairly plausible to believe this is the case with Buddhism. The Dalai Lama is not the only Buddhist to affirm that he has learnt from Christians much of vital importance about the importance of social justice and action for the poor, which the often-solitary practices of Buddhism have neglected. Moreover, there is in Buddhism the important idea that liberation does not have to be learnt from the Buddha. Buddhist scholar Rupert Gethin has argued that in the Buddhist scriptures known as the *Abhidharma* faith is not confined to explicit Buddhists but is present in all who live lives that are virtuous in Buddhist terms.[31] May a Buddhist not then learn from the "text" of such people's lives? Note that in the idea of the *Pratyekabuddha* Buddhism affirms the possibility that one might work out for oneself all that one needs for salvation. If it is possible to learn this by oneself independently of the Buddha and his teachings and *sangha*, why would it not also be possible to learn it—albeit by another name—from non-Buddhist traditions? Conversely, if the Buddhist who is still immersed in samsaric delusion, having yet to achieve nirvana, cannot conceive fully what nirvana will be like, why might those of other faiths—despite being partly deluded too—not deepen her insight?

Despite their historical hostility, there are also grounds for an open mutual inclusivism in the case of the Abrahamic faiths, because of their historical interconnectedness. There is a sense in which Judaism includes Christianity as one of its possible fulfillments, the sect of first-century Judaism that survived alongside what later became Judaism itself. The way that "sect" interprets the scriptures it shares with Judaism may have things to say to the Judaism that interprets them differently. Conversely Christianity "includes" Judaism, as being a globally successful variant of that faith, which also survives, in a specific form much more aligned with the traditions of a particular people; it too can expect to learn, and has learnt, much from the faith that provided the context of its founders, and the greater part of the scriptures on which it draws.

The case regarding Islam is similar. Judaism and Christianity are among its Abrahamic roots, and it shares with them many traditions, which are often slightly different versions of its own stories. The categories in which Islamic theology has developed—prophecy, apocalyptic, and Hellenic thought—are again similar. Islam may be thought of as including those earlier traditions from which it can learn much as it defines its own. The converse—the inclusion of Islam by Judaism and Christianity—is more

31. Gethin, *Buddhist Faith of Non-Buddhists*, 179ff.

problematic, since there is a real sense in which those faiths have yet to comprehend the rise of Islam. Their stories are partly its own, but most of its stories are not yet theirs. Christians for example have yet to make sense, in Christian theological terms, of the rise of a new faith some six centuries after Christ, who for them is the fulfillment of all faiths and the definitive embodiment of God. Nevertheless, in practice many Jews and Christians would affirm that they have learnt much from Islam, enriching their own beliefs.

Regarding other dialogues, such as Christianity in relation to Taoism, Confucianism, and so forth, the situation is probably more complex. There is neither the historical interdependence we find with the Abrahamic faiths nor the strange sense of complementarity in parallel development that often motivates dialogue between Christians and Buddhists. But in the case of the dialogue between Christianity and secular modernity, again, an open mutual interdependence may apply. It is obvious that on one level present modernity includes Christianity as one of the many "options" within its multicultural ideal. But the converse also needs to be acknowledged: that, as John Milbank has argued theoretically and Charles Taylor historically, secular modernity has developed as an option *within* Christianity. Though modern secularism has taken root in most cultures, it was Christianity that first gave rise both to the notion of a created order that could be explored scientifically, *"as if* there were no God," and to a natural law ethics that could be grasped and worked out universally, irrespective of faith. It was but one more optional step to change the quote to read *"since* there is no God." Christians have reason to believe, as the Vatican 2 documents encourage, that they have much to learn about Christ through the Spirit's work within secular society; conversely secular society has much to learn about its own rationale and basis through dialogue with the Christian "option."

Mutual inclusivism may seem paradoxical, since logically if A includes all of B, B cannot include all of A. But we are not speaking of a total inclusion here, but rather, of a sense in which A fulfills B or helps B to understand itself. The logic involved is, again, that of interillumination, where two things shed light on and interpret each other; this book will say more about interillumination than mutual inclusivism as such.

CONCLUSION

Those are matters to which we must return, as we develop two main theses. The first, developed in the following chapter, is the philosophical thesis that truth is apprehended primarily, neither in the individual's isolated contemplation of the world, nor in a society's own special "language game," but in dialogue between persons and societies. The second, argued in chapters 3 and 4, is the theological thesis that dialogue based on open mutual inclusivity has deep Christian theological roots and has characterized Christian theology at its best. Only in the light of these two lines of argument will we be in a position to return, in chapter 5, to the task introduced in this chapter, that of sketching a practice of interfaith dialogue that collapses neither into exclusivism nor into relativistic pluralism, but involves a genuine process of discovery.

CHAPTER 2

Do We See the Same Things?
Relativism and Reality

THE PREVIOUS CHAPTER DESCRIBED the collapse into exclusivist pluralism: how interfaith dialogue has, to a considerable degree, lost heart in the wake of a postmodern, relativistic perspective that makes tolerance easy and disagreement well nigh impossible, because we are each talking a language the other does not understand, and inhabiting a conceptual world to which the other has no access. The chapter described how the pluralist assumption that we believe in the same Ultimate or pursue the same ultimate goals "collapses" into a relativism in which each faith pursues the God and the goal its language game has constructed. In the absence of a reality referred to by our language and giving meaning to its terms, how could we possibly know our goals are "the same," when manifestly the words we use about it and the cultural context of those words are quite different? In this situation we can tolerate one another, but only because we have renounced the claim to understand what each other are talking about. In that sense our tolerance inevitably falls short of respect, if by respect we mean something that involves understanding and valuing what is believed by the other, even if we do not fully agree.

The exclusive pluralists have a point. Certainly it is valuable to see religions not as thin belief systems corresponding with "Ultimate Reality," or grand metanarratives describing how the universe is, but as thick, richly textured and embodied arrays of stories that evoke meanings, invoke the imagination, and impel ways of living. The second half of the book will explore in greater detail what various postmodern theologies—postliberal, narrative, liberation, and post-metaphysical—have contributed to the enrichment of our understanding of scriptural and theological texts, before

23

examining their inadequate analysis of theological truth in relation to apologetics and dialogue.

But at this point the urgent question is whether relativism is right: whether we simply have to accept that religions are incommensurable systems, in which case we also have to accept that dialogue between them—whatever its pastoral benefits—is indeed at an end as a search for understanding. Or is there yet a possibility that the different religions might be about something: something we might contest, dialogue about, be converted or changed by, or at least come to respect, rather than merely tolerate as unintelligible "other worlds." Or is the mutual inclusivism advocated at the end of chapter 1, in which religions somehow complete what is lacking in one another, futile, because there is no common language in which completion and lack might be assessed?

This chapter will distinguish kinds of relativism and constructivism and argue that the argument that religions constitute incommensurable "worlds" cannot be sustained. A more moderate epistemological constructivism remains true, but allows dialogue. Various kinds of dialogue are then explored, and a dialogue-based constructivism is expounded which, while defying the key dogmas which modernity has seen as the basis of realism, allows for a critical realism. This dialogical realism will form the epistemological basis for the rest of the book.

RELATIVISM AND CONSTRUCTIVISM

First, a word needs to be said about the terms "relativism" and "constructivism." Relativism is a term opposed to "absolutism" and denotes the idea that there are no absolute truths valid at all times and places, but that the truth of a statement or belief has to be evaluated with reference to something more particular—a culture, a religion, a worldview, or even an individual. Constructivism denotes the view that truths are in some sense "constructed" as opposed to "discovered." According to constructivism we make truths as we construct, for example, a mathematical system, or decree a new dogma, or apply our language and concepts. Relativism is therefore mainly a matter of ontology—the question of whether there really are absolutes "out there" independent of us, or whether all things vary according to our point of view—while constructivism is more about epistemology—how we come to know truths, whether by invention or discovery.

The two concepts are therefore not identical. I shall argue for a position that is constructivist about ways of knowing reality without being relativist about reality itself. (The converse position—non-constructivist

relativism—does seem much more paradoxical, but maybe not a contradiction in terms.)

This subtle difference, however, is often overridden by a more pervasive one that has to do with evaluation. In the 1960s and '70s relativism
became quite the vogue, and almost a dogma in certain academic circles,
while many conservatives made a point of criticizing relativism, and in
those circles to be found out as a "relativist" was to be discredited. For
reasons worth exploring in intellectual history, the conservatives have in
a sense prevailed, in that very few these days welcome being dubbed "relativist." Even Thomas Kuhn, who in the 1970s was the arch-relativist, has
since rejected the description. Constructivism—which sounds much more
positive than relativism—is now the term of choice for those who would
once have called themselves relativists. So the terms have become in effect
synonymous in terms of concept, the subtle difference just mentioned being overridden by a much more powerful difference between positive and
negative connotations.

WHICH KIND OF RELATIVISM?

In an early writing[1] I distinguished three kinds of relativism. I used the example of the "saligrams" that we found while trekking in the upper Kali
Gandaki valley which cuts through the Himalayas in Nepal. There is something magical about these dark stones in which, if you split them open in
just the right way, you find a spiral of ribbed gold. The local people regard
them as holy symbols of Vishnu, and will pile them onto the *gompas* (religious cairns) along with the carved images of the Buddha and the Bodhisat-
tvas and the holy texts. A geological scientist will see something entirely
different: a fossil laid down in the Jurassic period when the mountains were
under the sea before India collided into Asia and thrust the Himalayas into
the sky. Each is shaping what he sees according to his own story, his own
text. For one, the text is religious, while for the other the key texts are scientific ones belonging to the canons of what could be called the secular faith.
Do they see the same saligram or something different, or is one right and
the other wrong about what he sees?

According to what I called *semantic relativism*, the peasant and the
scientist see the same object but simply describe it in words that have different connotations. The difference between the stories they each tell about
the saligram will lead them to have different things "in mind" when they
look at the stone, and this may lead to confusion. But the confusion will

1. Thompson, *What Kind of Relativism?*

be easily cleared up because the difference has only to do with words and meanings, not realities. There is no fundamental incommensurability inhibiting dialogue between Vaishnavites and scientists; on the contrary, the lines of the dialogue will be clear if the scientist wishes to uphold his worldview and disprove the Vaishnavite's, or vice versa. It will be clear where the contradictions in their accounts of the world lie, and they will be battling for truths about the same saligram and the same world. In philosophical terms, the meaning or connotation or sense of words varies, but the denotation or reference does not vary with it. To use the famous example the philosopher Gottlob Frege used in a seminal essay,[2] the terms "morning star" and "evening star" have *different senses, but the same reference*, namely the planet Venus. The fossil and the sacred symbol have different "senses," but both terms refer to the same thing.

But according to *ontological relativism*—relativism of being, or metaphysical relativism—they do not. According to this view, the Nepali and the geologist inhabit different universes: one a world in which Vishnu scatters his holy symbol throughout the Himalayas, the other in which creatures evolve over millions of years while continents collide and mountains grow. In ontological relativism, the reference of words as it were disappears into the sense. The "fact" that snow is white (to use the famous example from the philosopher Alfred Tarski[3]) moves from being what upholds the truth of the statement "snow is white," to being seen as a projection of that statement. The way there seem to be facts out there so neatly corresponding to our statements gives the game away: for if we had no language to say "snow is white" there would—it is argued—be no fact that snow is white.

So, according to Ludwig Wittgenstein, the meaning of our words is not to be found in their reference but in their use in the conceptual "language games" of our culture. Meanwhile Jacques Derrida pointed out that meaning, determined by structures of "difference," was always "deferred" to the meaning of other words.[4] His term *différance* expressed this "deferral" involved in "difference." We define red in terms of "color," but color is then defined in terms of other terms, including "red." There is no firm foundation on which language is founded; rather language spins its own meanings in ever-deferred webs of context and definition, in which we never get to any stable and assured referent. So trying to get words and thoughts to mirror things in exact correspondence is, we might say, like trying to see your

2. Frege, *Sense and Reference*.
3. Tarski, *Semantic Conception of Truth*.
4. Derrida, *Writing and Difference*.

reflection in a stormy, ever-changing ocean. Building a stable story of the real world is as easy as walking on water.

For ontological relativism, there is no longer a way to distinguish actuality from story or mythology. The truth of mythical statements is decided not by looking at reality but by looking at the mythological corpus: whether that of science or that of Vaishnavite Hinduism. The result is something quite strange to common-sense, namely, a philosophical idealism for which the "world" is a particular culture's collective idea, a kind of corporate myth. From a sense of the difficulties of dialogue with alien cultures and religions, we have come through to a feeling of the impossibility of such dialogue, because we cannot be sure what those who inhabit those religions and cultures are referring to even by terms that seem on the face of it to translate readily and smoothly.

Ultimately there is something self-defeating about ontological relativism. For it ceases to be possible to speak of the two visions as ways of seeing the same saligram. The referent—the actual stone "out there" with its glittering kernel, which is what both the Nepali and the geologist *seem* to be trying to account for—has simply disappeared. The object looked at has disappeared into different ways of seeing.

The idea that there can be different visions of the same thing is what makes interfaith dialogue both possible and challenging. It implies a relativism more than semantic—more than the idea that religions differ on the level of the imagination of meanings—but less than the idea that they construct incommensurable worldviews. The crucial notion is that it is possible to construct *one and the same* world differently, that is, to embody different bodies of knowledge concerning the same (or at least overlapping) groups of knowables. This notion is what I call *epistemological relativism*. Because of the emphasis on epistemology, the term constructivism is also appropriate here. According to epistemological constructivism, the Nepali and the scientist are looking at the same object and describing the same thing, but they may know different things about it, and therefore see it differently. *They see the same thing, but see in it different things.*

It is important to distinguish this understanding, that there is one world, from the modern understanding that there is one set of criteria as to what constitutes knowledge of it, one foundational metanarrative of what the world is like. It would be a typically modern arrogance to regard our own current beliefs as the exclusive standard of knowledge. For other civilizations may have not just different beliefs, but different knowledge from our own. Ontological constructivism holds that language generates myths in the sense of illusions, merely projecting a culture's conceptual scheme upon the world. But according to what I call epistemological constructivism, or relativism of knowledge, other cultures may actually enable knowledge of the world different to our own. However, to constitute knowledge, and not just belief, there must be a way in which it could in principle become knowledge for those in our culture too. But the converse too applies; we can know that our own beliefs count as knowledge only if those in the other culture might in principle be able to come to know them to be true. According to epistemological constructivism, therefore, cross-cultural dialogue lies at the heart of knowledge.

If this is the case, then epistemological constructivism treads a tightrope. On the one hand, knowledge is affirmed as embodied in local practices that may, in the first instance, be inaccessible across cultures. On the other hand, verification of knowledge is universal, cutting across cultures—though again, not by reference to some modern metaculture that has got its procedures for knowing right.

To return to Frege's simple example of the morning and evening star, which for us moderns refer to the same planet Venus. Let us suppose that there were cultures for whom the morning star and the evening star were not the same. A modern arrogance would describe such cultures as primitive, asserting that they had failed to discover what we now know, so that they were under an illusion as to the true nature of the morning and evening stars. But a moment's reflection is enough for us to grasp that there is after all a difference in the reference of "morning star" and "evening star." The former refers to a bright object that appears before sunrise, the other to a bright object that appears after sunset. We now possess new astronomical practices of knowing that those in that "primitive" culture did not. What we cannot be so sure of is whether those in that culture might have put their experience of the morning star and the evening star into different practices of knowing, which we can no longer access in our culture (though we might if we learnt the ways of theirs). Likewise, we do not know whether those for whom Venus also named a goddess knew things that we cannot, because we lack the practices of Venus worship. How do we know whether we, for whom Venus only names a rock, surrounded by suffocating gases, orbiting the sun, are not missing certain possibilities of knowledge?

Perhaps the biggest difference between, on the one hand, the view advanced in this book, and on the other, secular modernism, religious exclusivism, and relativistic postmodernism *alike*, is that it seriously allows such questions to be asked, and partly answered. It is modern arrogance to assume that our worldview (whether modern secular science or our religious belief) has got *the* world in its sights, and provides the standard of knowledge by which all other worldviews must be judged. It may seem humbler for postmodernism to hold that our worldview gives us *our* world, and that is all we can ever "know." But such a view still leaves us stranded with "our" world and renders us impervious to change. Truly open humility only arrives with the belief that our worldview gives us *some* knowledge of the world, but that we might be enriched by other perhaps seemingly incompatible worldviews. That belief is what I call epistemological constructivism, according to which we need to learn from one another by a reciprocal adoption of one another's standards in dialogue. Through such dialogue across cultures there can take place an interillumination of worldviews, which shows that we are not referring to distinct worlds but to *distinct views of the same world*. We do not have numerous "cultural worlds" but one world offering many "aspects," many trajectories of knowing.

Think how many trajectories of knowing might emerge from a tree. For a tribesman the tree might embody the generosity of the forest goddess. He will know when her fruit will be perfectly ripe and when to pick her leaves for the medicines he needs, and how to tap and treat her sap for the poisons he uses to hunt; and when to refrain so that she does not become exhausted or angry. For a landscape gardener the tree will focus a knowledge of where to plant and how to prune to maximize the beauty of the garden. For the botanist it will be the springboard for knowledge of its parts, how they resemble and differ from those of other kindred trees, and how the tree has evolved from other forms of life. For the ecologist the tree will hold a unique place in the ecosystem, and he will be acquainted with what insects feed on it and how they feed other animals, and how the tree takes its part in the great cycles of water, oxygen, and so forth. For the woodsman the tree will focus knowledge of its timber, how to shape it, and what it is useful for.

What is involved here is more than a difference in semantic connotation; each knows something different in the tree, and each in a sense sees and knows a different tree. But the difference is less than ontological: it is the same tree that is known in different ways. What the tree really is cannot be defined; none of the languages the different people use has a monopoly on the tree's seemingly inexhaustible reality. But that does not make the tree an ineffable Kantian "noumenon" or thing-in-itself beyond all the different ways of knowing it. It is not something to which different forms of knowledge approach more or less closely, such that we might one day have a perfect tree-knowledge that is better than what the tribesman, the botanist, and so forth can currently offer. The coherent identity of the tree has to do with the fact that the languages that describe it are in principle commensurable. Different people might learn another's language and come to see how it correlates with their own. That way new understandings of the tree might develop, but without surpassing or making redundant the current range of understandings.

Imagine two cultures, one has the concept of a circle as a geometric construction, a locus of points equidistant from a center; but like the Incas it has not discovered the wheel, its coins are oblong, and it regards the circle as a purely theoretical idea never instanced in the real world. The other is more practical; it has no geometry, but has the idea of a circle as the shape it carves its wheels to make its vehicles run smoothly. Here seems a clear case of incommensurability between different concepts of circle.

But along comes the latter culture in its smooth-wheeled chariots and "discovers" the former. When the battles subside, then chariot culture learns the reason why its wheels run smoothly: because the circumference stays equidistant to the axle at the "center." And the geometry culture learns that its geometrical constructions have technological applications. The mutual inclusivism described at the end of chapter 1 applies here. The chariot culture can see the geometry culture as prefiguring its technology, seeing itself as the culture that fulfills abstract theory though technological application. Meanwhile the circle culture may see itself as refining the crude intuitions of the wheel culture in a more general theory that may have other applications. This way of including the other is only arrogant if the symmetry is denied: the fact that *both* societies have learned something, and have had to stretch their concept of circle to do so. Each culture has come to share the knowledge the other has, embodied in its practices, whether or not this finds expression in new words. Moreover, the cultures have not needed to resort to some higher meta-language in order to bring their knowledge together.

WHICH KIND OF INCOMMENSURABILITY?

But if this is really possible, whither incommensurability? Are all the arguments that have been marshaled in favor of incommensurability invalid? To clarify this matter it is worth noting the careful distinction made by Paul Griffiths between issues of incommensurability, comprehensibility, and cognitive content.[5] Each represents a kind of obstacle that may arise in dialogue between those of different faiths, cultures, or conceptual systems, and significantly for us, the different kinds of obstacle give rise to the different kinds of relativism just described.

The problem of *comprehensibility* arises from the way terms derive meaning from the context in which they are used, so we cannot be sure as to the meanings of terms used in a different system. Different terms may be used for the same reality and the same term for different realities. This is the semantic problem that gives rise to what I have called *semantic* relativism,

5. Griffiths, *Apology for Apologetics*, chapter 2.

and as argued above, it poses no insurmountable problem for dialogue or (as he argues) for Griffiths' own main concern, the apologetic attempt to explain and argue for one's faith in terms the other can understand.

The problem of *cognitive content* denotes the fact that sentences in a religious or other system "are capable of being true or false, and that this cognitive content extends beyond the bounds of the community that produced them."[6] Doubt about this real world beyond our separate languages represents what we discussed, and criticized, as *ontological* relativism. Once again, Griffiths himself concurs in affirming a cognitive realism in the face of relativistic trends that in his own day were immensely strong.

For Griffiths, *incommensurability* concerns neither the issue of comprehensibility and meanings of words, nor the objective claims of our language to refer to "cognitive content" across the borders of different conceptual systems, but rather to the means of assessing those claims. Commensurability means that "at least some criteria for the assessment of these claims must also be applicable across those borders."[7] In other words, incommensurability implies *epistemological* relativism, the notion that our ways of assessing our beliefs and knowing whether they are true vary from one culture, religion, or conceptual system to another. I have conceded probably more than Griffiths does to incommensurability and hence to epistemological relativism, while yet arguing that epistemological relativism is of its nature something we can overcome by learning one another's practices of knowing. Clearly it is incommensurability, rather than comprehensibility or cognitive content, that requires further exploration, to see how this overcoming may be possible.

The term "incommensurable" means "no common measure." In a rectangle whose sides are 9 and 12 feet long, for example, the length of the diameter will be 15 feet. It is possible to find a common measure (in this case 3 feet) of which one side is a multiple of 3, the other of 4, and the diameter of 5. If, however, we consider a square with sides of 10 feet, then there is no such common measure to express the length of the diagonal. (It is actually the square root of 20 feet, but this number cannot be expressed as a fraction of the length of the sides.) The diameter and the side were said by the Greeks to be incommensurable. The consequence of incommensurability was for them irrationality. If the side of the square were taken as the unit, the diameter could only be expressed by an irrational number, not by a "ratio" or fraction. If, on the other hand, the length of the diagonal was taken as the unit of measure, then the length of the sides became "irrational."

6. Ibid., 31.
7. Ibid., 27.

In Kuhn,

> the phrase "without common measure" is converted into "without common language." To state that two theories are incommensurable means that there is no neutral language, or other type of language, into which both theories, conceived as sets of statements, can be translated without remainder or loss.[8]

As in the Greek geometrical example, there are no concepts they share in common, by which each can understand and "measure" the meaning of the other. Consequently each looks "irrational" in terms of the other.

Incommensurability for Kuhn arises in the context of "scientific revolutions" when new paradigms replace old ones: for example, when sun-centered Copernican astronomy replaces the old earth-centered system, or Einstein's physics replaces Newton's.

> Within the new paradigm, old terms, concepts, and experiments fall into new relationships one with the other. The inevitable result is what we must call, though the term is not quite right, a misunderstanding between the two competing schools.[9]

There is no common language to decide between two different scientific systems; in other words, they are incommensurable. Kuhn says we have to forgo the widespread idea that "successive theories grow ever closer to, or approximate more and more closely to, the truth. . . . There is, I think, no theory-independent way to reconstruct phrases like 'really there.'"[10] Yet Kuhn explicitly denies being a relativist,[11] and affirms that science makes progress and relates to reality, though it can never arrive at a definitive theory of what is real.

It is the same with the incommensurability of religions. Make one religion the measure, and the other makes no sense, but also *vice versa*. So it is not just that one is right and the other wrong. In interreligious dialogue it is rare to find a shared "common measure" in the form of a concept of reality or salvation or whatever that both parties can agree on. There is seldom any way around the abyss of incommensurability: the deep divergence in ways of knowing and assessing truth between different religious systems. But I shall argue that it is possible for a religious believer to learn what the believers in another religion know, and sometimes to find a way of expressing and

8. Kuhn, *Road since Structure*. The quote is familiar online but without page reference.

9. Kuhn, *Structure of Scientific Revolutions*, 149.

10. Ibid., 206.

11. Ibid., 155.

evaluating this in terms of her own religion. For epistemological constructivism implies a critical, interactive realism.

The next section clarifies what I mean by "interactive," while the remainder of the chapter describes the kind of "realism" that is meant and establishes that, while rejecting the dogmas of modernist realism, interactive realism is real realism nonetheless.

WHAT COUNTS AS DIALOGUE?

In verbal dialogue a verbal event is followed by another verbal event that falls within a range in relation to that first verbal event, such that it can contribute something new—but not wholly unpredictable or unrelated to the opinion expressed in the first event. I say "Nice weather for the time of year," and responses like "A bit too hot for me!" or "Not very good for the allotment, though," fall within the range and continue the dialogue, whereas a response like "Thucydides was Greek" does not. What determines the range is the process of development of understanding through interchange. Interchange includes both agreement—which affirms the understanding proposed, but maybe adds a new aspect—and disagreement, which forces a rethinking of the situation. What is lacking in the "Thucidydes" example is precisely this intended world: the sentence, while true, refers to an entity impossible to link to the world of weather described in the first sentence.

It is this element of intended understanding of a world that defines dialogue and makes it, in principle, a means of knowing. It is crucial to epistemological (as opposed to ontological) relativism that, though our dialogue can be said to form and shape our understanding of the world, the belief in a world there to be understood is prior to, and conditions the possibility of, meaningful dialogue. Belief in reality precedes and conditions the possibility of making sense to each other, though as we make sense to each other in dialogue, the content of that belief may change.

Most language is dialogue, but perhaps not all. We do not call it dialogue when someone commands another to do something and they do it. Yet performing the action, or failing to do so, could be called the response to the command, which could lead to a further piece of language—"Thanks for doing that," or "Why do you never do as I say?" There is a kind of dialogue between words and actions going on here, which fulfills the criteria for dialogue just stated. Conversely, not all dialogue is linguistic. I shall argue that actions and things can exhibit the essential features of dialogue as just described, so that we can speak of a dialogue between things, or actions, or—as just noted—between words and actions.

This analogical way of speaking of dialogue is essential if we are to base knowledge on dialogue, since not all knowledge is verbally expressed or even expressible. It is not only in discussion of religious knowledge that we need to include a notion of ineffable knowledge. Quite simple knowledge, like knowing what the color green is like, may be impossible to communicate in words, for example, to a blind person who has never seen it. Our position is that even in the cases where words are inadequate to express our knowledge, that knowledge rests on some non-verbal kind of dialogue.

It will be helpful at this point to list some of the analogical forms of dialogue upon which knowledge may be based.

1. *Dialogue between two objects.* When objects are compared, immediately they may begin to question and answer each other. Likenesses and unlikeness may emerge. They may come to be seen as different instances of the same kind of thing, as when we see a bull terrier and a cocker spaniel as different instances of the kind of thing we call a dog. Or conversely different kinds of thing may suddenly evoke similarities, as with metaphor, when the movement of a ship through the sea may suggest the likeness of the movement of a plough through the earth, suggesting the metaphor, "the ship ploughs the ocean." Elsewhere I have written of "interillumination"[12] as the process whereby two things interrogate each other and suggest likenesses and contrasts, or if you like, nonverbal agreements and disagreements. Or one thing may be deliberately constructed to interilluminate with another, as a map is constructed to interilluminate with the terrain, standing in a kind of dialogue with it, such that when we see (on an Ordnance Survey map) a square with a cross on the top we ask, where is that church with its tower in the landscape, or conversely, when we see a church, we ask "where is that on the map?" In these cases the interillumination generates a picture of the world, which was just noted as an essential requirement in dialogue. If the map and the landscape cease to answer to each other in this way, no guiding image of reality emerges: I literally do not know where to go.

   Interillumination itself has likeness and unlikeness to the notion of correspondence. There is likeness in that both concepts refer to a pairing (or what mathematicians call an "isomorphism") between elements between the interilluminating or corresponding realities, for example my mind and the world. But there is a difference in that thoughts and things both precede the correspondence that is drawn

12. Thompson, *Holy Ground*, 48, 67-75.

between them. In correspondence theory, there are already thoughts in here and facts out there and the task is to bring the thoughts into line with the facts. An interillumination, on the other hand, picks out and shows us how to divide each reality into elements. A fact is not then a pre-digested parcel of the world that my thought attaches to, but rather my thought picks out the fact and the fact picks out the thought. The interillumination between thought and world is a way of seeing or knowing the world; an "aspect" of the world is brought to light.

These notions were found to be essential concepts for epistemological *relativism* (what we know about a thing will depend on the our way of investigating and knowing it) and show why it goes hand in hand with critical *realism* (these really are ways of knowing the object). Without the intention of interaction with the world our language does not make sense. It is the experience of successful description of the world by the use of terms like "nice weather" and "too hot" in dialogue *with other people*, that enables us to identify certain experiences *of our own* as an experience of weather and heat. The mistake of correspondence theory is not in believing in a real world but in limiting this real world to something that corresponds with *my* words, omitting the part dialogue with others plays in arriving at the words that happily "correspond."

2. *Dialogue of self and object.* What surely convinces us that we are encountering a reality that is not entirely of our own making is a kind of dialogue between ourselves and the objects around us. Reality, like a person in dialogue, bears a relation to the "questions" we ask of it, without being simply predetermined by those questions; for reality is always capable of surprising us by the "answers" it gives. As I turn a cube in my hands, for example, I build up a range of expected "answers" to the "questions" my actions make. If I turn it this way, I expect to see a flat square face. If I then turn that 45 degrees in that direction, I expect to see a vertex facing me surrounded by three faces. Once I have got my range of questions and expected answers "right" so as to predict what will happen when I do this or that, then I have a grasp of what the cube is as an object over against me. I can make the cube behave in various ways, but I cannot make it behave as a tetrahedron or a sphere. It responds to my imagination and execution of possible actions in its own cubical way, not in an octahedral or spherical way. So I cannot just be imagining it or making it up as I go along; I am engaging in what I have termed "*diousia*"[13] a dialogue not of words

13. Ibid., 123–26, 133.

(*logos*) but of being (*ousia*), in which the "questions" are my actions and the "answers" are what happens in my experience as a response. And these "answers" may in turn pose further "questions" for me, or invite them from me.

Such correlation between our actions and their *objective* is, I have argued, the root of our sense of an *objective* world, and at the same time the root of our sense of our subjective selves.[14] Self and world emerge simultaneously through interaction, as the ocean landscape gives answers to the "questions" my actions with the rudder and sail pose, and offers in turn further questions, further challenges to respond in action.

Science, in essence, does to the world as a whole what I do to the cube as I turn it. The world is infinitely more complex than a cube in my hand, but the scientist expects it to respond to his actions—called "experiments"—in a manner that can ultimately be predicted. Scientists need imagination, to frame the experimental "questions" to which the world will answer in ways that reveal its ultimate symmetry and structure. They also need a disciplined perception so as to hear or see and record the answers the world is giving. There is nothing as simple here as simply finding things in the world that passively correspond with my words or ideas; both word and thing are much more interactive in the process of discovery. And just as with the map, so with the scientific search, sometimes we find the world is failing to respond to our questions and we need to relocate where we understand ourselves to be, so as to ask different questions and do different actions. It is not just that the scientist interrogates nature; sometimes (as in Kuhn's scientific revolutions) nature questions his questions.

The process of interrogative dialogue takes us beyond the world of passive facts just lying there, as it were, waiting to be discovered by our language. It hollows out the world of indicative fact, necessitating the use of all the verbal moods. (More on this in chapter 4.) It makes us ask not only, "What is this?" or "What is going on?" but "What might have happened instead?" and hence "Why is it just this that is going on rather than that?" and "What might we hope to happen instead, and how could we make it come about?" Interrogative questions, hypothetical possibilities, and even hoped for optatives enter the field alongside the actual, making what actually happens just one trajectory within the range of the possible, and so provoking the need for explanation.

14. Ibid., 123ff.

3. *Nonverbal dialogue with others.* Watch two people in conversation and you will witness the "body language" of stance, gesture, and facial expression, engaged in a reciprocal dance, sometimes mirroring, sometimes opposing, sometimes engaging and sometimes expressing disengagement. And non-visual senses like touch, smell (through the mysterious pheromones and the like), and sound (through tone of voice) likewise communicate. We seem to exist in *diousia*, creating a tacit world between us, prior to and around our explicit dialogues. This is surely not a factor to be neglected in interfaith and other dialogues.

4. *Games* represent a particular kind of nonverbal dialogue between two or more "players." Whether it is a physical game like tennis or a board game like chess, games involve one player making a "move." This move is like a question that narrows the field of options available to the other player. Whatever move the other player makes must be an "answer" responding to this move. But this response in turn represents a question to the other to which the other must respond with his own move, which represents a further "question" to the other. In this way moves serve to build up strategies, which consist in arrays of possible sequences of moves. Though constructed by the players and their moves, strategies become givens, contexts within which future moves take on significance. Strategy is perhaps the aspect of games most seriously neglected by those who emphasize the 'language game' as a basis for relativism, since though constructed, strategies have a real life of their own. Games (like many good dialogues) are typically adversarial, but also convivial in that they require both players to accept the same rules and to concede defeat when appropriate.

5. *Inner dialogue.* Thought seems to constitute an inner dialogue in which we debate with ourselves in much the same way as we do with others, putting forth ideas, confirming and criticizing them, and quite often internalizing the voice of a familiar other. Speech has been regarded, from Descartes onwards, as a bodily externalization of a previously existing mental reality, thought: "I think, therefore I am." But it seems more likely that inner thought evolves as an internalization of outward dialogue. Dialogue with others exists, therefore there is dialogue with myself. Thoughts are always dialogical thoughts, that is, thoughts about something offered for consideration and response by a recipient, even when that recipient is the self itself. Certainly, though there is no serious reason to follow Descartes in doubting that the higher animals have some kind of consciousness (for example, they express pain and pleasure in ways we can immediately recognize), in the absence of

external linguistic dialogue, we have no reason to suspect that these animals have thoughts.

6. *Intracultural dialogue.* What we call a culture could be regarded as built up, constituted, and sustained through a multiplicity of inter-acting dialogues, some of which are verbal, others sustained through cultural activities like art and sport and theatre, which consist of verbal and non-verbal dialogue and interaction. One of the many reasons we chat so much may arise from a need to sustain the culture and sub-culture from which we get much of our own sense of identity. The kinds of dialogue we sustain—whether its subject matter is art, sport, or the weather—and the subtly varying modes in which we partici-pate, reveals the culture or subculture to which we belong, whether it is English or French, working or middle class, Christian or Buddhist, white or black . . . .

     Dialogues are dual or multiple partner exchanges proceeding ac-cording to tacitly agreed rules. In this they are like games based on language. However, when theologians and philosophers use the notion of a language game to suggest that our dialogue actually creates its own world, Christian or Buddhist, English or French—a world that thoroughly envelops us—they are failing to develop the analogy ap-propriately. Most of us engage in a variety of literal games, and it is the same with language games. The dialogue we sustain at church will be different, using different terms and following different rules, and often different non-verbal aspects, from that which we sustain in the pub or at home with the family. But this does not mean that I myself am more than one person, or that I inhabit a different "world" in the pub from that which I inhabit at church. There is perhaps a metaphori-cal sense in which that is true, but the dialogues and the selves and worlds that flow from them interact and transform one another. There is no worldview mystically attached to a culture or a language game; the worldviews are generated much more piecemeal in the dialogue between those within the culture, between people's inner dialogue and these outer dialogues, and between people from different cultures too. So while a culture is a powerful influence on all of us, it is not a condi-tioning or wholly defining one.

7. *Intercultural dialogue.* In that sense interfaith and intercultural dia-logues are far from being special cases. We already engage in a variety of linguistic and other dialogue games, yet manage to retain a sense of being one person in one world. When people from different cultures engage in dialogue, arguably the mutual adjustments and challenges

that need to take place do not need to be wholly different in kind. Intercultural dialogue is something we have already engaged in when we step from the church to the pub or the home, and enter the different kinds of dialogue that sustain those different cultural worlds. In postmodern, multicultural society, of course, meeting and dialogue across cultures becomes the rule rather than the exception. Hence, if they wish to retain the strong control they once had, religions and cultures sometimes resort to moral blackmail and even physical terror.

8. Hence such dialogues can become *inner intercultural or interreligious dialogues* in which two or more faiths interrogate and transform the thought of an individual. The limit of the interreligious case, where the two or more faiths are equally strongly represented, is dual or multiple religious belonging. As with any other dialogue, such dual belonging will need to be sustained by a third term, the reality each faith is striving to express or to which it is seeking to draw the individual's allegiance. But it will not be necessary for the individual to have some language to describe this reality independently of the religions involved. (If she does have such a language, it really represents a third, dominant dialogue partner in her soul.)

The question we now need to face is whether these many kinds of dialogue, between them, suffice to create realism. Could it be that reality is not something grasped by the solitary subject, as in much of modern philosophy from Descartes onward, but constructed/discovered in the dialogical triad of self, other, and intended world.

DIALOGUE AND CRITICAL REALISM

> I propose a form of critical realism. This is a way of describing the process of "knowing" that acknowledges the reality of the thing known, as something other than the knower (hence "realism"), while fully acknowledging that the only access we have to this reality lies along the spiralling path of appropriate dialogue or conversation between the knower and the thing known (hence "critical").[15]

So the Bishop of Durham—biblical scholar and theologian—expresses the core paradox of critical realism, combining as it does realism regarding the existence of realities outside language, with a critical regard for the "spiralling" complexities of dialogue involved in coming to know this reality.

15. Wright, *New Testament*, 35.

"Critical realism" is a widely used term denoting various distinct but related developments. The American epistemological critical realism pioneered by Wilfred Sellars[16] is perhaps the least relevant to our purposes as it remains fundamentally immersed in correspondence theory. Developments in the philosophy of science, associated with Roy Bhaskar,[17] Rom Harré,[18] and others, are much more to the point, arguing as they do that science, including the human sciences, engage with real generative mechanisms in the world, but these generative mechanisms need to be picked out by suitable models which will vary according to the reality of the object, those in the social sciences for example needing to be very different from those involved in say subatomic physics. Meanwhile theologian Bernard Lonergan has developed a theological method that began, like science, with empirical data and rational reflection, leading to insight, but proceeded further toward the point of conversion defined as "being in love in an unrestricted manner," which is for him the basis of all theology.[19]

Critical realism as realism, affirms that reality transcends language, but as critical, it allows reality to have different "aspects" or "perspectives" which different language use and different conceptual systems can pick out. Use is often made of Wittgenstein's famous shape,[20] which can be "seen as" a duck or as a rabbit depending on how we describe it. As critical, critical realism allows for the fact that our perceptions of reality are always already shaped by language and concept, but as realism, it does not allow the language and concepts we first bring to bear—or any particular "language game"—to have the last word on how reality is, but demands an ongoing process of dialogue in which we explore the other's ways of "seeing as," and build up a rich concept of reality in its many aspects.

The aspect or perspective analogy is significant. Perspective is something I can change. I can move my body in order to see the object from a different aspect. I can, so to speak, move my mind—through the use of empathy and imagination—to see the object as something different, as when I move from seeing the diagram as a duck to seeing it as a rabbit. This sometimes happens as a response to my will and sometimes the change just happens. Critical realism and epistemological relativism hold that the differences between different peoples' ways of seeing through different conceptual systems, including different religions, are not in principle greater

16. Sellars, *Empiricism and Philosophy of Mind*.
17. Bhaskar, *Realist Theory of Science* and *Possibility of Naturalism*.
18. Harré, *Principles of Scientific Thinking*.
19. Lonergan, *Method in Theology*, 106, 116, 242–43.
20. Wittgenstein, *Philosophical Investigations*, 2.6.

than differences I can make to my own ways of seeing. As noted above, it is a test of the validity of a belief in a conceptual system that others who do not share that system might be able to come to see how it is true. It is a test that you really can see x as a y that others may be able to see x as a y too, even though in their system it is a z. It is this fundamental tenet that distinguishes critical realism and epistemological relativism from the kinds of relativism that are anti-realist. It is what makes critical realism demand dialogue in the search for truth, while for other forms of relativism truth can only be found exclusively within a system.

But by the same token the notions of aspects and "seeing as" also move us beyond the kind of realism that is based on a correspondence between my concepts and reality itself. We allow for an interillumination in which my concepts throw into relief aspects that are "really there" in the object, but not as discrete already-existing segments of reality to which my descriptions merely correspond. Other language may divide up and throw into relief different aspects that are also "really there" and which I may learn to discern and interact with also. Thus, as well as picking out aspects of reality, interillumination allows the process to work the other way, from reality to language. Reality itself may impact on my language positively, by enabling me to know what I mean and perhaps what the other means. But reality may also make itself felt negatively, by throwing my descriptions into confusion and enabling me to realize that I am simply not (to use a momentously significant phrase to which we shall return) *doing justice* to how things really are. And this, as much as the positive process of interillumination, is also a process in which the other can help me.

I have described dialogue as involving a trinity of factors: the self and the other who are communicating, and that which is other to us both, the putative world we are engaged with. But in positing three elements that are already clear and distinct, this way of putting it is an oversimplification. In reality the "world" only emerges—for us at least—out of the interillumination between our understandings generated by the dialogue. This interillumination appears to be direct and immediate, and not simply a matter of working out the different correspondences the other is making between his private experience and the world we share. French philosopher, Merleau-Ponty explains this with reference to two onlookers regarding a landscape:

> Paul's finger, which is pointing out the Church tower, is not a finger-for-me that I think of as orientated towards a Church-tower-for-me, it is Paul's finger which itself shows me the tower that Paul sees, just as, conversely, when I make a movement toward some point in the landscape that I can see, I do not imagine

> that I am producing in Paul, in virtue of some pre-established harmony, inner visions that are merely analogous to mine. . . . In reality the other is not enclosed in my perspective of the world . . . [rather, my perspective] slides spontaneously into that of the other, and they are gathered up together in a single world in which we all participate.[21]

Merleau-Ponty speaks here of a "mutual inclusion" of my perspective and the other's, co-discovering our shared world. The other's perspective is fulfilled in mine and mine in the other's, and together we share in being. At the end of chapter 1 I suggested that interfaith dialogue involves essentially the same mutual inclusion, writ large. It is not clear whether the common world pre-exists the dialogue through which we *discover* it, or whether it is *constructed* out of it; both are in some sense true. For there is in dialogue what the Buddhists beautifully call an "interdependent co-arising" between self, other, and world. (The next chapter will relate this trinity to the theological Christian Trinity.)

But, it will be questioned, is this the basis of a tenable realism, or does it fall far short of that solid and secure "reality" modernism always hoped to engage with?

IS THIS REALLY REALISM?

In modernity, broadly speaking, commitment to realism has been sustained by three pairs of beliefs:

1. *Skepticism and foundationalism.* From Descartes onwards, a methodology of doubt has been applied so as to extract what is indubitable. These non-doubtable truths become the foundations on which to build sure and certain truth. Skepticism and foundationalism thus belong together. The root analogy is that of demolishing an old rickety building, digging down to firm rock that will not shift, and then building up from there.

2. *Deductivism and methodology.* If we are to build up, not only must the foundations be sure, but also the building materials and methods. Hence modernism focuses on epistemology and methodology, to supply a sure means of building on sure foundations. Knowledge is implicitly or explicitly equated with provability and certainty, arrived at through universally accepted methods of rational proof.

21. Merleau-Ponty, *Phenomenology of Perception*, 405–6.

3. *Correspondence theory and epistemological dualism.* Knowledge is held to consist in an exact correspondence between our statements, or beliefs, or what we hold to be true, and what is factually the case in the world. Descartes was famously dualistic, believing in mind as a non-extended substance existing in parallel with the spatially extended substances that make up the material world. Such metaphysical dualism has often been held in modernity but also widely challenged, but epistemological dualism seems to lie behind the correspondence theory, since it posits that knowledge consists in an exact mirroring between two worlds, a mental or linguistic world of beliefs, thoughts, and statements that may or may not correspond with the material world of things and facts.

Within the modern period debate raged between the empiricists, who emphasized pillar 3, ensuring we build on foundations (sense-data) that correspond with realities out there in the world, and the rationalists, who emphasized pillar 2, the power of reason to deduce new truths on the sure foundation of the old. In terms of pillar 1, empiricists were skeptical about reason and foundational about sense-data, while rationalists were the reverse. What empiricists and rationalists had in common, however, was their optimistic "modern" assumption that it was possible to bring about a good fit between our words and concepts and how the world was. They were also broadly agreed that science and mathematics offered the best examples of how to achieve this good fit.

In postmodern times these three pillars have been challenged, but rarely all at once. In what could be called *deconstructivism* (or nihilism) modern skepticism fails to find the indubitable foundations it sought, and eats up belief in method and a world corresponding to our ideas. In *neo-traditionalism*—manifest theologically in Radical Orthodoxy and postliberalism—the same despair of rationally indubitable foundations leads to an assertion of the need for faith in certain traditionally affirmed foundations, which can then be used to deduce the rest of what is felt to be true: so the modern faith in deductive method remains. In *relativism* the belief that there is a uniquely valid set of foundations is abandoned, and a plurality of possible worldviews is accepted. But ontological relativism (as described in the previous chapter) arises when mind-world or language-world correspondence theory is retained, so that there has to be a "world" corresponding to each language game or conceptual system.

A dialogical reason, on the other hand, Samson-like, destroys all three pillars. (For the analogy to work we need to imagine a somewhat Hindu, three-armed Samson!) It thereby, arguably, effects a more complete transit from modernism than the aforementioned forms of postmodernism. But does this demolition process bring realism itself crashing down upon our heads? It would seem so.

1. *Uncertainty.* Pillar 1—indubitable foundations—is destroyed. I have denied that we can often, if ever, be absolutely certain of anything. The possibility that dialogue may undermine what seemed sure and certain always remains. If there are no facts—nothing that can be said with irrefutable certainty—in what sense can realism be retained?

2. *Provisionality.* Pillar 2 is gone. I have argued that there is neither a sure and certain ontology, from which a sure epistemological method could be deduced, nor a secure epistemological method, from which we can deduce in advance what realities can be known. We have to start from the middle, from interaction itself, and build our knowledge and ontology out from there. But does this not leave us bereft *both* of anything we could call reality, and of any way to knowledge of reality?

3. *Non-correspondence.* Pillar 3—correspondence theory and dualism—has been destroyed. I have argued that words and ideas never refer in isolation to items or facts "out there." Our ideas are physically embodied, and physical reality is mind-informed; we can never disentangle this circle into a linear set of correspondences between word and world. What does realism mean if not correspondence between our affirmations or our ideas and reality?

Let us deal with these issues in turn, to see if an interactive realism without the three pillars is possible.

1. Realism implies Uncertainty plus reasonable Trust

I suggest that realism and certainty vary in inverse, not direct proportion. The more we believe our thoughts and language relate to something beyond them, the more we will affirm the possibility that they may be inappropriate or inadequate to that reality. In a closed system like arithmetic or a game perhaps we can be absolutely sure that we have got the right answer or made a legitimate move, so long as we are sure we have followed the rules. We can make mistakes, but if we are very careful we can be sure we have got it right. That is why the view of language as a kind of game is so attractive to the neo-traditionalists who wish to reaffirm old certainties.

Even in a reasonably complex game like chess, however, we may never be able to calculate whether we have made the best possible move; we can only find out if we have made a reasonably good move by continuing with the game. And if language is seen as a way of engaging us with real possibilities and actualities "in the world," the whole business of getting it right becomes much more complex. Most significantly it no longer depends just on us as individuals or a society following the right procedures. There is something we rather inadequately call "out there" or "other than language" which our words may do justice to, or fail to, and this business of doing justice is a more complex matter to assess than procedural correctness, such that we can never be quite sure we have got it all right. It is rather akin to those other (we shall see, related) matters of "doing justice," which are similarly intractable, and which our postmodern societies typically try to replace with the easier concerns over correct procedure.

Very often the religions (notably the Christian faith) speak not of certain knowledge, but of faith and hope, concepts that imply a degree of uncertainty. Certainty (or sureness) in such religions is replaced by a notion of "assurance," a degree of reliability in our words and beliefs that is good enough to base our lives upon. Reliability is a matter of trustworthiness; we rely on a set of concepts because the tradition from which they arise has proven trustworthy and not let us down or misdirected us. Sometimes we are led to trust people because we trust the tradition they represent, and sometimes the reverse is the case. Trust is a complex matter; it does not have to be blind, or irrational, but can be strengthened by criticism. But it is not built from foundations upwards, but rather by benign circles. When a belief turns out to be a correct guide to experience it strengthens the trust we place both in the belief and those who share it, and that encourages us to trust other things they (or their traditions) say. Trust is essential for dialogue to be possible, but dialogue also strengthens trust: when dialogue is ruled out by appeals to blind, authoritarian obedience, trust can be undermined, so that further dialogue becomes less and less possible.

Trust leads towards the "orientational pluralism" of philosopher Nicholas Rescher, which strikes a middle course between the notion that philosophy can gradually work out, through rational enquiry, what the truth is concerning the classic issues of the ultimate nature of reality, mind, matter, the existence of God, and so forth, and a sheer pluralism for which such issues are not just non-resolved so far but irresolvable, so that all views concerning the ultimate questions are equally valid (and equally invalid). Rescher argues that possible views are not completely random, but that once we have opted for certain fundamental "epistemic values" certain views follow, to the exclusion of others.[22] In other words, views come in clusters;

22. Rescher, *Strife of Systems*.

we choose the cluster, but that choice constrains further choice. It is rather like choosing a strategy in a game. Once we have opted for materialism, for example, belief in a substantial soul or a real God without "body, parts or passions" is ruled out. There are no indubitable foundations, but once we have opted for one fundamental understanding of the basis of knowledge, some things do genuinely follow to the exclusion of others. I would want to add the point that our "epistemic values" generally represent mutually reinforcing clusters of belief we have learnt to trust, usually because they tend to be held within a tradition of shared belief in which we trust.

Rescher argues that there is no way of determining—objectively and without an already existing bias—which belief cluster or tradition is true. But once we have made our choice, for example between Christianity and Buddhism, many other issues—in this case, the eternal existence of some realities including the soul, the existence of a Creator—and the value of some practices—for example, performing actions to make merit, and receiving Holy Communion—follow. Theologian Mark Heim argues that the Christian therefore cannot be certain that Christianity is right, but having made the Christian choice, for him, as a Christian, God and the soul exist, and receiving Holy Communion is his duty and joy.

> Orientational pluralism insists there is only one reality and we are trying to know it. It is not committed to regarding other substantive views as equally valid, only as tenable from different perspectives. What is fragmented is not truth but justification or warrantable certainty.[23]

In this connection, we note, it is better to speak of trustworthiness rather than certainty. It is not the case that first I choose the Christian tradition, and then I mysteriously become certain about God, the soul, and Holy Communion; rather that in committing myself to Christianity I place my reasonable trust in their reality. If the trust is reasonable, what is trusted must be reasonably sure to be real, though *this* (Christian) form of trust may not be the only way to relate to the trusted reality. Orientational pluralism squares well with epistemological constructivism, which allows for different ways of knowing (epistemic values or choices), and different ways of arriving at assurance and trust, without this implying a total relativism or pluralism regarding what is actually true.

It also suggests that the societies that relate best to reality will be those based on a reasonable trust; societies within which different traditions do one another justice as possible alternative ways to truth, in a manner that

23. Heim, *Salvations*, 137.

does not render them beyond dialogue and questioning. For this to happen there has to be the right amount of doubt, treading a middle way between, on the one hand, a totalitarian society in which a single tradition or party claims indubitable trustworthiness to the exclusion of all others; and a wholly skeptical society on the other, in which because no tradition is immune from questioning, trust in all traditions is undermined, and nobody can claim respect.

The Special Case of Dual Belonging

Now there is something that Rescher and Heim rule out, and I do not: namely the possibility of choosing to let the question of which tradition to trust remain unresolved. Could we decide that since both Buddhism and Christianity are self-consistent, and consistent with our experience, the reasonable thing is not simply to choose one belief system and "lose the truth" expressed in the other, but to retain both perspectives and refuse to choose between them. At first sight this might seem—as Heim argues—to result in confusion, both on a conceptual level and in our practice. God would for us both exist and not exist; we would seek to make merit, and refrain from doing so because we are justified by faith not works—and so forth.

But if what Rescher and Heim are arguing is true, the situation for this Buddhist-Christian dual belonger is actually more subtle, for two reasons. Firstly, he is making a choice to maximize the truths he can acknowledge at the expense of the coherence of their expression. If the situation is—as this book contests—that there is a trade-off between comprehensiveness regarding truth on the one hand and consistency and clarity of expression on the other, and (following Gödel) no one system is both completely comprehensive and confusion-free, then such a choice is not necessarily more irrational than the choice of the single-faith believer to choose the clarity and consistency of having one belief system at the expense of entertaining the truths another belief system might express.

And secondly, of course, our faith commitment is not, in any case, a simple matter of "choosing what to believe." What the dual belonger is refusing to choose between are not individual beliefs and practices, but two conceptual systems and ways of life. For the Buddhist Christian *as Christian* there definitely is a God whom he relies on by faith for salvation; for him *as Buddhist* there is no God (at least in the conventional sense of creator) and he has only his own effort to rely on in the pathway to nirvana. His Buddhism and his Christianity are both total perspectives, and he lives not by commitment to parts of one and parts of the other but commitment to the dialogue of perspectives between the two. Moreover, this is a dialogue from which new clusters of co-believable propositions and co-practical practices emerge. There is no reason to believe that the only possible co-believable and co-practicable clusters are those which the traditions have long ago identified. There may be new strategies for faith that develop traditional Christian and Buddhist strategies into a new strategy. Indeed, it is in this way that new forms of religion and philosophy have developed in the past: Sikhism, for example, from a reclustering of traditional Hindu and Muslim beliefs and practices; Zen and Ch'an Buddhism from a reclustering of Taoist and Mahayana Buddhist ones; arguably orthodox Christianity itself from reclustering of Jewish and neo-Platonic ones.

It may be in precisely this kind of development that the true aim of philosophy and theology lie: creating new alliances of ideas previously seen as inevitably committed to old forms of strife, rather than, on the one hand, developing some grand new synthesis that holds all the truth, and, on the other, scribbling tedious fragments of analysis and clarification. Dual belonging, as well as less even-handed mixes of traditional commitments, involve living with uncertainty, but not (as is sometimes claimed) the absence of commitment, or a random eclecticism; on the contrary, the uncertainty is countenanced as a means of apprehending truth more fully.

As Heim cogently argues, operational pluralism enables us fully to affirm a commitment to our own religion or worldview as—in our understanding—preferable to the others, while doing justice to the claims of those who find other views preferable. It allows for assurance in faith without pretending to more dogmatic certainty than is possible. It offers notions of what constitutes doing justice to the other, and what gives grounds for assurance, such that though we can never be completely certain, we can distinguish what we are justified in believing from what is, in terms of our belief system, completely mistaken.

This understanding of belief offers a *provisional* realism in the sense that our epistemic choices can be called into question by those who have made other choices. Conversion to another religion or framework becomes possible as a reasonable process of shift in trust, rather than a random groundless choice. But in the absence of convincing reasons of this kind to the contrary, it remains reasonable to stick with the assurances we have. And this kind of realism does not consist in asserting an exclusive one-to-one *correspondence* between our ideas and how things really are. The next two sections will explore these two connected points further.

2. Prophetic Realism

Our approach takes us beyond the merely subjective to the intersubjective; but the reader may be asking, can that move take us to the objective? Can we really move from "how it seems to you and me" to "how it really is"? Relativism does after all entitle us to move from how it seems to *me* to how it seems to *us*, defined as those who share my point of view or culture. With those in my culture or language game I am able to construct ways of understanding my experience that are not purely private, but shared within that culture. Within a language game I check how it seems to me against how it seems to you—and especially with how it seems to those bodies and texts that in my religious culture are given authority—so that sheer delusions of mine can be challenged and overcome. But relativism crucially denies all access to reality beyond our language games. When in doubt, it argues, ask the authorities. It does not allow us to ask of a whole culture or religion, or the authorities in charge of these, "How far does the way you see the world contain illusion and ideology, and how far does it do justice to reality and to people?"

But this chapter argues to the contrary, that this question *can* be asked. For dialogue is not only something that takes place between people within a given culture, *but also* something that works within people, and between cultures. Because intra-personal dialogue is possible, sometimes an individual comes to find dissonances between his culture's description and how it seems to him; dissent is a significant possibility. Of course, what distinguishes the prophetic dissenter from the insane person (with which his culture may well confuse him; the Old Testament prophets often seemed mad) is that the latter simply plays his own idiosyncratic language game, whereas the prophet's insights generate a new language game others may come to share, and so test those insights against their own experience. And because intercultural and interreligious dialogue is possible, the corporate delusions of a given culture may come to be challenged, while the insights of that culture may receive affirmation as something the other culture needs to learn.

Interfaith theologian Raimundo Panikkar emphasizes a

> universal principle regarding words and sentences. The moment that words say only exactly what you mean and do not leave room for what I may also mean, the moment that they become only signs and cease to be symbols, the moment that they only signal something else and are no longer the expression, the manifestation and with it the veil itself of that "else," in that moment they degenerate even as words. They become mere tools for transmission of coded messages, open only to those

who previously possess the clue. Words may then very easily become means of oppression, tools of power in the mouths or hands of those who dictate their meaning or know the key to decipher the signs.[24]

Within a given culture or language game, therefore, it can become easy to talk nonsense, and literally not know what you are talking about. Theologians of different religions, scientists, football fans, and the like readily develop their own jargon, which means nothing to an outsider. It is when people of different religions, or scientists and religious adherents, or even these and football fans, come together that they have to explain what they mean in the other's non-jargon terms. In the process they may understand afresh what they are talking about, or realize they have really been talking about nothing at all.

On this understanding, objective truth is prophetic, both in the sense of foretelling future hopes and (thereby) challenging present assumptions. Truth means that which would be comprehended by a consensus of all subjectivities. Or else it can be framed as a divine hope: all subjectivities may be thought of as converging in the mind of God, who eternally and immediately experiences all things as they really are; in which case, to put a Berkleyan thought in Kantian terms, God's mental phenomena are the noumena. In that case our strivings for objective truth are strivings for divine insight. More on this in the next chapter. But if what I have said is true, that insight is sparked by interillumination between *different* human minds. And that means we have to rest content with provisionality: the fact that what we believe contains partial insight and partial delusion, a state of affairs we can gradually improve on both through deeper inner dialogue and through dialogue with those who see the world in a radically different way.

Of course, modernism saw objective truth likewise, as a future hope and, for idealists like Berkeley, as that which is experienced only by the divine Mind. Where modernism differed was in having a master plan of how to get to that future state of knowing, a plan that was largely negative, involving the stripping away of all that was not measurable, leaving a world stripped of those secondary qualities that give life its meaning and joy. Our provisional realism has no such master plan. We cannot discern in advance the process that leads forward from our state of partial truth and partial delusion. There may well be things we regard as precious insights and rich experiences that prove to be rooted in a self deception that will not stand the test of dialogue. And this may be true, even if the religion I adhere to affirms those insights. But the converse is equally possible. Things that have

24. Panikkar, *Trinity and Religious Experience*, ix.

given meaning to my life may be such that will stand the test of dialogue, both inner and outer, and proceed to enlighten others whose perspective is very different from my own.

3. Reality without Correspondence

There is a Zen Koan that describes the experience of meditation:

> At first, the mountains are mountains and the rivers are rivers.
> Then the mountains are not mountains and the rivers are not rivers.
> Then finally the mountains are mountains and the rivers are rivers.

So far as I can remember, we begin life as naive realists, believing that the real world corresponds exactly with our perceptions. The world "out there" actually contains purple-headed mountains and brown rivers running between green banks under a blue sky studded with white clouds, just as these things appear to us. As we grow up, and as society grows up through its ancient and pre-modern periods, philosophers and scientists sow doubts. The blueness of the sky is an illusion caused by the way air molecules split light into different wavelengths, but actual air consists of nitrogen, oxygen, and other molecules that have no color at all. In the modern period philosophers, notably John Locke, began to distinguish between "primary" qualities like quantity, mass, size, shape, and motion, which science describes physical bodies as actually having, from secondary qualities like color, sound, smell, taste, and texture, which "correspond" with nothing real in things themselves, having to do only with the way things impact on our bodies and transmit impulses to our brains.[25] Modernism thus endeavored to establish what—as previously noted—philosopher Thomas Nagel called a "view from nowhere," a view of reality that does not vary according to the point of view or position of the observer, or require human consciousness to register So far all well and good for the correspondence theory: some words correspond with primary qualities—real things out there—while others correspond only with secondary qualities—things in our minds, or our brains.

However, science has progressively narrowed the range of what might be called primary. With relativity, time and space, and with quantum physics, mass and motion, turn out to be secondary constructs, products of our perception. How things really are—as described in the equations of quantum physics and more recent theories like string theory—corresponds with nothing we could describe or imagine. Some scientists have even advanced

25. Locke, *Human Understanding*, ch. 8.

"biocentrism":[26] the view that the "real world" exists only as information in biological systems, such as our brains. Mountains are not really mountains, and rivers are not rivers; both are merely brain events, or for the more idealistically minded (who might note here that the idea of a "brain" contains a residue of objective physicality) happenings in our mind or consciousness. Mind-world correspondence disappears because the world is "all in the mind."

Meanwhile, with his "critical" philosophy Immanuel Kant argued that all we observe, all that we take for the "real" world, and all that science can discover, is phenomenal reality: mental events structured by concepts of space, time, and causality. But he held on to the idea of the noumenon, or "thing in itself": things in their own intrinsic nature, which could never be captured by science or known as the object of experience. In a sense the noumenal represents a last fortress refuge for the primary characteristics, once all experience and all science is assigned to the secondary. The noumenal is now only accessible through rational argument, since all that we seemed to experience directly is secondary, phenomenal. The question that naturally poses itself is whether we cannot apply Occam's Razor to this noumenal realm that is theoretically so solid and in practice so ethereal and elusive, and place our confidence in the phenomenal world we all know.

What critical realism does is to restore faith in our power to experience the world as it is. If, as just suggested, the noumenal is allowed to vanish completely, the phenomenal world of secondary characteristics is rehabilitated. A kind of correspondence—and hence a kind of realism—returns, which is no longer a simple dualistic mind-world correspondence. It is now the correspondence between minds, and between events within minds, that secures realism. We ask no longer "what out there might correspond to this in my mind," but "what can I communicate, what in my subjective mind can be meaningfully shared, in verbal and non-verbal dialogue?' "What, when I shift perspective—whether simply through moving in relation to the object, or through talking to you and experiencing another perspective—endures or proves regular in its changes?" The real is not something I create through my thought, or which we corporately create through our dialogue; it is a kind of ideal point of convergence in our perspectives which we posit as waiting to be discovered, whether or not in fact we discover it. In that sense it resembles Kant's noumenon, which cannot itself be known but has to be believed for phenomena to be knowable. The real is that which we cannot experience directly apart from our perspectives, but which we have to believe in as beyond our perspectives in order to make dialogue between us in

26 Berman and Lanza, *Biocentrism*.

our different perspectives possible and meaningful. But the test of whether we have discovered this noumenon is whether we can both identify it as figuring for both of us in our different perspectives.

In this perspective a certain realism returns. Mountains are mountains again and rivers rivers, provided only that our talk and thought about these things can proceed in a meaningful way. The secondary characteristics return, in the manner Jacques Deleuze[27] and Don Cupitt[28] in their different ways have celebrated. For the characteristics we share or discover through our dialogue can be said to belong to them. Typically, you may notice a shadow of a particular purplish hue, or (like Polonius in *Hamlet*) a pattern in the clouds like a camel; and though I did not see it before, I may be able to grasp that it is truly there; or I may not, and may need to question my dialogue partner further. So the reality of the mountain unfolds through dialogue, such that we need not make an arbitrary distinction between what we know as "primary" or as quantity through measurement and what we know as "secondary" or as quality through contemplation of the immeasurable. The qualities we come to agree on from our disparate points of view—not only the brownness and the purple shadow, but things like awesomeness and beauty—can be affirmed once again as qualities there in the mountain, rather than springing just from you or me.

Consider awesomeness, for example. If I have a feeling that the mountain is awesome, that is a fact about me and my feelings; it does not necessarily say anything about the mountain. If after inner dialogue and reflection on my experience I identify things about the mountain that make it awesome, then there is a little more reason to say the mountain itself is awesome, but this is not conclusive. If all people in my culture agree the mountain is awesome then again there may be something about mountains my culture has keyed into; but it may be just a social convention, as when we refer to the countryside as idyllic, or lambs as cute. It is when people of vastly different cultures also describe this kind of mountain as awesome, that we have most reason to believe that in some sense the mountain really is so. (Needless to say, the "modern" standards of objectivity make no sense in this context; no amount of mountain measurement would establish whether a given mountain is objectively awesome.)

A crude formula for the objectivity or "really thereness" of a quality might be *consensus* x *diversity*: the degree of agreement among different people that the quality is there, multiplied by the degree to which their cultural perspectives differ. Here it is the correspondence between diverse

27. Deleuze, *The Fold*.
28. Cupitt, *Theology's Strange Return*.

perspectives that secures the likelihood that something "real" is at work constraining or surprising our perspectives. The big difference from old "mind-world" or "language-world" correspondence is that there is no ideal language in which the "real" out there can be perfectly formulated and tested for correspondence with what our crude actual languages describe. There is nothing describable outside languages, no real that can be felt except as an ideal constraint on our description, or to use an opposite but equally valid metaphor, an opening out of our always particular, always embodied, languages. That takes us back to our second issue, concerning the provisionality of our realism: the way in which realism in our descriptions means always being open to improvement and amendment through interaction with other descriptions and perspectives.

The goal to which we move does not have to be preconceived as a "view from nowhere," a barren world of mere quantity, mass, and motion, stripped of subjective resonance. It will rather be a "view from everywhere," a world of full intersubjective affirmation, a world characterized by fuller and richer subjective consciousness, about which I can only know that I have some insight now, but what insight I cannot yet know, as it is far larger and richer than anything I can now be aware of.

CONCLUSION

Of course that "view from everywhere" sounds rather like what some faiths call God, and others nirvana. That introduces the more theological questions of the next chapter, which considers the way all dialogue is implicitly a movement towards God, or the transcendent. Then chapter 4 will explore the converse point, that all theology is implicitly or explicitly a dialogue moving towards doxology; so that critical realism finds fulfillment in the return of religion and its notion of the transcendent.

This chapter began by criticizing two forms of relativism and establishing a valid kind of relativism, which I called epistemological constructivism. It is this kind of relativism, we saw, that relates to what is generally called incommensurability, and shows that the latter need not be an insuperable wall to dialogue. We went on to discuss various kinds of dialogue—between people, between objects, within people, and so forth—all of which both presuppose and further our engagement with reality. We argued that interaction and interillumination between dialogue partners forms the basis of a critical realism. (The "epistemological" element of epistemological constructivism gives us the "realism" of critical realism, while the "constructivism" implies the "critical" element.) Such a dialogical account takes us beyond the dogmas of modernist realism and its postmodern deformations, to offer the irenic possibility of an undogmatic, non-dualistic, and provisional realism. The next two chapters will show how such a realism is not only compatible with Christian theology, but grows from that theology's deepest roots in its demand that we do justice and worship God.

CHAPTER 3

Original Dialogue:
Trinity and Creation

THIS CHAPTER MOVES FROM the philosophical account of knowledge as dialogue, set out in the previous chapter, to see if it actually applies to theology. For however plausible our account may seem, it will be useless for the purposes of this book if it cannot shed light on or be squared with the authentic development of theology. After all, many postmodern theologians claim that theology rests on a faith, or a kind of knowledge, that has nothing in common with ordinary rationality, such that to ask theology to be rational at all is to subject it to a tyrannical monster called "secular reason."[1] This chapter will contend that theological knowledge always has arisen from some kind of dialogue, and ought to arise from dialogue if it is to be true to itself. And in particular it involves a dialogue between theology and philosophy. Combining as it does what might be called philosophical exegesis with theological epistemology, this chapter forms a bridge between the earlier philosophical and later theological parts of this book.

This chapter opens with an imaginative exegesis of the first creation story in Genesis. The second section develops this into an Trinitarian model of creation as arising from a kind of primordial Word and response. The following section unites these reflections with the suggestions of the previous chapter, developing a philosophical theology of God as mind and therefore Trinitarian dialogue. To broaden this and relate it more explicitly to interfaith dialogue, there follows an account of the Trinitarian theology of Raimundo Panikkar. The final section draws together the diverse threads. So three distinct theological approaches—biblical, systematic, and philosophical—converge to offer a strong affirmation of dialogue as central to God and to the doing of theology.

1. Milbank, *Theology and Social Theory.*

56

Chapter 4 will develop this normative account of theology into a descriptive reading of the development of theology through intrafaith dialogue. That chapter will then consider three possible criticisms of this account, so as to establish that it offers a real and positive alternative to exclusivism, inclusivism, and pluralism. Chapter 5 will develop a positive account of interreligious dialogue, and theology as dialogue, that might work in practice.

CREATION AS ORIGINAL DIALOGUE

The Bible begins (Gen 1:1—2:3) with the first of two narratives of the creation of the world. This story involves a week of seven days, each of which *approximately* repeats the same pattern. God issues a word of command, followed by a response in which the relevant part of creation appears or comes into being. This is then often followed by an act of separation and naming, and usually by an act of contemplation by God of his creation, seeing that it is good. We witness a repeated pattern: word → response of being → struggle, discernment, and naming → contemplative response of God. The pattern is like what is involved in dialogue: it is as if God *thinks the world into being* by an internal dialogue that passes through a period of work, struggle, and differentiation, but culminates in contemplative love on God's part. The simplicity of immediate response is followed by a period in which the simple intimacy of word and the other's response is complicated by the demands of that which is other to these others, but then again brought to rest in an encompassing affirmation.

However, as in any dialogue, there is no mere simple repetition, but variation. There are subtle differences between the events of each "day." Let us look more closely at the passage, ideally with a Bible near at hand.

Chapter 1 verses 1–2. We could call this Day 0, before the act of creation, prior to time as something measurable by "days" at all. There is a threefoldness prior to the existence of the universe: God, the "formless void," and the *ruach*-wind-spirit of God sweeping over what is now called "the face of the waters." It seems best not to interpret this "face" as a fourth reality, but rather as what the void or nothingness out of which God is to create becomes when the breath of God ruffles it. Sheer nothingness acquires a face when caressed by the active energy of God, and becomes "waters"—though this is not the created water we hear of later, but a water prior to creation and prior to the advent of light; something akin, perhaps, to the *chora*—the empty space or womb in which things have the potential to form—of Plato, which Heidegger and Derrida have revived in our awareness. The image that comes to mind is of an infinite sea that is neither lit nor shadowy, troubled by the wind, yet reflecting obscurely the face of God, the face of the wind. The abyss as it were becomes personal.

Verses 3–5. This is Day 1, the first day of creation. The command and response is clear and immediate. Uniquely, the contemplative response "that the light was good" follows straight away, before the separation from darkness. And uniquely again, this affirmative response applies only to the light and not to the darkness from which it is separated. In the creation story, light is the one thing God seems to prefer to its opposite, and there is perhaps something about light that makes it an appropriate image for truth, goodness, honesty, and even (notably in the Johannine writings) God. Darkness has come to denote untruth, concealment, sin; though there is also an apophatic tradition that sees God in terms of darkness, deriving perhaps from the preceding verse regarding "Day 0."

Verses 6–8. The making of the "firmament" and the sea on Day 2. At the time these verses were composed the "firmament" was a solid sky dome that separated two bodies of water—the terrestrial seas from the seas believed to be above the sky. Here, by contrast with the creation of light, the creation follows the word of command, not as an obedient response, but by God's own work of separation and naming. And there is no contemplative ascription of good. (Hebrew thought tended to poise the inhabitable world precariously between the threatening, chaotic, watery realms above and below; that may be why they are not seen as obedient or called "good.")

Verses 9–13. Here again, on Day 3—in both the gathering of the waters and the growth of plants—there is command and response, followed in the first case by separation and naming, and in both cases by the ascription of good. Land and sea, and all kinds of plants, are good.

Verses 14–19. The same pattern applies to the creation of the cosmic order: word of command followed by response, then separation and naming, and declaration of good. Only now with the sun and the moon—which create a second separation of light from darkness—can we make sense of the separation of time into days that has prevailed throughout that chapter. Of course, we moderns find it strange that the seas and the plants are created before the sun, on which we know they depend, though the animals are created after it as we would expect. And the notion of divinely ordained days before there were cosmically measurable days seems equally strange to us, and should again forewarn us against any literalist understanding of the creation story.

Verses 20–23. On Day 5 the sea creatures are created (like the waters themselves on Day 2), with a command that is followed not by direct response but by God's own labor. There are many kinds of sea creature created, but no binary separation; and the ascription of good is amplified into a blessing and a further command to go on creating.

Verses 24–31. The sixth and immensely important day. First the land and air animals are created by a command (to the earth) and response; again there is no separation, but there is an ascription of good (but not a blessing—that is just for humankind).

Then there is the creation of humankind. This takes place, uniquely, by God's command to Godself ("let us make . . ."), and the humans so created are, male and female, in God's image. We cannot here explore the immense theological reflection this phrase has provoked, save to note that the sense of plurality in God, and the sense of imaging, reflection, personhood, recapitulate themes we have traced in the opening two verses. The creation of humanity echoes what was before creation, the primordial tri-unity of Godself. It is the *us*-ness (or perhaps more precisely if barbarically the "I-you-and-it-ness") of God that humans image. Indeed, as noted, the whole story evokes the image of a thinking mind: a matter to which the next section returns.

God issues a second, stronger blessing and a command to have dominion (variously interpreted) over creation. The contemplative ascription is intensified: the whole of creation is now seen as "very good," and we might note that it is the presence of humanity, God's image, co-thinker and co-feeler, that enables the creation to be contemplated and affirmed by God as a unified whole. Humankind is not so much the summit of creation (there are creatures more beautiful, less sinful, more peaceful, more perceptive, and perhaps even more intelligent than "humanity") as the brush stroke that enables God to know his work is finished—or the signature by which he declares the whole picture his own.

Chapter 2 verses 1–3. The Sabbath rest on the seventh day. After all the work, a rest and a "making holy" which is a third, even stronger form of blessing. There is no further speaking, working, differentiating, naming, or contemplating; all is done. If God has made the world through an internal dialogue of word, response, differentiation, and contemplation (and it is these processes through which our thought too apprehends a world) the story tells also of an end to dialogue, a final "day" given solely to doxology, the word of glory.

The main variations in the pattern of creation concern the means of creation, and the ascription of goodness. God creates

1. *directly:* "let there be . . ."—light, "dome," stars, sun and moon, birds.

2. *through separation*—light from darkness, waters above and waters below, water and dry land.

3. *through things already existing in creation:* "let *x* bring forth . . ."—plants (from earth), sea creatures (from the sea), land creatures (from the land).

4. *through Godself:* "let us make . . ."—humankind in God's image.

We shall see in the next chapter that these four patterns have parallels in the patterns that dialogue assumes, and in particular, the way theology evolves as the Trinitarian, and necessarily dialogical, unfolding of the creative Word of God.

Also worthy of note is the way in which goodness is ascribed to everything except the waters above and below (though the seas separated from land are later called good) and the primordial darkness from which the good light is separated. The cosmic darkness of night separated from day is, by contrast, deemed good. So we have to think of the primordial darkness in a non-cosmological way, perhaps as representing a primal delusion or evil, which by definition is not good. Yet—perhaps as the shadow of primordial clarity, goodness, and light—even such evil is part of God's creation: as Isaiah 45:7 puts it, in words nearly quoted at the beginning of Jewish daily prayer, "I form light and create darkness, I make weal and create woe." The primordial waters may be taken likewise as a symbol of a chaos, not good in itself, but an indispensable part of creation that becomes good when separated into its proper place as the life-teeming sea.

Many parts of creation are given a benediction or declaration of goodness, though only the whole, completed creation is declared "very good." The sea creatures and birds, and humankind, are blessed and bidden to multiply. The rest after creation is hallowed. Benediction . . . blessing . . . hallowing: in the course of creation the affirmation of goodness steadily intensifies.

TRINITY AND DIALOGUE

In view of the preceding discussion a playful rewording of the opening of John 1:1–2 suggests itself:

> In the beginning was the Dialogue, and the Dialogue was with God, and the Dialogue was God. Dialogue was in the beginning with God. All things came into being through Dialogue, and without Dialogue not one thing came into being . . . .

The notion of dialogue (in the broadest sense, as explored in chapter 2) as something primordially internal to God, entails some kind of plurality—or more specifically Trinity—in Godself, such that God is at once speaker, hearer, and communication, or initiator, responder, and response. The world may then be seen as coming into being by, and as, the self-proliferating dialogue of the Trinity.

A Trinitarian-cum-dialogical reading of the creation story is not hard to construct. Of course, an understanding of the Trinity in terms of three beings, or a threefold being, would offend against the divine unity and simplicity cherished by all three Abrahamic faiths; but the Trinity, understood in an orthodox manner, asserts neither that their are three Gods nor that the one God has three parts, or modes, or a threefold internal structure.[2] At this stage let us just agree to read this Hebrew text for what it seems to present about God and the world, and leave the metaphysical implications for later.

Each "day" of creation involves, in varied manner, an originating agent or speaker, a word of command, and a response of transformation. This response then changes the situation for the agent or speaker; it is something that can be used in further acts of creation. The character of creation is not thereafter determined solely by the choice of the originating agent but also by the nature of what has already been created: what the agent now has "at hand," so to speak, to use.

Creation is conditioned therefore by both transcendent freedom of choice and immanent necessity, though this necessity has its origin ultimately in the transcendent choice also. By transcendent choice, for example, God commands the waters to appear, but the presence of the waters then conditions the following separation into sky and sea, and the presence of the sea conditions the generation of dry land and provides the medium for the creation of the sea creatures. All things are created by God and nothing else, so God is sovereign, but the created order, once created, means that God in his sovereignty cannot do absolutely anything. The answer to many of the old conundrums regarding divine omnipotence, creaturely freedom, and natural necessity are surely to be found by careful exegesis of this ancient text.

All this suggests that God in the work of creation is already what theologians call the "economic" Trinity. But even before creation there is the darkness that is on the deep, the face (reflection?) of the deep which the darkness is upon, and hovering of the breath or spirit. It would not be legitimate, concerning this stage, prior to the creation of reality itself, to speak of realities other than God: of a deep, or a nothingness, or a spirit, co-existing alongside God before all worlds. Rather, they must exist somehow in God. It seems reasonable to infer from this and other like passages the "immanent Trinity" that many theologians affirm for other reasons: God as Trinity in

2. Cf. Turner, *Christians, Muslims, and the Name of God*, 25–32.

relation to Godself and not only in God's work of creation and redemption. God as love entails God as beloved and lover as well as the love itself.

God is not seen, then, as a self-existent monad, nor are the three persons seen as existing independently in themselves (which would imply the kind of tritheism that Jews and Muslims ascribe to Christians). The third alternative is that followed by Thomas Aquinas, for whom the persons are distinguished not in their essential nature but in their relations: the persons are subsisting relations, relations that are themselves real and logically original, rather than relations between previously existing individuals. This reverses our conventional understanding, whereby things first exist in their own right and then we are able to determine their properties and relations. First I apprehend the beer, the glass, and the table, and then I determine that the beer is *in* the glass *on* the table. For Aquinas, in the Trinity on the contrary it is the relations of begetting and breathing that first subsist ("really exist"), and determine that there is a Father begetter, a Son begotten, and a Spirit breathed.

For analogies here we might look to quantum physics, in which it is the relation of observing that determines and fixes the particle as having a real position (and if the analogy is to hold, that there is an observer observing); or to the whole of "reality" as conceived in the non-dual systems of Advaita Vedanta Hindu thought as well as Madhyamaka Buddhism, for which subject and object exist only in their relationship, out of which they co-arise in mutual interdependence. The Mahayana Buddhist Thich Nhat Hanh uses the word "interbeing" to translate the concept of *pratitya samutpada* (more often translated "dependent co-arising"), which refers to the way things exist in and for their interrelationship. Arguably too our experience of love and interchange with other persons imparts a sense of how far we are constituted, as the people we are, by our relations with others, from our parents onwards. Though Christian theology, with its Greek philosophical inheritance of strong realism regarding substances, has not tended to apply this notion of the priority of relationship to the created order, Aquinas does seem to apply it to the Trinity, and a close reading of Genesis might seem to justify applying it to God's work of creation too.

If so, theology has further reason to regard dialogue, relation, and exchange as constitutive of reality and of any account we may give of it.

> A God who himself exists in a self-communicating manner, in
> Trinity, engages in conversation with his creatures, one by one
> and all together, and they in turn exist in order to converse with

him. . . . He moves right inside their being to give it its very own mind, voice and life.[3]

The Trinity, then, is God in dialogue in Godself and in creation. The next section explores the implications for our "mind, voice, and life."

THE VIEW FROM EVERYWHERE

The story of creation has implications for what it means to be. It encourages us to venture into a dialogue between the theological story of God and the philosophical story of being. If God creates directly, through his word and the response of being, through separation, through what God has already made, and through his own inner consensus, then God must analogically at least think, speak, and act. Whether or not we wish to hold on to a materialist and/or determinist philosophy regarding God's creating *through what has already been made*—such that created things follow their own laws and do not always spring immediately from the divine activity and will—the ultimate perspective will be idealist, the source of all things being the divine mind.

And this idealist perspective will enable us to ascribe subjective matters like value to things in creation. "God saw that it was very good." Goodness will apply to things not as labels we humans apply to indicate our personal preferences, but as the response to them of the One who causes, knows, and loves them. They will be good-in-God, and that is to be good in their ownmost God-created being. For all things possess what Gerard Manley Hopkins in his poem "God's Grandeur" called "the dearest freshness deep down things": something we shall call "Edenic."

The end of chapter 2 introduced the suggestion that dialogue moves toward an ideal "view from everywhere," a world of full intersubjective affirmation, characterized by fuller and richer subjective consciousness. This was contrasted with the modern ideal of a supposedly objective "view from nowhere" stripped of all non-quantifiable personal experience. If we piece together the above exegesis of the creation narrative and a dialogue-based critical realism it is possible to arrive at a convincing account of God as the view from everywhere in which dialogue is grounded and towards which it moves. But what needs to be asked now is whether such an idealist understanding is just something we tease out from what many would regard as a primitive and obscure Bible story, something that flies in the face of all respectable philosophy. I shall argue to the contrary, that idealism is in itself

---

3. Tsakiridou, *Icons in Time*, 176, cited in Wirzba, *Christian Theoria Physike*, 223.

a more coherent understanding than its philosophical alternatives. Far from being an awkward but necessary extension of our argument, philosophical idealism forms one if its independent supporting pillars.

The argument for idealism begins with the strangeness of consciousness. As David Chalmers has argued,[4] the world could be just as it is in physical terms, and yet contain no consciousnesses other than my own, which of course I directly experience. His "zombie" argument posited that given any organism or functioning system that is believed to have consciousness, it is always possible to conceive of and describe a physically identical "zombie" that lacks it. The fact that an organism is conscious therefore cannot be reduced to or identified with describable facts about its physical make-up or structure. It is something we know we have in our own case and believe to be possessed other human beings and probably many other beings. But we cannot identify features or degrees of complexity whereby we know that consciousness is present. Consciousness, therefore, is irreducible, not definable in physical terms alone. This argument has yet to receive a convincing refutation.

This problem is one among several faced by a materialist perspective that sees matter as foundational, and consciousness as an emergent property arising when material structures get sufficiently complex. There is the notorious "problem of qualia": what in the physical world explains the *greenness* of the experience of green? (This is a different question from what explains the *occurrence* of such experiences, which may well have a physical explanation in terms of light rays.) There is the problem regarding what counts as sufficient complexity to necessitate the presence of consciousness—that of an amoeba, a dog, or only a human . . . ? Finally, what is the magic whereby just this degree of complexity conjures up a consciousness? According to Chalmers no such magic is conceptually possible. It is not that one day we may find the answer—as many scientists still hope—because given any degree of complexity, or any physically observable structure, it is conceptually possible both that consciousness is present and that consciousness is absent. Nothing in nature necessitates, or causes, the presence of consciousness.

Chalmers himself describes several ways of conceiving of the relation between mind and body, or consciousness and the natural world.[5] His arguments lead him to reject the three materialistically reductive ones. He does not favor the two possible dualistic accounts, though he admits, for reasons "largely grounded in aesthetic considerations whose force is unclear."[6] He

4. Chalmers, *The Conscious Mind*, further developed in *Character of Consciousness*.
5. Chalmers, *Character of Consciousness*, ch. 5.
6. Ibid., 138.

favors what he calls "panprotopsychism," according to which—following the "neutral monism" of Bertrand Russell—there is one kind of reality with aspects that are physical and mental, or at least "proto-psychical" that is, having qualities that when assembled into larger organisms take on the character of consciousness. Consciousness in his view "goes all the way down" from humans and humanoids through fish and amoebae to—perhaps—all information-bearing matter, even perhaps thermostats!

This continuity has an admitted elegance, but Chalmers' account is hampered by a lack of clarity regarding precisely how simple units of consciousness assemble into bigger ones. Consciousness has a kind of unity. The experience of my keyboard and desk right now is identifiable as my experience because, among other reasons, it is part of the same field of consciousness that includes other experiences and memories of mine and excludes those of other sentient beings. It is hard to see how proto-psychic consciousnesses could both have their own unity (hence excluding the contents of other such consciousnesses) and be parts of a wider consciousness that includes them.

The other form main of monism—philosophical idealism—is only mentioned briefly by Chalmers, though it has had far greater prominence in the history of both Western and Eastern philosophy. If panprotopsychism tries to construct consciousness "bottom upward" out of smaller units, idealism starts at the top—with a single universal Mind—and sees our minds as fragmented and limited versions of this. Such a view has—I would argue—three main advantages over the alternatives.

Firstly, it would seem (somewhat) easier to understand our own human consciousness as a kind of fragment of the larger whole than as something built up from smaller atoms of mind. Certainly many religions have seen it that way: Advaita Vedanta Hinduism sees the *atman* or soul as a fragment of the universal *Atman*, which is Brahman, the divine Spirit, to which it is destined to return; and many religions repeat some form of this myth of our emanation from and return to the divine Mind. There remain problems regarding the exact relation between the infinite consciousness and our finite ones, and how what we experience relates to what God experiences. For example, many of our experiences, such as sins and temptations, are constituted by a lack of completeness, or even an ignorance or self-deception. In that sense the unlimited Mind cannot experience all that we as limited minds do, and must fall short of the total omniscience traditionally ascribed to it. But at least we are not attempting, as in Chalmers' favored view, to *constitute* the divine consciousness out of our fragmentary ones. The causality flows the other way, from the infinite consciousness to finite beings with their finite consciousnesses. What flows from the finite to the infinite consciousness is purpose or aim.

Secondly, we noted Chalmers' argument that consciousness cannot logically be reduced to matter. But the converse—the logical construction of matter out of consciousness—would seem to be possible. This does not mean that matter is ontologically built of units of mind, of course, but rather that matter reduces epistemologically to experience: that we have no reason to assert the existence of something physical unless there are some possible or actual mental experiences associated with it and evidencing it. To show this was the central endeavor of the British empiricists—pioneered by Locke, Berkeley, and Hume—and though the endeavor has been criticized (by myself among others[7]), it now seems to me to possess a large element of common sense. Such empiricism notoriously faces a problem in the form of the many objects that inhabit the worldview of modern science—from superstrings through quarks and neutrinos to dark matter, dark energy, and black holes—that are not and cannot be perceived. But the answer proposed by Berkeley seems valid: such things, and the physical world as a whole, exist because they are perceived by God, an eternal and infallible Mind that includes all consciousness of all possible and actual things. God can then be regarded as the consciousness in which our noumena (things which really exist, unknowable to us) are experienced as phenomena.

Thirdly, God conceived of as a Mind in whom all possible realities are thought or experienced has the singular advantage of explaining Godself. God so conceived is the kind of reality that can explain everything. As Keith Ward argues, "No question arises of why this consciousness is as it is, since it includes all possible worlds and states exhaustively. No reason needs to be given why one state exists rather than another, since all those states exist, though only as possibilities."[8] God in this sense is what scientists call the multiverse: not as the rather oppressive idea that all possibilities, including universes that are everlasting hells, must actually exist, but as the infinite array of possibilities held together in a Mind that can choose to actualize them or not. But this Mind also explains why it is this actual world that has arisen out of all the possibilities: namely as having meaning and purpose in the mind of God, who has chosen them to give rise to an amazing array of good things (as well as some admittedly problematic bad things.)

Such an account explains things both in terms of scientific lawlikeness, and in terms of something genuinely "protopsychic." Idealism

---

7. Thompson, *Holy Ground*, 29ff. and *passim*.

8. Ward, *Pascal's Fire*, 131.

shares with [panprotopsychism] the property that phenomenal states play a role in constituting physical reality, but on
the [idealist] view this happens in a very different way. Rather
than believing that each physical state has a corresponding
"microscopic" phenomenal state of its own, each such state is
constituted holistically by the perception of a "macroscopic"
phenomenal mind.[9]

So atoms and the like exist, not as *subjects* of perception (as in panprotopsychism), but as the *objects* of a true knowing, inhering as they do in the
mind of God. On such a view there is an "inwardness" or subjective aspect
to atoms and all things, in addition to the physical aspect studied by science.
But this consists not their own primitive consciousness, but rather God's
perfect—or as we shall now see, "Edenic"—consciousness of them.

Finally, as well these philosophical advantages, the idealist view possesses great ethical and theological benefits, including a fundamentally dialogical bias and a coherence with the biblical account of creation.

In the Garden of Eden, we had unmediated contact with the
world. We were directly acquainted with objects in the world
and with their properties. Objects were presented to us without
causal mediation, and properties were revealed to us in their
true intrinsic glory.[10]

Thus Chalmers describes a mythologically original state where a naive
realism held true, and our perceptions coincided perfectly with things as
they really are. But then—the myth continues—we ate from the tree of illusion, and learnt that our perceptions could often deceive or mislead us as to
how things really are, and we ate from the tree of science, which described
a world markedly different from the world as we perceive it. We lost our
Edenic consciousness. Yet Chalmers believes the ideal of Edenic consciousness is still necessary, guiding us in our perceptions, even if it has strictly
speaking become invalidated. We need to believe in the possibility of Edenic
perception if we are to have perceptions that are valid in any sense at all.

I suggest it is possible, given the idealist view just described, to take
this further and chart a pathway to restore what we lost when we partook
of the two trees, which we might regard as the two typical trees of modernity. The notion of God as the bearer of a perfect "Edenic" subjectivity—the
ground of all objective reality and causality—is precisely what enables us
to pass beyond a modernist, imperialist yet desiccatingly minimalist "view

9. Chalmers, *Character of Consciousness*, 137.
10. Ibid., 381.

from nowhere" towards a genuinely postmodern, dialogue-based, and richly intersubjective "view from everywhere."

The key points about the divine "view from everywhere" are these.

1. As an Edenic subjectivity, God's consciousness affirms the potential of our subjectivities, our minds, to move towards an Edenic state. *Qua* consciousnesses—created as the Genesis story says in the image of the divine—our subjective minds are the kind of thing that could approach perfect knowledge (which as we shall shortly see, involves a perfect love) of things in the created world. A prophetic realism, hopeful for the future as described at the end of chapter 2, holds sway. This contrasts with the modern "view from nowhere" which systematically roots out the qualitative and subjective in favor of a supposed quantifiable objectivity.

2. On the other hand, because the Edenic consciousness is ascribed to the divine, not to any individual human or group of humans, it transcends any partisan mind's apprehension. Divine, Edenic consciousness is something we can grow towards, but never perfectly realize, and in that sense such consciousness sets a question mark against individuals' making excessive claims as to how things "really are." Our realism accepts uncertainty. We accept that our vision of things is partial and full of distorting illusions, created not only by the distorting lens of our egocentric desires and wishful thinking, as well as the distorting corporate ideologies of the societies we belong to, but also by more ethically neutral factors such as the selective, instinct-governed, and imperfect nature of our senses and nervous systems. The Eastern emphasis on *maya* or illusion is important in this respect, as is the Christian notion that "after the fall" our view of things is partial and distorted by egocentric desire. All this is in profound contrast with the "view from nowhere," which is something that an individual or a party of humans can claim to possess, providing they have performed the required feats of exorcism of all that is merely and subjectively qualitative.

3. Because of both 1 (the fact that our minds are capable of moving closer to an Edenic state) and 2 (the fact that no individual or group can claim to possess such a state), the view from everywhere demands more than a mere correspondence between "observer" contents and world contents; it demands dialogue, as a way of building our subjectivities towards an intersubjective Edenic ideal. That is why we describe it as a "view from everywhere," on the understanding that a

view that encompassed *all* subjectivities would in no way differ from God's perfect knowledge, there being by definition no further view that could challenge or expose it as illusory. By contrast the modernist view from nowhere encourages imperialism, inviting us to struggle for the victory of the true view, whether by neo-conservative conquest or liberal assimilation.

In this context the kinship and difference between my understanding and that of authors like John Hick and Wilfred Cantwell Smith becomes clearer. Like Smith I am unashamedly utopian, prophetically looking forward, in the very long term, to an increasing unity and coherence between views that at present are diverse and divisive, until all share in the divine "view from everywhere." The difference is that I do not see this in terms of an elusive, mystical faith that is a common theme contrasted with the diversity of embodiments in different religions. Nor do I connect the arrival of this unifying "faith" with the application of modern paradigms that presuppose the triumph of skepticism and the stripping away of "accretions." Rather, it is the in the very diversity of religious embodiments that people's real faith lies. People's faith is not a pure essence over against religions, or merely "expressed" in the religions, but the inward or subjective aspect of which the outward objective aspect is the religious practice itself. It is the material religious embodiments that need to interrelate to generate the rich Edenic view from everywhere, as their subjective and intersubjective side. Though we cannot exclude an element of rational debate in which the attempt is made to arrive at logical consistency between the religions, that is not the essential core of the process I advocate, because believers' different religious subjectivities may co-exist and interrelate even when there is no rational consistency or correlation between them.

PANIKKAR ON THE TRINITY AND WORLD RELIGIONS

The idealist understanding just sketched does not, of course, necessitate the creation account or the doctrine of the Trinity. There are a number of ways in which an idealist account can unfold in religious terms. We can emphasize either the integrity, or the universality, of the divine mind. If we emphasize the integrity, then indeed the divine mind becomes a personal agent, as sketched in the creation story, creating beings that, though ultimately produced by mind, have a physical, law-like integrity of their own that constrains God's further acts of creativity. If, on the other hand, we emphasize the universality, we might be led to speak of the divine mind as the Advaita Hindus speak of Atman, the Yogacara Buddhists of Mind, and Mahayana Buddhists generally of *Sunyata* or Emptiness: a less personal space, prior to any God-world duality, within which all things co-arise and subside. Chapter 8 will discuss a little more fully the different "grammars" whereby God and beings may be related.[11]

There is metaphysical room here for accommodating a rich dialogue between faith perspectives. One writer has suggested that the Trinity itself offers a template for such dialogue between the religions. Raimundo Panikkar argues that while the Christian religion includes a more explicit reference to the Trinity than any other, Christianity is here witnessing to a deep structure that is not limited to the Christian faith. This structure is unravelled in his seminal yet much neglected work *The Trinity and the Religious Experience of Man*, which represents a slight reworking of an earlier text.[12] These books argue that three core spiritualities are to be found in all faiths, in differing balance.

Firstly, in *iconolatry* (or to use the Hindu term, *karmamārga*, the path of duty) the transcendent God is worshipped through humanly created symbols. Though the monotheistic faiths Judaism and Islam condemn idolatry—the worship of the divine through material symbols—Panikkar argues this is because their own worship is primarily of the iconolatrous type: it is just that Yhwh, or Al'lah, are worshipped through non-physical, mental, or imaginary symbols to which the physical ones are seen as crude rivals.[13] Worship here consists in performing liturgical and moral duties to the deity following the laws and procedures he or she has revealed. Secondly, in *personalism* (or *bhaktimārga*, the path of devotion) the focus shifts to a more intimate personal relationship with the divine, who is now envisioned as revealed, embodied, or incarnate in human form. Finally in *non-dualism* (*advaita*, or *jnanamarga*, the path of wisdom) the duality between the deity and the worshipper that is implied in the other two pathways is overcome, in a wisdom or nirvana in which there is no longer a separate self and no longer a separate God, but one blissful consciousness of divinity immanent in self and all things.

Panikkar believes that the doctrine of the Trinity allows of this threefold diversity in pathways to God. "Father" names the ineffable transcendence of God, which icons strive but ultimately fail to capture. The Son names not only Jesus but the other incarnations. The Son is the God whom Greek

---

11. See also Thompson, *Creation, Dependent Arising and Dual Belonging.*

12. Panikkar, *Trinity and World Religions.*

13. Panikkar, *Trinity and Religious Experience,* 11–12.

theology names "he who is" (*ho on,* always inscribed on the halo of Christ in the icons):[14] the God of revelation, who appears to us. The Father transcends appearance, while the Spirit is too thoroughly immanent in life to need revealing;[15] the Son is God as revealed, with whom it is possible to have a personal relationship.[16] Finally, the Spirit is God immanent in consciousness and in all things: "what is the Spirit but the *atman* of the Upanishads?"[17] Iconolatry, personalism, and non-dualism represent the pathways prioritizing what Christians call Father, Son, and Spirit respectively.

Authentic faith in all traditions balances the three ways, being at once prophetic, humane, and mystical. But when people approach God exclusively through one "person," distortion results: either nihilism (when the transcendence of the Father becomes a total unknowability), humanism (when the "theandric" unity of Christ is eclipsed and leaves merely "human values"), or "angelism" (an elitist, "gnostic" spirituality seeking a disembodied and often asexual purity).

In a more recent essay[18] Panikkar presents the same threefold pattern in a striking geo-historical format: the three pathways—or something similar to them—are now represented by the Jordan, the Tiber, and the Ganges respectively, and also to three different phases of Christianity. The Jordan represents the prophetic, conversion-demanding iconolatrous faith centered on Christ, characteristic of early Christianity (and also, we might note, attempted revivals of it since). The Tiber, the river of Rome, represents the more institutional and culture-centered faith of Christendom, which approaches other faiths through a mix of apologetic, crusade, and mission (gradually shifting from the first of these to the last). Finally the Ganges, which arises in many places and divides into many estuaries, represents what Panikkar calls "Christianness," which sees Christ neither as an individual revelation nor as embodied in the corporate church, but as a hope for humanity as a whole, still largely to be discovered by Christians as well as others through dialogue. We may be reminded at this point of D'Costa's approach, also Trinitarian in basis, discussed in chapter 1, where though Christians have the name of Christ there is still much for the Spirit to teach Christians about him, not least through dialogue with and learning from other faiths.

14. Ibid., 51.
15. Ibid., 59.
16. Ibid., 52.
17. Ibid., 63.
18. Panikkar, *Jordan, Tiber and Ganges.*

Panikkar's model is not uncontroversial, of course, and the next chapter we will consider the obvious criticism that it represents, not pluralism as Panikkar claims, but just another kind of Christian inclusivism.

DRAWING THE THREADS TOGETHER

Very often theologies derived from philosophical reflection are dissociated from those derived from revelation and its interpretation. In traditional Catholic theology a hierarchical model was adopted that placed theologies described as "natural," "philosophical," or "fundamental" below, and revealed theology above. The latter was based in part on the former and built on it, as a rational foundation allegedly accessible to Christian and non-Christian alike, but reached much further into the sky because it incorporated what the tradition stated, things revealed only to the Christian's eye of faith. In the narrative and postliberal theologies discussed in chapter 6 and the post-metaphysical theologies discussed in chapter 8, a much more polarizing position is held: philosophical theologies are regarded as the enemies of true theology. In my own terms, it is an advantage of the account now being offered (though in terms of those traditions it is obviously the reverse) that philosophical and theological reflection as well as biblical exegesis converge. This convergence can be seen as a case of the piecing together of diverse starting viewpoints into the view from everywhere, or at least the view from more places than one: from philosophy, from the Bible, and from Trinitarian theology.

Panikkar's Trinitarian understanding itself represents a commendable example of this kind of convergent approach. It seems to represent the outworking of a "view from everywhere" among the religions. By contrast the essays other than Panikkar's in *The Myth of Christian Uniqueness* tend towards a view from nowhere, imposing a modernist structure that represents the standpoint of no particular living religion.

Taking up points 1–3 above in the section on "The View from Everywhere," Panikkar's "Father" and the path of iconolatry could be argued to follow from point 2, the transcendence of the Edenic view, which means that we need to smash any idols, physical or mental, that claim to represent a total understanding. The Spirit and the path of non-duality then represents the working through of point 1, the potential of the development of consciousness: the possibility that if we purify our minds of particular attachments they have the potential for an Edenic view, seeing reality as it truly is. Finally, the Word and the path of personal relationship carries forward point 3, stressing that the way to this perfection is through relation with others, and that the Logos unfolds through dialogues between persons, and between people and the incarnations of the divine that intimate Eden. The Trinity therefore names the way all religions strive to express the divine consciousness through working out in balance the three aspects of the Edenic view. And when one aspect is exalted at the expense of the others, distortion results: atheism, which only affirms the non-attainability of the divine perspective; angelism, which thinks that a solitary purification of consciousness is all that is required; or humanism, in which dialogue with other humans in "personal relationships" is pursued in the absence of either the thrust towards transcendence or inner transformation.

But as well as indicating the pattern of the pathway, the Trinity also names the process, offering an interpretation of our exegesis of the creation story. It has often been noted that this story is at variance with a scientific account of the evolution of the cosmos. This divergence has been used to argue either that the physical account is mistaken, or that the biblical account is purely mythological; or else botched attempts have been made to reconcile the two. But our understanding enables us to see the Genesis account as neither a poor, primitive, and superseded attempt at cosmology, nor a charming but naive myth, but a subtle alternative, idealist account. If the argument of the preceding section is true, the Genesis story represents an account of how the mind of God might conceive creatures, what it would have to be like to do so; and what it is therefore like for us to arrive at the knowledge of beings.

It shows us a God who is Trinitarian dialogue in Godself, and necessarily so as infinite and all-encompassing Mind. Consciousness always involves three: that of which we are conscious, the act of being aware of it, and the one who is conscious and holds this act in a unity with other contents of consciousness. These are neither three co-existing entities, nor just three aspects of the same entity. But of the all-encompassing consciousness that creates the universe, more can be said. In our own case, there is a separation between knowing, creating, and loving. In time our consciousness *precedes* the making of the thing, which brings what we think of into actuality; our knowing *follows* the existence of the thing, being an apprehension of what is already there prior to our knowing it; our loving *accompanies* the existence of the thing, being a kind of welcoming affirmation and wanting of what is there alongside us. But if God (following Augustine and the mainstream Christian tradition) creates time, these temporal distinctions cannot apply to the act of creation itself. It would then be a mistake to think of God first creating the world, then loving it, then sitting back and knowing it. God's making, loving, and knowing the world are all aspects of God's making-cum-loving-cum-knowing.[19] God knows the world in his making and loving it; God makes it by knowing and loving it into existence: as Julian of Norwich famously said concerning the hazel-nut in her palm:

> It is all that is made. I marvelled how it might last, for methought it might suddenly have fallen to naught for littleness. And I was answered in my understanding: It lasteth, and ever shall, for that God loveth it. And so All-thing hath the Being by the love of God.[20]

But conversely God loves the world because he made and knows it. God's knowledge, love, and desire are a perichoretic interdependent Tri-unity.

Such thoughts enable us to correlate the Genesis story with Panikkar's understanding of the Trinity. "Father" names the source, the darkness, the nothing, that which God creates out of or from, the one whose voice we hear but remains transcendent, the face not seen. As creation emerges first of all in obedient response to this source, so the pathway of the Father is that of obedient response.

"Son" names the Word of God and the face of the deep, communication and embodiment, that by means of which God creates, which is at once God and other than God; not a second God but God rendered present, in the cosmos itself and in incarnations within it. The path of the Son involves a spirituality of both imitating and relating personally to this embodied reality.

"Spirit" names the other to this other, the breath or wind rippling the surface, matter's response, God immanent in the inwardness of things, that which God creates through and for: God as what it is like to be me, you, *atman*, or atom. If the Son represents difference *within* God, the Spirit integrates *into* God, overcoming duality: the Spirit's pathway is that of non-duality and the opening up of our closed consciousnesses to their always-already Edenic divinity.

These three persons and pathways co-exist in a fullness of interaction, analogous to the three-body interaction of Newton that, unlike a dual interaction, can never be reduced to the readily predictable. As the Genesis account concludes, the interaction reaches ever onward to the transcendent Sabbath. Doxology—"glory word" or praise—represents the end of dialogue, both in the sense of the end to which all dialogue moves, and in the sense of that which brings dialogue to an end. In doxology dialogue passes into

19. Thompson, "Creation, Dependent Arising," 65.

20. Julian, *Revelations*, 9.

harmony, words into music, as what were partly opposed, partly agreeing proclamations become partly dissonant, partly resolved voices in relation to one another. The unity that dialogue aims at therefore is not a monolithic agreement, but a mutual interrelation, *perichoresis*, in which diverse and perhaps, on a logical level, contradictory visions nevertheless contribute to one whole that cannot be stated without them. Panikkar's Trinity seems to offer a pattern for such a musical inter-participation in worship, but perhaps multi-religious musical works such as John Taverner's *Requiem* provide another model (whether or not you actually like the specific music).

Doxology is a further step forward from dialogue, whereby the creation that God has contemplated ("saw") and called "good" responds contemplatively to what it cannot see or differentiate in any way, and calls God. Doxology is what the Anglican priest William Vanstone called "the response of being to the love of God";[21] it is the answer to the word that calls us into being as dialogue partners with God. It involves doing justice to beings, grasping their "Edenic" nature as made/known/loved by the Triune God. It is the only act of ours that can do justice to God: the equable and fair vision of all things by all things everywhere, in which all things realize their true nature as words and thoughts of praise offered in God by God to God.

21. The subtitle of Vanstone, *Love's Endeavour*; cf especially chapter 5.

CHAPTER 4

Interfaith Dialogue: Theology

THE NORMATIVE ACCOUNT OF theology as dialogue, developed in the previous chapter, needs testing out in a descriptive account of theological practice. Does the history of theology in fact show that theology, insofar as it has been authentic and true to itself, has always been dialogical in the broad sense developed in chapter 2? If not, our theoretical account can scarcely be sustained. The first section of this chapter offers a template for theological development based on the creation account from chapter 3.

But even if our account can be sustained in that sense, still it might be argued that it represents no real advance on the threefold paradigm described in chapter 1. The succeeding three sections therefore address these critical questions:

1. Does the emphasis on dialogue and openness secretly superimpose a rationalist secularism, as argued by D'Costa (see chapter 1), John Milbank, and other writers? If so, it represents just another kind of pluralism masking an exclusivist modernity.

2. Does the Trinitarian account of creation and dialogue in chapter 3 imply a Christian attempt to fit other religions to its template? If so, it is just another kind of inclusivism.

3. Does our emphasis on "truth" and apologetics in dialogue mean that only one religion can really be true? If so, we are committed to exclusivism after all.

The focus of the argument here shifts because how we do theology as an intrafaith dialogue and how we conduct interfaith dialogue clearly must interrelate. Interreligious issues therefore begin once again to raise their head. The conclusion draws the answers together in an appeal for a liberal, dialogue-friendly, and reasonable yet rooted and embodied theology, and leads into the next chapter, which explores how this might work out in the actual practice of dialogue.

THEOLOGICAL TRADITION AS DIALOGUE

Chapter 3 noted the four ways in which God was presented as creating the world in the first creation narrative.

1. Direct command of a name and response: "Let light be . . . and light there was" (Gen 1:3). The Word of command is a bolt from the blue, eliciting not a dialogue of equals, but a spontaneous response of being where before there was nothing.

2. Separation and subsequent naming: "God separated the light from the darkness; God called the light 'day' . . ."(1:4). A more subtle process of discernment, distinction, and description.

3. Using things already created and named:—"Let the waters bring forth swarms of living creatures" (1:20). Here God does not create from nothing, but by harnessing the potential of what already is.

4. Creation out of God's own nature: "Let us make humankind in our image" (1:26). God creates not through the potential of what is already made but through a kind of command to Godself ("let us . . .") to bring forth something that bears the mark of Godself ("in our image").

I suggest that these cases of creation find their parallel in the ways in which theology has developed as a creative, essentially dialogical process: through what I shall call proclamation, discernment, incorporation, and apologetic. Though theologians can be found to exemplify primarily one or the other mode, and in the teaching of Jesus too we can find such examples, all good theology involves all four, as indeed does the teaching of Jesus. In the following I make use of the grammatical moods that will be further explained in chapter 5.

1. Proclamation

Sometimes theology speaks with authority, both in the sense of original authorship (*auctoritas*) and in the sense of power and right to command. Such theology seems like a bolt from the blue, creating as if *ex nihilo*, making little attempt to persuade, or engage with what goes before. Jesus himself is described as having a reputation in his teaching for "having authority (*exousía*) and not as the scribes" (Mark 1:22), who were presumably much more interested in reference to tradition and the careful drawing of distinctions. Collections of teachings like the Sermon on the Mount (Matt 5–7) bear this out: the tradition is remembered, but only to intensify it with moral commands that are often not argued for, but challengingly stated: "You have heard it said . . . , but I say to you . . . ." There have been times in theological tradition more appropriately described as rupture than development—perhaps most notably at the Reformation, and again with the "Barthian Thunderbolt" in the early twentieth century. In the spirit of Panikkar's "Jordan," theology undergoes a baptism of fire.

These instances are not obviously cases of "dialogue," and certainly not the kind of thing polite interfaith dialogue encourages. But more careful reflection reveals the contrary. Commands, after all, are not soliloquies; they are always addressed to others who are called upon to make a response. And Jesus' authoritative teaching had a context, standing in a relation to tradition, even if this relation is often challenging and far from irenic. That is made explicit in the "You have heard it said" of the Sermon on the Mount. But even where there is no such explicit reference, Jesus' teaching often implies a context of tradition that hearers would recognize. In the same way, Luther and the other reformers were engaged in a bitter dialogue with the tradition of their day, and with hindsight we can see how far their theology was shaped by current controversies over indulgences and other "works" designed to accomplish salvation. Likewise, the theology of Karl Barth was shaped by his rejection of the nineteenth-century liberal assimilation of idealist philosophy, and though he presented it as a rejection of any assimilation to philosophy, it has been argued that it made the very same anti-metaphysical movement as philosophy was making at the same time with the Vienna circle and the like. "His whole purpose was . . . to put an end to the old refined intelligent culture of the nineteenth centuries, with all its 'progressive' tendencies, its faith in human reason, human culture, or the knowledge of God acquired through the strivings of human piety."[1] Rather than moving away from philosophy, Barth and his successors were in (hostile) dialogue with nineteenth-century philosophy and therefore unwittingly in league with the twentieth-century philosophy that likewise rejected it. Unlike God, theologians never really create *ex nihilo*; nevertheless, their theology may present itself as, and have the authoritative force of, such a creation.

1. Fuller, *Theoria*, 171.

2. Analysis

A very different kind of theology works through the drawing of careful distinctions and the development of apt concepts, analogous to God's work of separation and naming in Genesis. It is not a mode we find much of in the teaching of Jesus; we find more of it in St. Paul with his many distinctions, some subtle, some stark, some both. And we find a great deal of exhaustive analysis in the teachings ascribed to the Buddha. The scholastics, pre-eminently Thomas Aquinas, exemplify this process, which presupposes Panikkar's "Tiber": an established Christendom that does not need to shout, but can develop through a kind of inner dialogue between different ways of developing the tradition in which the primary mood is indicative or descriptive. Aquinas and the scholastics saw themselves as developing a tradition, but the tradition was a broad, open-ended one that included, alongside the Bible, pre-Christian philosophers like Plato and Aristotle, Jewish ones like Moshe ben Maimon ("Maimonides"), and Muslim ones like Ibn Rushd ("Averroes"), all of whom could be cited as authorities or sources of useful concepts. At the same time there was scope for disagreement, notably with those regarded as heretics. The drawing of distinctions and development of new concepts remains important in theology, even though the broad consensus that the medievals could rely on no longer exists, and the process is generally therefore subordinated to a primary motive of proclamation, incorporation, or apologetic.

3. Incorporation

Different again is the kind of theology that starts from what precedes it, like God creating new things out of what already exists. Jesus' own teaching in the parables typically starts not from the traditions of the elders but from everyday matters already familiar to his hearers, using these to expound his own often stranger message. In contrast with the analytical mode of theology, which takes an already defined block of tradition, and subdivides and clarifies it, this mode is synthetic. It draws on sources that may seem diverse, including already existing informal folk wisdom, and harnesses and uses them, synthesizing them with the Christian tradition. For obvious reasons this is the easiest model with which to approach interfaith dialogue, lending itself as it does to a pluralism ("Gangetic" in Panikkar's sense) in which the primary mood is speculative, imaginative, and hypothetical—putting ideas together to see what results—and also perhaps optative, motivated by the development of hope for humanity and the cosmos. In the light of the other it works towards a rich but possibly contradictory "lowest common multiple" or "LCM." It is a theology of mutual inclusion and listening rather than one of proclamation or persuasion: teasing out the potentialities of the other, learning what the other knows that I may not, and translating it into my own context. It is often criticized for being "eclectic," yet the term "eclectic" covers a multitude of virtues as well as sins, since theologians from the patristic period onward have drawn on ideas outside the Christian tradition to express Christian concepts.

4. Apologetics

Whereas incorporation starts from the alien, and assimilates, apologetic starts from what is ordinary and familiar in the tradition, and teases out its meaning and defends its truth in response to questions the other might or does pose. Like God's creation of humanity out of God's own nature, such theology is primarily intent on developing the tradition for others' use, rather than assimilating what the other may say. The primary mode is interrogative or question-and-answer, and the search is not for a rich "LCM" but for a highest common factor or "HCF," narrowing the faith down to the core of truth that can be communicated and that will withstand the onslaught or the other's argument. In the teaching of Jesus the arguments between Jesus and the authorities—developed particularly in the Gospel of John—illustrate this mode, though very often Jesus does not so much respond to questions as take them to a higher level in his answers. The "apologists" in the patristic period engaged in debate with Hellenic philosophy, defending the strength and truth of Christian claims against skeptical questions. Aquinas' *Summa contra Gentiles*, with its question and answer approach, illustrates an apologetic mode contrasting with the discernment and analysis of his *Summa Theologiae*. Friedrich Schleiermacher sought to defend the truth of Christianity against its "cultured despisers," initiating a century of liberal theology against which Barth's proclamatory approach subsequently resounded. Paul Griffiths has usefully distinguished negative and positive apologetics. Negative apologetics "is designed to show that a given critique of . . . the central truth claims [of a religious discourse] fails," while positive apologetics "is a discourse designed to show that the . . . doctrine-expressing sentences constituting a particular religious community's doctrines is cognitively superior, in some important respect(s), to that constituting another religious community's doctrines."[2] As Griffiths notes, apologetics has become widely suspect in the circles that study and discuss theology

2. Griffiths, *Apology for Apologetics*, 14.

and religion, and as noted above, this trend has if anything increased in the quarter century since Griffiths mounted his challenge to this status quo. It has by no means been banished from the academic theological scene, though it is perhaps most apparent and successful in works like those of C. S. Lewis and Keith Ward, written with sound scholarship and argument, but for a wider than academic audience.

Summary

From this overview, the following points emerge. Firstly, theological dialogue is not necessarily irenic. Doing justice to the other involves both empathetic identification and a sense of the other's otherness; so a tension between inclusion and exclusion is of the essence of true dialogue. If there is no inclusion there can be no *logos*, no communication; if there is no exclusion there is no *dia*, no reaching across genuine difference. So theology may involve a peaceable process of mutual inclusion, enrichment, and discovery: seeking the "lowest common multiple." But equally, it may emphasize a pursuit of truth and discovery, seeking out, with a certain ruthlessness, through apologetic critique and argument, the "highest common factor" that withstands mutual criticism. And at its best, theology involves both.

On this broad understanding of dialogue, theologies are always engaged in a kind of dialogue with a Christian or non-Christian "other," whether irenic and incorporative or proclamatory and hostile; whether apologetic and engaged with the other or analytical within a self-contained tradition. When this element of dialogue is lost or occluded, so likewise is the sense that theology is engaging with reality.

DIALOGUE AND APOLOGETICS:
CAN THEOLOGY BE TRUE AND NOT EXCLUSIVE?

Many are wary of claims, arguments, and judgments regarding truth in theology and especially in interfaith dialogue. Such claims are central to the apologetic enterprise, as just described. Relativism, as we have seen, has undermined the sense of a truth beyond our different religious concepts and languages, thereby rendering apologetics in both negative and positive senses either irrelevant or impossible. But as discussed in chapter 2, Griffiths argued strongly against such relativism and its threefold assumptions of unintelligibility, incommensurability, and lack of objective reference. He defended a NOIA (Necessity Of Interreligious Apologetics) principle:

> If representative intellectuals belonging to some specific reli-
> gious community come to judge . . . that some or all of their
> own doctrine-expressing sentences are incompatible with some
> alien religious claim(s), then they should feel obliged to engage
> in both positive and negative apologetics vis-à-vis these alien
> religious claims and their promulgators.[3]

("Representative intellectuals" are simply those qualified by their understanding of and faithfulness to their own tradition to represent their faith
in dialogue.) The obligation to engage in both kinds of apologetics derives
partly, he argues, from the demands of the religions themselves to promote
the truth they contain, and partly from the demands of intellectual integrity.

Suspicion of truth-claims and apologetics comes from two opposing
quarters. One is that which advocates dialogue on the basis of some kind of
pluralistic openness to other faiths. The feeling here is that claims to truth
are, or at least sound, exclusive and alienate dialogue partners.

> If the Christian or Buddhist or believer in whatever religion ap-
> proaches another religion with the a priori idea of defending his
> religion . . . we shall have . . . no religious dialogue, no encounter,
> much less a mutual enrichment and fecundation. . . . We must
> eliminate any apologetics if we really want to meet a person
> from another religious tradition.[4]

Thus Panikkar would eliminate what he calls "particular apologetics"
(arguments for a particular religion) from interreligious dialogue. He goes
on to eliminate "general apologetics," that is, arguments on behalf of the
religions against irreligion or atheism: interreligious dialogue must not have
as its aim a reconciliation of religions against a common enemy.

The other quarter is what I have termed exclusivist pluralism, often
of a neo-traditional kind. Here there is much more caution about dialogue,
because of the insistence that truth can only be found within particular religious systems, which often claim unique revelatory status. This renders
redundant the apologetic attempt to persuade the other in her own terms, or
mutually acceptable terms, of the truth of an element of one's own tradition.
For the other will only see our truth if she is persuaded to participate in our
system.

> Once one acknowledges that one's religious faith is rooted in
> a God-given revelation—however offered—then it would be
> fruitless to try to demonstrate that tradition to be true. One will

3. Ibid., 3.
4. Panikkar, *Intrareligious Dialogue*, 62.

> always be tempted to show "the primacy" of one's tradition, to
> be sure, but such "showing" will proceed at best rhetorically, by
> "out-narrating" the other, as John Milbank puts it.[5]

Milbank's term refers to the notion that religions are not primarily propositional systems that can be assessed by universal shared criteria for truth, but narratives. To out-narrate is to include the other's story within one's own, and more, reaching out to narrate what the other fails to narrate at all, or well. He sees theology therefore as primarily an exercise in rhetoric, rather than dialogue, seeking mastery over the other through the splendor of the tropes and paradoxes of Christian language rather than the apologetic persuasiveness of its arguments. And "as regards the furtherance of the critical understanding of discourses (the minimum that religions can truly share in common) it will be better to replace 'dialogue' with 'mutual suspicion.'"[6] (Extreme as this may sound, we will later see that there is a place for suspicion in dialogue provided it is mutual and welcomed as such.)

Now both quarters of criticism cannot be right. We cannot oppose apologetics both because it generates a suspicion by the other and so rules out mutual trust and "fecundation," and because it renders us insufficiently suspicious of one another, enabling too much reliance on a supposed common framework and too much cross-fertilization. One strategy for us would be to withdraw and let the two opposing sides fight it out, and then, when the enemies have defeated each other, advance again to claim the reasonable middle ground. In a sense this is the strategy this book has pursued all along, in charting a critical realist course between uncritical realism (too easily assuming shared standards of what counts as truth) and hyper-suspicious relativism.

Critical realism and epistemological relativism involve an affirmation of religions as embracing truth claims, and a consequent welcoming of apologetics, even in the arena of dialogue. They pose questions for both the opposing ways of rejecting apologetics just described. For those who reject apologetics because it raises suspicions in dialogue, our position questions whether truth claims in religion inevitably commit believers to exclusivity. And for those who argue that apologetics assumes too much common ground, it questions whether truth claims in religious dialogue necessarily have to be assessed by universally accepted criteria for truth, in the form of a third set of beliefs and standards—probably liberal, secular beliefs and standards—which are external to and probably inimical to the religions themselves.

5. Burrell, "Response to Davies," 156–57.
6. Milbank, "End of Dialogue," 190.

According to Mark Heim, as discussed in chapter 4, Rescher's "operational pluralism" enables us fully to affirm a commitment to our own worldview as preferable to the others, while enabling us to grasp and understand why those who affirm a different worldview will, with equal necessity, hold their views as superior in the same way. This is not because of arrogance, but logic: the fact that to believe in something is to believe it is true and reliable, and to reject as false those positions that contradict it. "Rescher argues . . . that we necessarily assert the validity of our own perspective in the process of exercising it. It is both irrational and dishonest to argue otherwise."[7] So if, for example, I believe in the Christian faith then, though I may believe there are some areas where Christianity needs to learn from superior Buddhist understandings, I cannot believe that Buddhism offers completely or mainly better accounts and ethical standards than Christianity. I believe in Christian statements of faith because I have found them, on reflection, better or truer than their alternatives.

On the other hand, my Christian faith, if it is humble, will include an awareness of the fact that it is *as* a Christian that I make such judgments. It is because my standards of truth and morality have been formed and shaped by long-standing (perhaps lifelong) Christian practice that Christian beliefs and standards are likely to seem the best to me. There is a circularity at work here, not a vicious one but a humbling one: namely that by my Christian standards I judge the Christian standards to be the best. It is certainly not the case that I have leapt into some detached void or "view from nowhere" where, by standards totally objective and unbiased by any religion, I have come to see that Christianity is the best. What Milbank should enable us to see, however, is that if I judge in advance that Buddhism and Christianity, or all religions, are equally valid, it can only be by a similar assumption of a "view from nowhere." Chapter 1 noted how Hick, Knitter, and others all seem to assume some such objective stance as the (exclusive) basis of their pluralism.

So the role of apologetics in dialogue is subtle. Because religions involve truth claims that in many places contradict those of other religions, apologetics is necessary. But because claims make sense only within clusters and systems of propositions, including systems based on particular faiths, the apologetic enterprise can only proceed after a hermeneutical enterprise in which we enter deeply into the assumptions of the other faith and endeavor to understand what makes believers in that faith make the claims they do. And finally because, on our understanding, the objective emerges from the subjective via the intersubjective, dialogue can never work on a

---

7. Heim, *Salvations*, 136.

purely propositional level. Before any mutual apologetics based on appar-ently opposed truth claims, it will be necessary to do more than understand what the other is meaning in terms of their own religious framework. We will need to understand not only what it means for the other to believe x, but what it is like to believe it, or how x functions in terms of the other's phenomenal world.

If then the other's belief in x and my belief in y, which entails "not x," are opposed on a propositional level, three scenarios are possible. It may be that once I have understood how x functions in the other's religious context, I realize that it does not after all contradict what I understand by y in my be-lief context. But even if the contradiction persists at this level, it may be that what it is like for a believer to believe x in her context and what it is like for me to believe y in mine can interilluminate or generate an intersubjective rapport, in which new realities and new ways of thinking and feeling about them emerge. This possibility is not so often recognized, or distinguished from the first possibility. Finally, though, there is the possibility that our divergence persists at the most intimate level: that there is a clash of subjec-tivities, such that we really not only believe different things, but accordingly experience the world in ways that cannot be reconciled. If we are realists, albeit critical, that possibility cannot be ruled out, as it is in those forms of pluralism in which it is believed *a priori* that we must be experiencing the same ultimate reality. Convergence in understanding of one another's posi-tions in context, and interillumination between our subjectivities, are for us a prophetic hope, not a given.

Apologetics therefore is not out of place in dialogue, but the critique of the hold we each have on reality is a much more subtle affair than traditional apologetics often recognized. A simplistic apologetic can only be destruc-tive, if it simply judges the other wanting by my standards, as if the latter are neutral and objective. When Christians argue, for example, that Buddhism is inferior to Christianity because it is not a religion of love, they are mak-ing two mistakes. The first is not sufficiently attending to the presence of loving practice in Buddhism, but making a superficial judgment based on the *relative* absence of explicit reference to love in Buddhist teachings. The second is the assumption that the Christian teaching on love is an objective norm by which all religions must be judged. To say more cautiously, "to me as a Christian there seems to be less emphasis on love in Buddhism than in Christianity, which is one reason why I opt for the latter faith," would be much more humble and much more likely to invite an appropriate re-sponse. On the other hand, to assert dogmatically that Christianity as a religion of love and Buddhism as a religion of detachment are equally valid pathways to the same Ultimate would be as dialogue-stopping as the first approach. Good, enriching apologetics, and constructive debate over areas of disagreement, is predicated on an empathetic listening, a real attempt to understand what the other is saying in his context, and honesty in asserting the strength of one's own root convictions while humbly recognizing their conditioning context in turn.

In other words, apologetics has to follow from what Marianne Moyaert terms hermeneutical openness (see chapter 1). But at the same time, hermeneutical openness needs to be followed by an epistemological openness in which, having understood what each other is saying in their own terms, we come to consider what the other may be knowing through their claims, and whether it contradicts what we are knowing through ours, and if so, who is right. We need to not assume that we are saying and knowing the same things in different ways, but to allow what each of us knows to be genuinely and perhaps disturbingly different, such that the other may know realities we do not, *and vice versa*. Dialogue needs to move on from hermeneutical to epistemological openness, in which having ascertained that we understand each other and the context of commitment that underlies each others' beliefs, we begin to challenge each other, thus opening up the possibility not only of understanding but also of learning and discovery. Finally, we need to return to our own faiths and examine whether or not what we have learnt can be expressed in the context of our own belief system, or whether it is a reality that our religion cannot express without doing violence to itself; in which case we have learnt, not something expressible, but a quality of humility, a realization that our faith, however worthy it remains of our total commitment, cannot be viewed as a final word encompassing all the truth there is.

Griffiths' book ends with a helpful example of how his proposals might work in the case of dialogue between Buddhists and Christians on the existence or otherwise of the self.[8] Relativism would simply say that we cannot know what the other tradition means by the self (the problem of intelligibility), or that there is no shared way of evaluating the truth of Christian statements about the self vis-à-vis Buddhist declarations of its non-existence (the problem of incommensurability), or finally that there is no real world out there in which we either do or do not have selves (the issue of objective reference). Griffiths argues to the contrary that despite initial differences we can come to a common understanding of what we mean by the self, and why we do or do not believe in it; that we can therefore construct positive and negative apologetics regarding our own and the other's concepts of the self or no-self; and finally, that if this is done carefully and respectfully,

8. Griffiths, *Apology*, 99ff.

there is no reason to suppose we are not discussing an issue about the real world. So the three barriers can in principle (if not necessarily in practice) be overcome.

Real dialogue therefore is a tall and demanding order. It might seem impossible, but the next chapter will consider how it might actually work out in practice.

DIALOGUE AND TRINITY:
INCLUSIVISM BY ANOTHER NAME?

Though our conviction that religions make truth claims therefore does not represent a barrier to dialogue in the form of a new exclusivism, the criticism might obviously be made that the Trinitarian understanding sketched in chapter 3 represents just a new form of inclusivism. Though Panikkar presents his case as an argument for pluralism, and writes in a volume of essays with a similar aim,[9] an obvious query is whether it in fact represents, as D'Costa's Trinitarian approach explicitly does, the case for a kind of inclusivism, in which the Christian Trinity forms the template that includes all other faiths and even atheisms.

This criticism is more simple to counter. Panikkar's retort is along the lines that the Trinity names something that Christianity does not possess exclusively; that the teaching has its analogies in many faiths; and that historically Christianity has itself seldom been the best representative of a balance of the three pathways. And if there remains a sense in which the Christian Trinity "includes" all faiths, there may be other senses in which other faiths "include" Christianity, resulting in a *perichoresis* or mutual indwelling (and what I described as a mutual inclusion) of the faiths analogous to that believed to hold in the Trinity.[10]

In a later work Panikkar implicitly criticizes pluralist positions like those of John Hick, Wilfred Cantwell Smith, and Paul Knitter, and the familiar underlying image of the many religious paths up to the one mountain peak. Panikkar radically transforms this in a postmodern way:

> It is not simply that there are different ways leading to the peak, but that the summit itself would collapse if all the paths disappeared. The peak is in a certain sense the result of the slopes leading to it. . . . It is not that this reality *has* many names as if

9. Hick, *Myth of Christian Uniqueness.*
10. Panikkar, *Trinity and Religious Experience,* 60.

there were a reality outside of the names. This reality *is* the many names, and each name is a new aspect.[11]

The Trinity is therefore not the name for the Ultimate Reality to which all the diverse religions are subordinated as means to its end, but something more like the shape of the pathways themselves. If this is so then Panikkar offers an inclusivism that is neither merely a reiteration of Christian inclusivism, nor a kind of inclusivism by Western secular rationalism. Panikkar is an inclusivist, or a pluralist, with a difference: a difference that leads both D'Costa and Rowan Williams[12] to single his article out from those that stand alongside it in Hick's co-edited *Myth*. What is uncertain is how far this constructivist account can be reconciled with Panikkar's position,[13] which seems to rely on a realist understanding of the Trinity that precedes and transcends the constructions of Christianity.

In the previous chapter Panikkar's positing was expanded with reference, on the one hand, to the biblical account of creation, and on the other to a philosophical understanding of God as the view from everywhere. While obviously the biblical account is specific to two religions, the philosophical "expansion" of it offers something much less religion-specific; indeed we noted the idealist position it represents could be interpreted in a non-dual Buddhist or Hindu way. The Trinity therefore is not presented as Ultimate Reality—the common goal that includes all religions within Christianity—but rather as the Christian name for that which all religions, as patterns of knowing, loving, and being, must in their different ways represent and embody.

It might of course be criticized that this still represents a "something"—constructed out of a mix of Christian theology and rational dialogue—that "includes" all the faiths. Now if what we were claiming was that the Christian Trinity, or philosophical idealism, defines the reality that the other religions approximate to, then the criticism holds valid. But if all we are saying is that the different religions participate in reality, and then (lest this affirmation be a vacuous piety) try and say something about that reality from the limited and non-definitive perspectives of our Christianity or philosophy, then our inclusivity looks like something much more humble, tender, and potentially mutual. But this introduces our third area of critique.

11. Panikkar, *Unknown Christ*, 19 and 24.

12. In D'Costa, *Christian Uniqueness Reconsidered*.

13. In, for example, *Trinity and Religious Experience*.

DIALOGUE AND SECULAR PLURALISM:
BEING LIBERAL WITHOUT LIBERALISM?

> One can only regard dialogue partners as equal, independently
> of one's valuation of what they say, if one is already treating
> them, and the culture they represent, as valuable mainly in
> terms of their abstract possession of an autonomous freedom
> of spiritual outlook and an open commitment to the truth. In
> other words, if one takes them as liberal, Western subjects, im-
> ages of oneself.[14]

We are forced to ask whether the criticism John Milbank applies here
with characteristic vehemence to pluralism applies to our account too. Does
our or any commitment to religious dialogue commit us to acknowledging
a shared framework for it? Might it be argued, moreover, that our commitment (distinct from standard pluralism) to mutual apologetic and discussion of truth claims, commits us all the more to an impartial standard of
what counts as true? If not, by reference to whose standards are we claiming
to speak the truth?

In response, I argue on three fronts. Firstly, I distinguish the mini-
mal rules of reason that *are* the universal framework of argument from the
hegemony of a maximizing Enlightenment rationalism. Secondly, I argue
that when Enlightenment ideology, "secular reason," and the like figure in
theological thinking, it is as another "religion" in dialogue, not as a privi-
leged arbiter to whom religions are obliged to give account. Finally, I point
out that, apart from the basic constraints of reason, the criteria by which the
faiths assert their truth in dialogue are internal and particular, not external
and universal. Truth criteria are not "prolegomena" settled in advance of
dialogue but "dialegomena" discovered and tested in the dialogue itself.

Regarding the first point, we note that in the attacks on liberalism by
postliberal and Radical Orthodox theologians, it is not always asked what is
meant by liberalism. Arguably the term can mean two different things. One
is primarily an adjectival and adverbial qualifier of something else: we can
be or not be a liberal *x*, or do or believe *x* liberally or illiberally. Here our
primary identity or allegiance is defined by *x*: we are a liberal *Christian*, or
a liberal *socialist*, or whatever. The opposite of liberal is here something like
dogmatic, or fundamentalist, or ungenerous; "liberal" means holding our
beliefs in an open-minded, flexible, and reasonable way, with a readiness
to argue for them and defend them, but also to modify then in the light of
contrary arguments and criticisms. The other is primarily a noun. A person

14. Milbank, *End of Dialogue*, 178–79.

is no longer "liberal" so much as "a Liberal" or someone who believes in Liberalism. Here liberalism has come to denote the content of our beliefs and values, rather than our manner of believing something else. Liberalism now denotes an ideology. This difference in meanings means there is no contradiction in describing someone as a dogmatic liberal, for example, or a liberal conservative.

Now when the postliberals and Radical Orthodox theologians criticize liberalism it is quite clearly the second sense that is meant. Liberalism in this sense represents the ideology of what Milbank terms "secular reason," the ideology that tries to construct all knowledge on the limited kind of foundation considered to be "rational" or "empirical." Much of modern philosophy—from British empiricists like David Hume and A. J. Ayer to the grander and more reason-based constructs of Immanuel Kant and Friedrich Hegel—did indeed involve a great attempt to base belief and ethics, not on religious doctrine or "revelation," but solely on human reason and experience (in varying proportions), limiting belief to what they could verify, and constructing a worldview that applied universally and objectively whatever your personal or religious stance—Nagel's "view from nowhere."

Now it is clear that a participant in interreligious dialogue needs to be liberal in the first sense. Dialogue will be a very wooden affair unless participants hold their beliefs in a flexible way that is open to challenge and modification in the light of the dialogue. That does not mean, of course, a total openness. Unless participants are substantially committed to their respective faiths they can hardly participate as trusted representatives of those faiths. But someone who is committed to their faith in a dogmatic, exclusive way is hardly likely to be motivated to engage in dialogue in the first place, and if they do so engage, what ensues will be a dialogue of the deaf.

The critical realism and epistemological constructivism that I have advocated as the basis of dialogue, it must be noted, counsels us to be liberal in the first sense, since it commits us both to rational argument and critique and to the allowance of perspectives and ways of knowing other than one's own; yet this kind of liberalism actually undermines liberalism as an ideology, since it denies that we can arrive at definitive certainty on the basis of experience and argument.

It is very doubtful that, to participate in dialogue, liberalism as an ideology is necessary or even helpful. To believe that all one's claims, and those of one's partners, need to be based on rational argument and experience, to the exclusion of any appeal to revelation or any leaps of faith, is likely to limit dialogue on both sides.

And this brings us to the second point. Liberalism as an ideology is by no means to be despised. But it is best regarded as another faith, another cluster of Rescher's "epistemic values," and as such, another possible dialogue partner. In the case of Christianity, the dialogue with some form or other of the liberal rationalist religion has been going on since the early apologists of the second century, being renewed in thinkers like Aquinas, and again with the Renaissance humanists, and again in the dialogue with the Enlightenment that gave shape to the liberal theology of the nineteenth century, from Schleiermacher onward. And though theologians like Barth and Milbank mightily contend against subordination to, or theological accountability to, liberal ideology, it is obvious that they continue the dialogue with it, albeit in a characteristically hostile mode.

Theologian Robert Jenson makes the same point with reference to attempts to see "philosophy" as a distinct enterprise prior to theology. "Philosophy" here stands approximately for what I term the liberal rationalist ideology.

> We usually refer to the work of Greece's theologians with their own name for it, "philosophy." We have thereupon been led to think this must be a different kind of intellectual activity than theology, to which theology perhaps may appeal for foundational purposes or against which theology must perhaps defend itself. But this is a historical illusion; Greek philosophy was simply the theology of the historically particular Olympian-Parmenidean religion, later shared with the wider Mediterranean cultic world. The Church fathers, in direct contact with "the Greeks," were usually clear about this. In the view of most of them, the doctrines of the philosophers were simply the theologoumena of a different faith, with some of which it might be possible to agree, some of which had to be rejected, and some of which offered occasion of further discussion.[15]

Now if ideological liberalism is to be seen as a dialogue partner rather than the arbiter of dialogue itself, what should arbitrate and structure dialogue? This brings us to the third point: namely that in interreligious dialogue, the standards by which arguments and constructions are assessed need to be internal to the faiths in question, not some third, external set of criteria such as those provided by liberal ideology. Approaches like that of Cantwell Smith, for whom believers should only believe what is in principle believable by any "rational" person, are ruled out as excessively limiting, reducing faith as it does to a bland HCF acceptable to the rationalist skeptic.

My proposal needs qualifying, in the light of the need, just noted, for dialogue participants, not to be Liberals, but to be liberal; or as we might put

15. Jenson, *Systematic Theology 1*, 9.

it, not to be rationalist, but to be rational or reasonable; or, to use another concept presented in this book, to be concerned to do justice to one another. In this context there surely are criteria for what constitutes a rational debate, such as readiness to follow the basic rules of logic, for example, not being happy with self-contradiction, being prepared to follow arguments to logical conclusions, and recognizing a *reductio ad absurdum* when one sees it. In applying this kind of criterion, we are only applying what most religious traditions have applied to themselves in their internal debates, as when Christians have debated with other Christians, and Buddhists with Buddhists. (This is not to say that we should not allow mysticism in the religions, embracing, if need be, paradox and seemingly "absurd" tenets contrary to common sense. But mystics themselves have not been as irrational and self-contradictory as is commonly supposed: witness the writings of St. John of the Cross, Eckhart, Jalal ad-Din Rumi, or Bodhidharma.) So this kind of criterion is not external to the religions.

And beyond this requirement to be reasonable, I am suggesting that when say Buddhists and Christians engage in dialogue, it needs to be by reference to Buddhist and Christian criteria, not some third allegedly impartial adjudicator. At first sight, of course, this looks like a recipe for disaster, since by the Christian criteria all the Christian tenets would "win," and by the Buddhist criteria all the Buddhist ones would. But we need to move away from two implicit models here: that of dialogue as a kind of game or contest in which both sides aim to win, and an impartial referee is needed; and that of criteria as separate and prior to the act of dialogue, constituting a kind of "prolegomenon" that determines in advance what moves are legitimate and illegitimate. If we apply these models to the dialogue in which each side sets the criteria, then the result is indeed absurd: rather like a team of American footballers playing by the rules of America football on the one side, playing against a team of Englishmen playing by the rules of cricket on the other, each with their own referee!

But of course interreligious dialogue is not a contest, nor is it a game in which we know the rules in advance. We do not start life—or lively dialogue—with solemn "prolegomena" that we proceed to put into practice; we come to understand the rules we are following in the act of playing. In dialogue we do not merely apply what is fundamental to us, we discover more of it. And the dialogue itself needs to include the rules, such that in a Buddhist-Christian dialogue the criteria, insofar as they can separated from the dialogue at all, need themselves to be in dialogue, challenging or reinforcing one another. In other words, in dialogue it is not just our beliefs that are brought into relationship with those of the other, but our reasons for believing those beliefs. It is that which makes such dialogue so painfully challenging, but transformative.

In a Buddhist-Christian dialogue about the soul—for example—a little more needs to be said than was said above. The dialogue needs to move beyond the propositional contradiction between belief in the soul and belief in *anatta*. The Christian begins to ask himself, Why do I believe so passionately in the self? What work does this belief do in Christianity? What does it connect with? Where does it come from and where is it aiming to get us to? What are the criteria by which I affirm it as true? And the Buddhist likewise with the belief that there is no self. Out of this process we move beyond sheer contradiction to a possible convergence (or possibly to an even more fundamental divergence). The process is at one and the same time a move toward greater abstraction (from the question of whether the soul exists to the metaquestion of why the answer matters) and greater concreteness (from the general question of whether the soul exists to the subjective question of what it is like, and what it means for me as a Christian, to believe in it). It is by this movement—from the question in general to the metaquestion for me—that there arises the possibility of interillumination between our subjectivities: a view from both places that anticipates the divine "view from everywhere." Only in that context can the more rational discussion described by Griffiths above take on its full significance.

If there is no such view from everywhere, of course, this move would not be justified; there would in dialogue only be the possibilities of imposing my criteria on the other, or submitting to a third party "referee" to arbitrate between us. True interfaith dialogue involves relinquishing the prior convictions either that my position must be true whatever we say, or that both must be in some sense true. It involves an act of faith in what lies beyond us both—as yet—so leaving the partners quite open and vulnerable to whatever reasons to believe the dialogue itself may discover. In the next chapter this vulnerable but fundamentally adventurous and hopeful process will be explored.

CONCLUSION

This chapter has shown that theology has itself proceeded, and discovered realities, by a mixture of kinds of dialogue: proclamation, discernment, incorporation, and apologetics. It then showed how this mixed kind of dialogue that is theology offers, as we turn back to the issues of interrreligious dialogue, something new and distinct from the threefold paradigm, It affirms truth—even exclusive truths—without excluding other faiths as valid ways of knowing; it is Trinitarian in its approach to faiths, but not in the sense of including all faiths within the Christian model of the Trinity; and it is liberal and open, without being committed to ideological Liberalism.

But this discussion has been somewhat abstract; it remains to be seen whether it might work in practice, and if so, how in detail. That is the task for the next chapter.

CHAPTER 5

Interfaith Dialogue: A Model

THE PAST FOUR CHAPTERS have argued on philosophical and theological grounds for an epistemological constructivism, arguing that realism in religious belief involves us in an open dialogue. But the discussion has been broad and abstract, and the reader may by now be questioning what a reality-searching interreligious dialogue would actually look like. Can we really imagine that a common search for truth or knowledge beyond the framework of our particular religion forms a viable basis for interreligious dialogue, and vice versa?

The previous chapter also argued that dialogue characterizes the internal development of theology as much as its external relations with other religions. In this chapter we shall find that interreligious dialogue can learn a lot from long-established discussions of the intrareligious dialogue that is the reading of a religious text. The reading of the texts, whether of one's own or another religion, sets up a virtual dialogue in the reader's mind. Both text interpretation and dialogue involve three factors at work.

The first two factors are, in the case of interpretation, the reader and the text, and in the case of dialogue, the two partners who are endeavoring as it were to "read" each other. As human beings we each constitute what has been memorably described as a "living human document."[1] Each of us inhabits a conceptual world that is more or less different from that of the other, and in the light of that there takes place the effort of what is called hermeneutics, the attempt to interpret and understand. In reading a scripture or text, the hermeneutical effort can only be one-way: the reader is trying to understand the scripture but it is not trying to understand her.

---

1. Gerkin, *Living Human Document*.

In interreligious dialogue of course the hermeneutic effort is, or should be, mutual.

However, epistemological constructivism, as we saw, suggests that we cannot have any hermeneutic without an epistemology or theory of knowledge: an idea of what might make what is communicated true or false, or what might be learnt or known through the dialogue. This introduces a third element to the process: "reality": that is, an actual world that cannot be identified with either of the conceptual worlds of the dialogue partners (or the worlds of the reader and the text), though of course it can only be described through *some* conceptual world. Understanding the other therefore involves both bringing our conceptual world to the understanding of the other, and reframing our own conceptual world in the light of what we come to understand of the other. The language and conceptual worlds of each partner must be assumed to gain significance from their relation to reality.

This relation to reality may be of various kinds. Modernism has tended to prioritize the descriptive relationship, seeing the function of language as being primarily to provide a description that corresponds exactly with reality. But in practice language has many functions in addition to description. Language may deliberately conceal or lie about reality, and that too is a form of relation to reality. It may express as truth what is in fact a distorted or deluded picture. It may ask questions, express hopes and wishes, entertain hypothetical possibilities, or issue imperative commands. In each case two people are communicating with each other in the context of, and with a view to, how reality is or might come to be.[2]

So language opens to the real, not only by cognition, but also by imagination and volition. It is tautologous to say that language cannot directly convey perceptions about reality in a pristine, pre-linguistic state. But language is well suited to imagining, exploring, forming, and communicating a desire to produce a reality within the range of the possible. We cannot directly compare words with realities, but ideally we want our words to touch, explore, share, and bring about engagement with reality.

To adopt Gilbert Ryle's famous distinction between "knowing how" and "knowing that,"[3] the ideal of being detached desire-free observers who know the full range of facts—for whom "*knowing that . . .*" is fully mastered—proves unrealizable. The "view from nowhere" leads us nowhere. But in the full range of its grammatical moods, language explores and expresses ways of *knowing how* to live, including what to hope for. It issues from us—who are agents before we are speakers—as we survey the range

2. Cf. Ford, *Christian Wisdom*, 45ff.
3. Ryle, *Concept of Mind*, ch. 2.

of possibilities, hope for outcomes, and choose to, and perhaps command others to, act to produce something like those outcomes.

Our words, be they about buses or big bangs or Vishnu or God, grope toward realization. The term "realization" expresses several things we want to say at once at this point: making something that was only imagined before really happen; accomplishing an objective; and grasping a truth that was there before, but not noticed. It is the thrust towards realization in all three of these senses—imaginative, volitional, and cognitive—that makes language what it is, communication, and energizes language and drives it along. Text interpretation and dialogue both involve all these modes of relating, in a complex mutual process, not only of sharing of vision, but of exposing of delusion, engendering of hope, and many other aspects. It is this complex process that this chapter will unravel.

FOUR ELEMENTS OF ENCOUNTER

I propose that the encounter with reality through dialogue with the other contains four key elements, because—as will become clear at the end of the chapter—both I and the other, in our beliefs and conceptual schemes, embrace knowledge and ignorance, and insight and illusion. Here I flesh out the potential methods available to the account developed in the previous three chapters, and especially the four kinds of intrareligious dialogue argued to be the creative basis of theology. The previous chapter considered four processes involved in the *making or writing* of theological texts; all four processes were seen as a mode of dialogue analogous to the dialogical process whereby God is described as creating the world. The four methods described here relate to the *reading and interpreting* of religious texts and of the religious speech of the other. The four processes therefore do not exactly correspond, though I shall suggest they are close to being mirror images of each other.

Though as chapter 2 noted this was not implied in the original development of the concept by Kuhn, incommensurability is sometimes presented as a kind of impermeable wall, analogous to the Berlin Wall or the West Bank Wall, dividing religions and cultures from one another. So I give each section a playful name, referring to the way, without denying the existence of those walls, our four elements can facilitate dialogue despite them.

1) Dancing on the Walls: Imagination

We must not underestimate imagination. I cannot entirely believe in the hierarchical, three-tier, faith-fired world of Aquinas and Dante, but I can imaginatively enter into it and identify with some of the things that mattered to them. The Nepali described in chapter 2 cannot make himself believe in the drifting continents and buckling mountains of the geologist's mythology, nor can the scientist make himself believe in Vishnu. But each can endeavor to imagine what it would be like to hold those beliefs. Our worlds are not transparently open to each other, but they are not hermetically sealed, and it is the imagination that opens us to other perspectives and enables us to use them to enlarge our own. Therefore, though we do not all inhabit the same universe of discourse, there is something like a continuum of conceptual universes we can step in and out of, through the power of imagination. Through imagination we can dance defiantly on the walls between our cultures, and see a view on both sides (even if we cannot know how far it really resembles the view from inside each culture).

But what is imagination? We might define it, provisionally, as a focus on the connotations of our words and thoughts—including the associations they conjure up—suspending concern about their denotation or what they refer to. When we read a poem like, for example, Blake's *Tiger*, we suspend concern with whether there are actual tigers "burning bright / in the forests of the night." Tigers are actually not, in point of fact, luminous, let alone ablaze, in forests at night time! But the image, the connotation of the word tiger, does cohere well with the startling image of something aflame in the darkness. When we respond imaginatively to a religion, in the same way, we allow its stories and images and art to stir up deep associations in our mental life, without concerning ourselves with whether it is true. Chapter 9 will expand on this provisional understanding of the imagination.

Our engagement with the text must begin with imagination: we must know what it means and suggests before we can evaluate its truth. I suspect it is often the case that our interest in another faith, or our conversion to the faith we now have, begins with imagination. In my own case, my interest in interreligious dialogue might well proceed from an over-heated imagination! As a six-year-old boy attending church, most of the conceptual content obviously went over my head, but the rich array of imagery in the Anglo-Catholic ritual, appealing to all the senses, gave me an imaginative sense of Christianity that would draw me back more intellectually and emotionally later on. And I remember how my first reading about Buddhism, and more especially later about the intricacies of Tibetan Vajrayana Buddhism, introduced me to an imaginary world that was wholly strange and yet curiously familiar too. In my youthful imagination, cold, wide Tibetan landscapes somehow fused with imaginary temples, the intricate arrays of cloud-riding Tibetan Buddhas, and the rarefied, expansive concepts of the Mahayana traditions. No doubt these mysterious worlds of the imagination have as much to do with us as with the religion in question; I was certainly naive. But the beginnings of dialogue with the other is bound to involve a naivety that cries out to be extended and deepened by critique. And dialogue can be killed if skepticism and criticism are brought to bear prematurely.

So Paul Ricoeur describes the "first naivety" of reading a text for the immediacy of its imaginative appeal, and allowing an imaginary world to be conjured up "in front of the text."[4] The text at this stage is mainly a stimulus to the imagination, and little thought is given to whether this corresponds to anything in the author's intention. The careful attention to what the images may have meant in the context of the author's culture are, at this stage, beside the point.

In the field of literature, pioneered by the likes of F. R. Leavis and Cleanth Brookes, the New Criticism of the 1940s and 50s rejected the preceding concern for history and context, and focused on the text itself, and especially the structures of symbolism and imagery within it. More recently this literary approach has been applied to the Bible, not least by those of the narrative school to be discussed in chapter 6. The concern to establish context was abandoned, and metaphysical issues of theological reality suspended, in favor of close attention to the text as literature. But of course, before the rise of critical method, the Bible had long been approached as a springboard to disciplines of the imagination, such as Jewish Midrash and Ignatian meditation.

Now it might seem that imaginative readings have, by definition, little to do with reality. Imagination is often defined as visualizing, or entertaining thoughts of, or framing stories about what does not exist or is not believed in. Or at least (as suggested above) disbelief is suspended, and the sense of words is enjoyed for its own sake, occluding any reference. Two points must be made in response.

The first is that the world of appearance is not sheer delusion. There is such a thing as how things really appear to me, and what it truly feels like for me to experience them. Phenomenology—the study of how things appear, bracketing out questions of what really exists behind the appearances—has been hugely important in twentieth-century philosophy, and significant in religious studies after the decline of the more abstract comparative religion approach. To be able to convey to a Buddhist, for example, what it is like to

4. Ricoeur, *Rule of Metaphor*.

worship and pray as a Christian, and for a Tibetan Buddhist to convey to a Christian what it is like to meditate or to visualize the meditation-Buddha Tara, and how the green Tara is experienced differently from the white—all this can set up real interillumination in defiance of our official accounts of reality.

Although science tells me a lot about the planet Venus, as a barren lifeless rock surrounded by suffocating gas, still the experience of gazing at the evening star as the golden sunlight recedes and the sky darkens and becomes more populous with stars: that is a *real* experience that science cannot take away, and only poetry better than mine can convey. Music too offers a real experience, conjured not by any reference to the world, but by pure interrelations between sound "images"—patterns of melody, harmony, and rhythm. We need, here, to speak of "phenomenal realities" or perhaps less paradoxically of phenomena we can experience and so know: imaginary experiences stimulated by sounds and words that can interact and resonate with one another as they are in their own right, irrespective of any objective reference.

The second point is that the entertaining of unrealized and perhaps unrealizable possibilities (the subjunctive voice) and the dreaming up of worlds to be desired (the optative) are surely preconditions for working for realizable and desirable goals, as well as for finding new ways of looking at the reality that already exists. Those predecessors of Copernicus who first conceived of the idea that the sun was the center of the universe must have wondered whether they were entertaining a wild fantasy. We know that Johannes Kepler, for example, entertained the heliocentric view because of his attachment to a Platonic poetic in which the sun was a metaphor for the form of the Good, and he imagined (in a beautifully imaginative mistake, expressed in his *Mysterium Cosmographicum*, 1596) that the orbits of the planets were correlated with the Platonic solids.

Chapter 9 will have more to say about the imaginative realization of experience as experience, and the conjuring of imaginary worlds, and especially, following Ricoeur, about the interilluminative role of metaphor in this. For now, I suggest that interreligious dialogue needs to be unashamedly imaginative. The Jew in dialogue might produce Midrash on the Buddhist texts, for example, while the Buddhist might explore the resurrection with Ignatian imagination. In the process an interillumination of experiences may take place, a suggestion on which chapter 9 will expand. In this process we emphasize *what I and the other both know* on the imaginative level, and explore likenesses and differences between what is it is like to be . . . a Jew, a Buddhist . . . . This is the first stage in our being able to realize worlds we can share.

But only the first stage. The imaginative suspension of the real differences may sparkle and rejuvenate, but for any sparks of interillumination to set our worlds on real fire, more work has to be done. For all their poetic and musical aspect, religions are not *only* invitations to imagine and desire, though they surely are that.

2) Circumscribing the Walls: Context

Language (whether written or spoken) is not something immaterial. The very reason Derrida prefers to speak of there being nothing "outside the text" rather than "outside of language" is that text denotes something physical, whereas language and speech can *appear* immaterial and spiritual.[5] But of course, speech itself is a physical event, an inscription in sound waves on the air, if you like. This means that language, or text, is actually in the world it describes. The world may be "in" language in the sense that language forms and shapes all the knowledge of the world we have. But this needs to be balanced by the other manifest fact that language is something that happens in the world; there is absolutely nowhere else for language to happen!

This offers a way of circumscribing the walls between cultures. We can learn how and when the walls got built, and write about the other culture as a materially arising entity. In doing so it is as if we go round the walls to look at the culture from an "objective"—or in the jargon "etic," meaning "outside"—perspective that purports to improve on the culture's "emic" insider view of itself. To do so, of course, we have to stay within a thoroughly "modern" way of doing things. But a case may yet be made for doing so.

Some of Derrida's interpreters have proposed a kind of linguistic idealism, denying the existence of an objective world or anything else except language. According to Don Cupitt, for example, "I am made of and by the torrent of words that spins through me each day, and you are made of and by the torrent of words that spins through you."[6] But this is not what Derrida seems to be saying. For him, it is precisely the objective, material existence of the text that is being emphasized, while the ideal or spiritual penumbra of meaning is subordinated to this textual materiality.

Hence in relating to the written text—or equally the living text of the human other, who is of course only manifest to me, communicating spirit and meaning, as a material being—it is vital to understand the other as a material production gaining meaning from its social origin and context. Modern times saw the advent of a wealth of new ways of approaching the

5. Derrida, *Of Grammatology*, 3ff.
6. Cupitt, *Revelation of Being*, 69.

biblical text, seeing it not (at least in the first instance) as divine revelation, but as a human artefact. Historical criticism sought to unearth the social conditions that gave rise to the text; textual criticism attended to clues of such context in the text itself; source criticism broke up the text into parts arising from different traditions with different historical origins; form criticism attended to the literary genre manifest in the shape of the text; and so forth.

In dialogue with someone of another faith, it is important to learn and know a lot about their own history, and the whole symbolic order that makes sense of their ideas and practices, so that we "hear where they are coming from." That phrase, though hackneyed and potentially patronizing, remains significant in that it speaks of the origins of the other's beliefs, and acknowledges a background space from which the other has, as it were, come into your foreground. Paul Ricoeur uses the same spatial analogy when he speaks of "going behind the text," reconstructing a world from which the text has, so to speak, come forward to meet you.

Such a learning of the other culture may precede the process known— especially in Roman Catholic circles after Vatican 2—as inculturation, in which we attend to and learn the ways of another culture in order to find ways of communicating what we believe in terms the other can comprehend. Interreligious dialogue cannot of course be a one-way process of inculturation, in which the text of the one simply adapts to the context of the other; this would be a one-way communication and not a dialogue. Nevertheless, we could say that *mutual* inculturation is an indispensable part of such dialogue. Each partner will try to express what she feels she knows in a form the other can understand, expressing her own faith in terms of the other's culture. The corollary, necessary if this is to work, is that she will also need to be willing to receive and acknowledge the other's faith—perhaps truth—expressed in the terms of her own culture.

But such a process has two limitations. First, it involves the "modern" arrogance described earlier as "the view from nowhere." The knowledge involved is "objective" knowledge in the weighty modern sense: the knowledge only accessible to the detached, neutral, omnipresent, and omnicompetent observer. The text interpreter or dialogue partner assumes the perspective that focuses on *what I know that the other does not (or not yet)*. I assume I know the other's cultural context objectively, and that the other participates in this context subjectively, being too much identified with it to understand it. I hold a typically modern scientific or historical set of well-founded certitudes and methodologies, which I insist must circumscribe and delimit what in the other's faith is believable.

So while seeing the other in context is an important aspect of encountering the other, "contextualising" the other may be a way of avoiding the other's otherness. The other becomes a fact in my conceptual scheme, an "it" I know all about rather than a "you" who offers me something different. The claim that I know why the other is saying what she is saying permits me to avoid listening carefully to what she is saying, and any challenges it offers to my perspective.

That is why modern, reductionist hermeneutics are often suspicious of all cultures but their own. Marxists explain away all culture "scientifically" in terms of class conflict and the laws of economics, but cannot explain the rise of Communism in feudal societies like Russia and China; feminists justly expose the blind spots and oppressive nature of patriarchy, but risk taking their own feminist assumptions as the last word, beyond a critique of power;[7] Nietzsche exposed the roots of Christianity in resentment and craving for power, but failed to anticipate the potentially fascist uses of his own account of the will to power.

On the other hand, religions often have an arrogance of their own. The truths of my faith can become the "objective" viewpoint, which I seek to inculturate in the other's context so that he will immediately want to convert. Even a mutual inculturation can involve a curious kind of mutual arrogance, in which each partner assumes she knows more about her own truth and the other's culture than the other does. This is bound to subvert the course of dialogue if not complemented by other, humbler approaches.

The second problem is the assumption of an easy divide between truth or belief and context. Content or meaning is assumed to be the hardcore indispensable thing, which can be clothed in any number of cultural forms, and easily "unpacked" from one cultural package and wrapped in another. Such is the assumption of a weak, "semantic" constructivism for which terms have a variety of possible connotations deriving from culture and context, but there is no serious doubt as to what they are about or what makes statements true or false.

Now in reality there is always a continuum between what people regard as more essential in their faith and what they regard as more dispensable. Many a Christian, for example, would regard the historical truth of the raising of Lazarus as dispensable, and the historical truth of the resurrection of Jesus as essential. This might be because the latter is a creedal belief, but more profoundly it would also probably be because if the resurrection of Jesus did not in some sense "happen," then the whole Christian faith would

7. Cf. West, *Deadly Innocence*.

require a radical rewriting, if indeed it could survive at all. The same is not true if the resurrection of Lazarus did not happen.

The continuum involved here applies to all bodies of belief, not just religions. In science, for example, if a particle moves faster than expected, that is no problem, but if a particle seems (as in the experiments in September 2011 at Gran Sasso) to go faster than light, that is deeply resisted. This is not because of some obscure scientific "creed," but for the same reason as applies in the Christian case: the drastic and total rewriting of a highly successful theory (Special Relativity) that would have to be done if a particle were found to go faster than light.

In any dialogue, then, there will be beliefs each partner sits light to, and others she will rightly resist giving up. But this does not amount to a hard and fast distinction between adaptable form and indispensable content. If epistemological constructivism is true, content and expression are much more intimately connected, because *all* the beliefs are interconnected with one another and with practice, so that we cannot differentiate an indispensable core from beliefs and practices more lightly dispensed with. In the game context, dispensing with or tweaking an apparently trivial rule (for example, the complex castling rules in chess) can have a huge unforeseen impact. May it not be the same for religious beliefs and practices?

Certainly religions vary across cultures, and some practices and beliefs are more obviously derived from local culture than others. But the question of origin should not be identified with the question of knowledge. Consider, for example the unique Latin American forms of the cult of the Virgin Mary, or friendship with Jesus in Southern Baptist Evangelicalism, or the adoration and visualization of Tara in Tibetan Buddhism. Who knows whether what particular Christians and Buddhists know to be true may not be bound up with these particular "cultural forms," rather than some identifiable and separable universal Christian or Buddhist "content"?

Interreligious dialogue is impossible, of course, if the partners are not prepared to stand by what they regard as essential to their faith, and without an element of wanting to inculturate these elements in terms the other can understand and ideally believe. An element of mutual conversion needs to be going on. Unless the dialogue partners are truly representing their faiths in this way there is no interreligious dialogue, only an open-ended discussion. In the same way, looking for context is an essential aspect of interpreting a text. On the other hand, dialogue that is *only* an attempt at mutual inculturation, and textual interpretation that is *only* an attempt to find the context behind the text, will sooner or later reach the double impasse of objectivizing arrogance and the indefinability of the boundary between form and content. To go further, dialogue and interpretation have to grapple with the text (living or written) itself, and enter the darkness.

3) Undermining the Walls: Deconstruction

It was Socrates who first pointed out the role of *aporia*—literally "wayless-ness" or "resourcelessness"—in our coming to knowledge. In the writings of Plato he teaches that we cannot move from the realm of mere opinion to true knowledge without first having our presuppositions called into question. Socrates saw his primary role as being to induce precisely such an *aporia*, so that people would begin to think and wonder, and reason their way towards genuine knowledge. He sought to undermine the conceptual walls of opinion with which people surround themselves, exposing how shallow their foundations were, and enabling them to collapse, to let in the light of truth.

To this day science develops through *aporia* and doubt. Philosopher Karl Popper has argued that falsifiability is what makes a theory truly scientific: theories can only embody knowledge if we are clear about what circumstances would make us abandon them.[8] Thomas Kuhn on the other hand emphasized that normally scientists do not doubt their theories but seek to extend them. But still he argued that it was anomalies that forced the revolutionary changes of paradigm thorough which science most dramatically advances.

> Normal science does not aim at novelties of fact or theory and, when successful, finds none. New and unsuspected phenomena are, however, repeatedly uncovered by scientific research, and radical new theories have again and again been invented by scientists. History even suggests that the scientific enterprise has developed a uniquely powerful technique for producing surprises of this sort. . . . Produced inadvertently by a game played under one set of rules, their assimilation requires the elaboration of another set.[9]

Religions, meanwhile, have a reputation for making a virtue of clinging to opinions regardless of the facts, and never allowing doubt. In this they resemble Kuhn's "normal science," proceeding by assimilating new truth to old, tried and tested traditions. However, religion like science has its revolutions and revolutionaries too. Jesus and the Buddha, in their different ways,

8. Popper, *Conjectures and Refutations*.
9. Kuhn, *Structure of Scientific Revolutions*, 52.

often used their discourse to shatter the opinionated complacency of their hearers, and get them wondering and pondering. And the mystics of many faiths speak of the need of a dark night of confusion—Jan van Ruysbroeck's "wayless way" and the anonymous English mystic's dark "cloud of unknowing"—in the ascent to ultimate knowledge. (More on them in chapter 9.)

Samuel Johnson famously refuted philosopher George Berkeley's notion that only ideas were real by kicking a stone. Just as when we collide with things we know they are physically real, so the experience of mental collision, the *skandalon* or stumbling block of *aporia*, assures us that we are grappling with a reality in our thoughts, something bigger than our preconceptions. When everything goes smoothly, on the other hand, it may be because we are merely projecting our theory onto the world and refusing to acknowledge discrepancies.

It is this that makes the "deconstruction" advocated by Derrida—currently a widely pursued approach to literary and cultural criticism—more than a purely destructive process. Deconstruction has been defined as

> a technique of literary analysis that regards meaning as resulting
> from the differences between words rather than their reference
> to the things they stand for. Different meanings are discovered
> by taking apart the structure of the language used and exposing
> the assumption that words have a fixed reference point beyond
> themselves.[10]

What deconstruction destroys, then, is the illusion of a stable world, fully grasped and clearly delineated in the language of the author. By showing how meanings in the text shift and self-contradict, deconstruction thrusts us back on the sea of meanings. It is as if we first think of ourselves as looking on the text as a calm sea that perfectly reflects the world, such that we hardly notice the sea but look through it to the objects in the world. But then we begin to notice the sea is in fact moving and flowing, distorting the objects that seemed so real. We begin to attend not to the world but to the "sea" of text itself.

The deconstructive approach differs from the contextual approach in three ways. The contextual hermeneutic looks (1) behind and outside the text for clues that can make for (2) a solid, definitive account of (3) the author's meaning in his context. The overall perspective is, as noted, the clear view from nowhere, something akin to the neutral and infinite sensorium of Newtonian space. The emphasis is on what I know that the text does not: on what I need, as it were, to inform the text about in order for its meaning to clarify; on "objective" knowledge as certitude produced by the

10. *Collins English Dictionary.*

appropriate method. The deconstructive hermeneutic looks (1) at the text alone to (2) undermine the illusion of solidity and (3) dissolve any definitive understanding of the author and her intention. The overall perspective is the confused and shifting view from somewhere in particular, namely the text itself. We are now in something analogous to Einsteinian space, a shifting space whose curve is generated by the objects in it. The emphasis is on what *neither I nor the author (yet) know*, the as-yet-hidden and unconscious motives of us both, whose collusion needs to be unraveled if the real is to appear. Reality here is more like Jacques Lacan's "real" or Freud's unconscious, or even perhaps the disturbing YHWH of the prophets: that outside our symbolic structure which moves and disrupts that structure, confounding methodological correctness.

The focus on the text is reminiscent of the imaginative approach, but in that approach insights and interilluminations are accepted and enjoyed "naively," at face value. With deconstruction we arrive at Ricoeur's "hermeneutic of suspicion," which he saw as pioneered by Karl Marx, with his exposure of ideology and false consciousness, Friedrich Nietzsche, with his account of the will to power in human communication, and Sigmund Freud, with his emphasis on the unconscious and its repressed motives and meanings.

Interreligious dialogue, to my knowledge, has so far failed to embrace such deconstruction. But I suggest that dialogue needs, at decisive points, to be prepared to enter the abyss of the incommensurable, and seek what neither partner yet knows, the immeasurable real. To this end, those in dialogue need to be prepared to unmask each other, and to be unmasked, in a process of mutual deconstruction.

We need to be asked by the other, for example, why we are so anxious to stick to certain formulae. What ego-investment or assertion of power is going on? Why is our energy so different at this point of the dialogue, from the confident and generous openness that marks true knowledge? Why, for instance, have we become bodily edgy and tetchy? And we may need to press the other on what seem to us to be contradictions or inconsistencies in their language, asking questions like, "If there is no self in Buddhism, how can nirvana come solely through self-reliance?" and "If the Christian God is all-loving, why can he not forgive us without his own Son being tortured and sacrificed to him?" These are naive, childlike questions; but we all know that children are adept deconstructors of our adult pretensions, expert at asking why the emperor has no clothes.

At times the mutual deconstruction may seem crude and destructive. But Derrida does not suggest that there is nothing that survives deconstruction. For him, what survives is the justice that emerges when the power and manipulation implicated in the text is exposed and brought to consciousness.[11] But what is expressed here negatively—as liberation from ideology—can be expressed more positively. It is arguable that what survives deconstruction is truth as lived, belief that is not merely entertained with the mind but goes to the heart and guts, being rooted in an active, practical apprehension of reality. We emerge from deconstruction believing in less but more strongly, with chastened, leaner faiths more fit for action. In that sense a mutual deconstruction can save us from the idolatrous attachments that most faiths contain yet actually counsel us against, and open the path to inter-action.

4) Leaping over the Walls: Interaction

The two imaginary "circle" cultures discussed in chapter 2 did not just have different languages or mythologies that somehow packaged their world up in different, irreconcilable ways. In each case their concepts related to practices: in the once case, the practice of designing wheels, in the other, the practice of geometry. Each represented tradition, not bare theory, but bodies of procedure: ways of living in the world, handed down from teacher to pupil or apprentice. It was these procedures that the hypothetical cultures could learn from one another, enabling them to pool their knowledge, leaping over the walls that had seemed to divide them.

Actual bodies of knowledge function in the same way. The religions are first and foremost traditions that have to be learnt, and the skills and virtues they instill passed on. This is perhaps clearest in Buddhism, where purely theoretical questions are discouraged and doctrine is firmly attached to the practical business of progressing toward the goal, through right life, right meditation, and the other components of the Eightfold Way. But Lindbeck and the other postliberals to be discussed in chapter 6, and the otherwise very different liberation theologians to be discussed in chapter 7, agree on this point, that theology is to be regarded as "true" insofar as it leads to right action. Orthopraxis is the test of orthodoxy.

But this is true of the sciences too. Michael Polanyi has taught us to see scientists as a community engaged in certain traditions of relating to each other, passing on traditions that are skills of interacting, through experiment, with the world. Each theoretical system of knowledge, according to him, is also a system of social interaction.[12] Chapter 2 discussed how Wittgenstein's concept of the language game likewise emphasized how sciences

11. Cf. discussion in Cornell, *Deconstruction and the Possibility of Justice*.
12. Polanyi, *Personal Knowledge*.

and religions alike are, like games, learnt by following in a tradition of social interaction; and that interaction is a major feature of games often neglected by those who advocate the language game model. [13]

However, there are at least two senses in which the language game is not a good analogy for the sciences and religions. First *language* is not the only thing we "play with" in science and religion. Science uses mathematics too, not to mention experimental operations. Religions use meditation and other practices that aim to go beyond language, and bodily and liturgical actions, which are more than only verbal. Kimberly Hope Belcher writes of the "efficacious engagement" of a baby with baptismal ritual; obviously the child cannot understand the words, but it can participate through bodily play and interaction.[14] Polanyi likewise writes about the tacit knowledge that cannot be put into words or theory, comprising a scientist's basic skills of experimenting and observing, learnt in the scientific community to which he belongs, guiding him toward discovery and the formulation of more explicit theory.[15] Ryle's aforementioned "knowing how" could be described as tacit knowledge of this kind.

Secondly, and more important, the *game* is something played for its own sake, for a mixture of the fun of the play itself, the social interaction generated, and the desirability of building on the basic knowledge of the rules to form wider strategic and sometimes bodily skills, so as to "win." The game does not embody knowledge of anything outside itself. But though science may involve "winning," the victory is that of discovery. And though social interaction and community building are important in religion, they are not important as ends in themselves, but in order to help save the world, or accomplish the distinct ends of the religion. Though religion and science can be profoundly playful activities, they are serious play, not carried out just for the fun of it.

Wittgenstein's own examples of language games do not imply either linguistic exclusiveness or triviality, but many who have taken on the analogy and applied it to science and religion have carried over these implications. The sciences and religions are then presented as being as self-contained and as oblivious of any world beyond, like chess or cribbage.

The truth is precisely the opposite. I suggest it is because they carry forward and extend the childlike and original way we know the world beyond us—namely play—that playing language (and other ritual) games is the best way we have of deepening our contact with reality. Some of the

13. Wittgenstein, *Philosophical Investigations*, 50ff.

14. Belcher, *Efficacious Engagement*, 44ff.

15. Polanyi, Personal Knowledge, 87ff, and *Tacit Dimension*.

best analogies for knowledge derive from sport and play, such as the sailing example in chapter 2.

It is interaction that takes us beyond the fixity of the indicative to all the other moods described above. Action generates, alongside this indicative (what is happening right now), the subjunctive (what might I now do, or might have done), the interrogative (what is it best to do, and how can it be achieved), the optative (what do I hope to do and where do I want to go), the jussive (what ought to be done or must happen), and the imperative (what must I therefore do). Language games, I suggest, serve to extend the range of these moods and widen the context of my action.

In games we learn different ways of playing with reality. Science is clearly built on the subjunctive and the interrogative as much as the indicative. The basis of experiment is the question, "What would happen if . . . ?" Religious language games involve questions and the hypothetical imagination too, but they also evoke the optative and invoke the imperative: learning to long for this (the kingdom . . . nirvana) we must do that (the ethical path). The whole of our life and universe is restructured around the deeply serious play demanded by our religious "game" (which is, as noted, not only a *language* game).

The previous section described how deconstruction can expose ideology, which we might now describe as a malfunction of the moods of our game. Typically—as exposed by the masters of suspicion such as Nietzsche, Marx, and Freud—ideological language ties indicatives, optatives, and imperatives together in a self-perpetuating contradiction or delusion. Because we see the world as x, we believe that in order to achieve y we must do z, but in practice z undermines y. Because, for example, we believe that only the triumph of our religion will liberate the world, and we long for everyone's liberation, we believe it imperative to persecute, imprison, or conquer all those who reject our religion. So our striving for people's liberation actually accomplishes its opposite. (One recalls the words of the American general in Vietnam, who declared that in order to liberate the village it had to be destroyed . . . .)

Ideological language is not necessarily false on a descriptive level (the religion may well have a liberating message). Ideology is false in terms of the passing on of encoded delusions about the world that reinforce bad practice, and hence, negative, oppressive societies. More on this in chapter 7. The religions need to ask, not only whether they are true, but whether belief in them is functioning in a liberating way, a way that enhances people's play with the real. The question of truth cannot be separated from the "metaquestion" of ideology: the question, raised at the end of chapter 4, of what it is that makes us cling to certain beliefs.

But the answer to the metaquestion need not always be negative. What makes me cling to a belief so fervently may be good possibilities of life it opens up, or the realities it enables me to engage with. The possibility of ideology entails the possibility of its opposite: a language game that actually does tie the moods together in a creative way, and enhance life and liberation. This is a question we can ask of the text we interpret. We need to ask, what practices of engaging with truth, and what self-deception, are being lived out within this text? But this is the kind of question that probably cannot be answered except in the context of a search for redemption or liberation. Having engaged in a painful mutual deconstruction, exposing one another's ideological tendencies, partners in dialogue can begin to ask, *what does the other seem to know that I do not (or do not yet)?* And this question—what does the other seem to know?—is primarily a question about knowledge embodied in practice. What truth is the other living, what reality is he inhabiting, what positive transformation of life is she undergoing, that I would like to learn and incorporate into my own play with the real?

DIALOGICAL WRITING AND DIALOGICAL READING

How do the four elements of encounter just described relate to the four modes of theological creativity discussed in chapter 4? That chapter considered four processes involved in the *making or writing* of theological texts, whereas the four elements of encounter just discussed relate to the *reading and interpreting* of religious texts and of the religious speech of the other. There are two differences here. Firstly, the concern in theological writing is primarily epistemological, and secondarily hermeneutical, while the concern in reading is primarily hermeneutical, and secondly epistemological. That is to say, in theological and other religious creativity, the goal is to create an account we can know, or failing that, in the context of our tradition, believe to be true. The creation and comprehension of meaning is a necessary means to that end, since if we do not know what we mean, we can hardly know whether we are right. But in dialogue with others and engagement with texts, the primary goal is make to sense of the other, and the question of truth arises because we cannot know what the other means unless we know what knowledge they are expressing, and what would make their claims true or false.

Secondly, the previous chapter's four categories related to the writing and making of religious and theological traditions, while this chapter has been concerned with their reading and interpretation. In the former case, the perspective is that of the writer trying to arrive at truth by means of an inner or virtual dialogue, while in the latter the perspective is that of the reader or the dialogue partner trying to make sense of an explicit dialogue. Our two fourfold patterns may therefore be looking at the same process from different ends, such that the four elements in each case are approximately mirror images of each other. Does this suggestion work?

1. *Proclamatory writing mirrors interilluminative reading.* The process concerns what both writer and reader already know, though the reader has to be reminded by the writing, which comes as a "bolt from the blue" casting light on the reader's predicament and calling forth a "naive," direct response as to an imperative command.

2. *Analytical writing mirrors contextual reading.* The process concerns what the reader knows and the writer naively embodies without explicitly knowing. The theological writer is here essentially the reader of a tradition, which is in a sense the original writer, from whose naive *stories*, by careful analysis and broad historical knowledge, she "*restores*" a description of how the world is and how we ought to live.

3. *Apologetic writing mirrors deconstructive reading.* Through a mode that is primarily interrogative, writer and reader expose what the other does not know. Theology anticipates its possible deconstruction and writes for whose whom Schleiermacher called its "cultured despisers." It endeavors to answer the profound questions set by the wider world, even as it asks that world questions of its own, in order to show what escapes deconstruction, leading to a purified clarity of message.

4. *Incorporative writing mirrors interactive reading.* Both concern what the writer knows and the reader learns by incorporation. The mood is mainly subjunctive and optative, as resources are gathered from all sources—Christianity, Socialism, Feminism, local religions—and set in interaction to provide active practical hope for human liberation.

A FOURFOLD PATTERN FOR DIALOGUE

But as well as being set in relation with the modes of theological writing, the four elements of encounter need to be brought into relation with one another. The question needs to be posed, are they rival or contradictory processes, or can they work together in a coherent process of interpretation or dialogue? It is possible to sum up the different processes in *Table 1*, which rather like the Johari Window, maps out what is known and unknown in my relation to the other.

Table 1: A Fourfold Hermeneutic for Dialogue

	What I know	What I don't know
What the other knows	1. *Imagination*: reaching an interilluminative imaginary. Mutual enrichment of phenomenal knowledge.	4. *Interaction*: Engaging with the liberating practices of the other, perhaps working together for liberation. Practical knowledge.
What the other does not know	2. *Context*: each learning the culture of the other and how each might express her belief in the other's context. "Objective" knowledge.	3. *Deconstruction*: bringing each other to *aporia*, unknowing. Knowledge as rupture: the Lacanian "real" beyond our symbols.

Out of this pattern it might be possible to trace a rich and plausible process for dialogue, consisting of . . . .

1. *Interillumination.* We each "naively" let the other inspire us, delighting in a piecemeal way in the imaginary world conjured up by the other, suspending questions of disbelief. For most, interreligious dialogue begins here, and here it often ends, with the intuitive affirmation of "what we share," bracketing out the deeper questions of what might be true.

2. *Mutual inculturation.* We learn about each other's historical and social contexts, so passing beyond the first impressions—what the other's imagery "does for me"—to a serious attempt to grasp the wider context of the "language game" the other is playing. We each then try to express the truth as we see it in the other's terms. A great deal of academic interreligious study focuses on this area.

3. *Mutual deconstruction.* Each submits to the searching critique of the other, until cherished beliefs may be exposed as ideological and dissolved. Needless to say, most interreligious encounter pulls up short of this.

4. *Practical interaction.* Each of us focuses on the knowledge embodied in the practice of the other: the way the other is not only to a degree deluded by his faith (as emerges with the deconstruction), but also in some aspects liberated by the practices of his religion in ways that I perhaps am not by mine. I may then try to adapt these practices as best

I can to my own religious context. Or there may arise a solidarity in the search for liberation, differently embodied in each faith.

1a. This then might lead to a return to piecemeal focus on the imaginary—an interillumination of faiths at a deeper level.

It might be possible to construct a hermeneutical circle for interreligious dialogue along the lines of this table. It would be encouraging if the four rather different modes of relating to other faiths involved can in this way be brought together in a singe process. It would be a demanding process, requiring partners to be both tough and tender with each other and themselves; critical but also empathetic; confident of their own beliefs yet also open to transformation by the encounter.

It seems to me that the "Comparative Theology" advocated by theologians like Francis Clooney and James Fredericks, and also the "hermeneutical openness" proposed by Marianne Moyaert—all discussed in chapter 1—contain elements of this circle, though the first two elements predominate and there is relatively little mutual deconstruction. And Ricoeur's hermeneutical scheme—his move from the first naivety of building an imaginary world "in front of the text" thorough serious analysis, including a hermeneutic of suspicion, to a second naivety—includes part of the circle. However, our scheme places more stress on the epistemological question: the real that may be known (in a different aspect—phenomenal, objective, aporetic, and practical—in different pathways within the circle). The emphasis on critique and deconstruction and also on practical knowledge introduces aspects that are not so clearly emphasized in Ricoeur and the others.

In practice, of course, interreligious dialogue will not—and need not—follow sequentially our neat methodological circle. And different parts of the process will come more or less naturally to different individuals. We need to be grateful that dialogue is not a machine churning out predictable results, but an ongoing process of often surprising mutual enrichment. What is important in any dialogue is that all the elements are there, and this implies quite a critique of much interreligious dialogue—including that involved in some of my own previous writings—which tends to focus on one or other area to the exclusion of others.

Summing up, it seems that each stage of interreligious encounter involves an apprehension of some kind of reality. And because the stages come together in a coherent way (a point that at this stage can only be a suggestion, becoming clearer as the book progresses), these modes of apprehension of reality in dialogue might also build on one another. This suggests a strong sense in which through interreligious dialogue we may encounter the real: as our interilluminating (not identical) experience; as our objective context (part shared, part not); as a disruption and confounding of our systems; and as purified and liberating practice. The second part of this book will try to deepen and test out this speculative hypothesis.

PART 2

Realism and Dialogue in Postmodern Theologies

T HE FIRST PART OF this book argued from a dialogue-based understanding of reality to what a theology in general ought to be like and how it ought to engage with dialogue. This second part evaluates strands of recent (in some sense postmodern) theology in the light of this understanding, working towards a conception of theology in which these strands might not be rivals or merely parallel approaches, but work together in intrafaith and interfaith dialogue.

These different theological strands embody, with differing emphasis, four theses.

1. *The Centrality of Narrative.* The Bible and (perhaps) other sacred texts are primarily stories that engage with the "story" of our lives.

2. *Doctrine as Grammar.* Where theologies do produce what look like propositions, these are to be interpreted as rules for the theological "language game."

3. *The Critique of Metaphysics.* Theologies do not primarily consist in propositions that correspond with a sacred or transcendent reality or "theological truths."

4. *The Primacy of Praxis.* Though there are no theological truths, there is "theological truth," which consists in the engagement with the reality of the whole form of life invoked by the stories and language games of

the religion. Ethical judgment therefore forms the basis of epistemological judgment: orthopraxis grounds orthodoxy.

These four theses are not wholly interdependent: one can hold one without the others, and this allows different strands of postmodern theology to focus on different theses. Broadly, the postliberal strand discussed in chapter 6 focuses on theses 1 and 2. However, 3 and 4 are accepted by most postliberals, 3 being the negative corollary of 1, and 4 providing a much needed way to stop narrative theology spinning off into neo-gnostic mythology, ensuring it has a way of grounding itself in reality and being tested for truth.

The liberation theology discussed in chapter 7 starts from a different point from postliberalism, namely from 4, the primacy of praxis, but this has generally, for the relevant theologians, entailed 3, critique of metaphysics, and 1, an emphasis on the story aspect of scripture (especially the exodus narrative). Many "grammatical" theologians, as noted, also welcome the emphasis on praxis. However, the converse does not hold, since the notion of theology as a language game tends to propel theology into an exclusivity that resists universal notions of justice and liberation, whereas for liberation theologians, these must apply to all humanity.

The theologies discussed in chapter 8 begin from 3, the rejection of metaphysics, driving a wedge between God and metaphysical "being." What makes sense of seemingly metaphysical claims can then be interpreted in terms of narrative and rules, but there are other strategies, as we shall see, so approaches to 1 and 2 vary. Generally, however, it is an emphasis on 4 that forms the basis for the rejection of metaphysics, as being incurably ideological or patriarchal or in some way or other standing in the way of human liberation.

Chapter 9 offers a positive vision for the future of theology in which story and metaphysics, and grammar and praxis, have their place, and each strand of theology moves from being a "school" or a self-referential tradition to being a mode in a rich, six-aspect process. The conclusion presents a theological exegesis of the narrative of the transfiguration of Christ, which occupies for this part of the book a similar role to the philosophical exegesis of the creation story in the first part. Theology is seen to involve the dimensions introduced in chapters 4 and 5, proceeding from a first innocence in the face of textual narrative, through metaphysics and deconstruction to a second innocence grounded in liberative practice, making way for an interreligious city of God, illuminated by the view from everywhere.

CHAPTER 6

Theology as Story: Postliberalism

This chapter, as just noted, considers a strand of theology that has been hugely influential well beyond the theologians and schools with which it originated, and which this book has already touched on several times. It is a very varied strand, but what the variations have in common is the view that theology, and religion generally, do not consist ultimately in propositions about the world—which might be debated with other religious and theological views—but in stories and practices. The main point is not to understand a religion, or its view of the world, but to participate in it and so be transformed into a better relation to the world. What look like propositions about the world must therefore be reinterpreted as parts of the religion's story or practice. The "truth" in religion is believed to lie not in the reference of religious utterances and propositions, but the imaginative evocativeness and transforming power of religious stories and practices.

These theologies, therefore, embrace all of the theses just noted: theology is quintessentially narrative; doctrine offers rules for reading and applying the narrative; metaphysical reference is outlawed; and liberated life or salvation is the criterion for a religion's truth. Not all postliberal and narrative theologians embrace or emphasize equally all four theses, but for these theologians the theses support one another like a stack of cards: take one away and the others fall too.

This chapter begins with a brief description of the three roots of this complex, tangled theological plant: the nineteenth- and early twentieth-century challenges to liberal theology in Kierkegaard and Barth; the much more recent (1970s onward) rise of narrative theology; and the account of theology as grammar deriving from George Lindbeck and the Yale School. The chapter continues with an affirmation of five kinds of benefits that flow from these theologies. However, the chapter goes on to question whether what is offered by these forms of theology is actually delivered. It draws on many of the subtle criticisms posed by Francesca Aran Murphy.[1] First, the question is asked whether categories like "story," "language," "grammar," and "rules" really do offer a sufficiently rich understanding of the Bible, religions, and even life itself: whether these categories do not represent, in some or all of these cases, a falsifying straightjacket or a new kind of abstraction. The second section asks whether, even on the basis that theology consists of story and grammar, metaphysics can be avoided, or whether story-reading always has a metaphysical aspect (and metaphysics always a storytelling aspect) that is best made explicit, so that it can be evaluated, rather than repressed. The section numbered 3 will then suggest that narrative and postliberal theologies present Christianity as a monological melodrama rather than dialogical theatre; or to change the analogy, an abstract rather than living and lifelike art. The final section shows that narrative theology fails to avoid modern rationalism, and is committed to a neo-traditionalist form of modern foundationalist methodology.

ROOTS AND STRANDS OF POSTLIBERALISM

The Barthian "thunderbolt," which shook the complacency of nineteenth- and early twentieth-century liberal Protestantism, has many aspects. It can be seen as a carrying forward of Søren Kierkegarrd's lonely attack on the "absentmindedness" of the great theological systems—pre-eminently that of Hegel—which conjure up massive worldviews, but take us away from the scandalously particular God-man, Jesus Christ. These authors argue that it is not abstract ideas that challenge us to change our lives, but the living person, Jesus Christ, who must be allowed to define who God is for us. The work of Barth resounds throughout with the claim that we are saved not by nice worldviews, which only reverse the movement of incarnation to one of abstraction and disembodiment, but by the person and work of Christ.

Or we can trace Barth's roots further back, to see it as a radicalization of the basic Reformation insistence that we are saved not by works but by faith. The apologetic attempt to make Christianity accessible by rational argument is seen as a "Pelagian" attempt to save ourselves by our own intellectual labors, when what is needed is the leap of faith and trust in the paradoxical work of Christ, which no intellect can rationalize. "In God's revelation God's Word is identical with God Himself."[2] God's revelation is

1. Murphy, *God Is Not a Story.*
2. Barth, *Church Dogmatics*, ii, I.

therefore not an appeal to a previously existing human reason; it justifies itself solely in its own terms. God does not give us *logoi*, words that persuade, but the Word made flesh, an unreserved giving of God's whole self, which we must either accept as such or reject. Thus, we do not begin with reason and argue our way—or, as in apologetics, argue others' way—to faith; we have to begin with faith, and theology consists in what Anselm called "faith seeking understanding" (*fides quaerens intellectum*). Understood in these ways, Barth's primary commitment is to our third thesis, a trenchant opposition to abstract religious and philosophical speculation, and a reliance instead on the particularity of Jesus Christ, who is the beginning, not the conclusion, of our intellectual struggles to understand.

But Barth can equally be seen in terms of what followed from him and claimed his inheritance. His emphasis on the particular can be seen as anticipating narrative theology and its emphasis on the *story* of Christ. Barth can be seen as the first narrative theologian. In reality Barth's emphasis was broader; it is not just the biblical narrative that is emphasized in his theology, but the *person* of Christ and the saving *events* that lie—he believes—at the Bible's center. Barth has a subtle theology of revelation, lacking in narrative theologians such as Frei.[3] As an orthodox Chalcedonian, Barth interprets the person of Christ in the traditional metaphysical way; it is this that enables him to understand the revelation in Christ as God's gift of Godself. Francesca Murphy comments on the two major strands of postliberalism in a manner that questions whether Barth was himself a "story Barthian":

> In the expressions "story Barthianism" and "grammatical Thomism," "Barthianism" and "Thomism" refer to *principles* which narrative theologians have considered these writers to yield. . . . Our typology relates to certain types of Barthian*ism* and Thom*ism*, not Barth and Thomas.[4]

With Hans Frei, we certainly move to a much more exclusive focus on story as the key category for understanding the Bible. He argued in his seminal 1974 work that the narrative core of scripture had been "eclipsed" in the modern emphasis on apologetics and historical criticism. Both tendencies sought to find in the story something else—a factual basis or an authorial intention or a universal meaning—from which theology could then be built, discarding the original narrative husk. Frei drew on the advent in the mid twentieth century of the New Criticism in literary studies, which rejected the search in literary works for social contexts, authorial intentions, and

3. Cf. Demson, *Hans Frei and Karl Barth.*
4. Murphy, *God Is Not a Story*, 5–6.

universal meanings, and focused on the literary text itself, its narrative, imagery, and structure, as the place where the meaning of the text must be found. Frei argued that we should study the Bible in the same way, for its images, narratives, and structures, not finding its meaning outside itself in contexts, intentions, or grounds for apologetic argument. Just as Barth urged us to see Christ in his own terms, not as the answer to our preconceived questions, but the one who questions us, so Frei urged us to see the Bible in its own terms, as the story of salvation.

This emphasis on narrative, however, is only half of the postliberal story. If there is much in religious traditions that is obviously narrative, the question remains what to do with all that is not like narrative at all. What, for example, do postliberals do with elements that are propositional in form, for example, doctrines? So alongside what Murphy neatly styles "story Barthianism" there has arisen a "grammatical Thomism" pioneered by Lindbeck. Lindbeck compares three approaches to doctrines, which he calls cognitive-propositional, experiential-expressive, and (his own preference) cultural-linguistic.[5] In this last approach

> emphasis is placed on those respects in which religions resemble languages together with their correlative forms of life and are thus similar to cultures (insofar as these are understood . . . as idioms for the construing of reality and the living of life). The function of Church doctrines that becomes most prominent in this perspective is their use, not as expressive symbols or as truth claims, but as communally authoritative rules of discourse, attitude, and action. This general way of conceptualizing religion will be called in what follows a "cultural-linguistic" approach, and the implied view of Church doctrine will be referred to as a "regulative" or "rule" theory.[6]

The three approaches might be clarified by looking at how they might interpret the Christian doctrine of the Trinity: namely that God is one substance and three persons—Father, Son, and Holy Spirit. On a cognitive-propositional understanding this would be a statement about God, to the effect that though not identical with each other, the persons called Father, Son, and Spirit are God. Most pre-modern theologians from the Cappadocian fathers though Augustine, Thomas Aquinas (*pace* the grammatical Thomists), Luther, and Calvin would have understood the doctrine in this way, and endeavored to clarify it by reference to analogies like memory,

5. Lindbeck, *Nature of Doctrine*, 16ff.
6. Ibid., 17–18.

love, and will in Augustine, or concepts like the persons as being relations in Aquinas.

On an experiential-expressive understanding, on the other hand, the statement would not correspond with any such transcendent reality, but it would express or direct people to some kind of immanent psychological or spiritual experience. Such understandings of religious language have abounded in modern times, from Schleiermacher to Jung and on into the "social Trinity" that allegorizes the nature of human love. An excellent example is to be found in Anglican writer Harry Williams' interpretation of the Trinity, as arising from our two primordial fears, of absorption into the Whole on the one hand and isolation from it on the other. The Trinity points to the possibility of being in a perfect relationship that neither absorbs us (since in the Trinity the persons are each themselves, not confused with the others) nor leaves us lonely (since they are share fully and equally in the divine nature).[7]

Finally on Lindbeck's own cultural-linguistic understanding, the Trinity is a rule telling us how to use the words "God," "Father," "Son," and "Holy Spirit" correctly as we tell the Christian story. It would enable us, for example, to say things like "God (in Christ) suffered on the cross" because the doctrine asserts the identity of Christ with God. But it would not enable us to say, "The Father suffered on the cross" because the persons Father and Son are non-identical. "Identical" here means something like "substitutable in the Christian story." On this understanding, to say the Father suffered on the cross (a view traditionally condemned as "patripassionism") would not be objectively false, but rather, a case of "bad grammar," going against the rules of the Christian language in the same way that to say "He suffer on the cross" goes against the rules of the English language.[8]

Lindbeck would not call himself a Thomist, of course, but in taking the grammatical approach he was following a trend among some Thomists, for "[b]y the late 1960s, the American Thomist school had begun to interpret Aquinas' idea of 'God talk' as referring, not to a real analogy of creaturely and divine things, but to the logic of our language for God."[9] Thomas' Five Ways, for example, are not really intended as proofs, but as reflections on the logic of Christian discourse about God. Lindbeck's distinct move is to replace "logic" with the Wittgensteinian notion of "rules" for language games. For Lindbeck, Christianity with its stories, rituals, and ethical forms of life makes up a language game, while Christian doctrine is a second-order

7. Williams, *True Wilderness*, 125–28.

8. Cf. the notion behind Hauerwas' *Working with Words*.

9. Murphy, *God Is Not a Story*, 19.

discipline exploring and expounding the rules of this game. This second-order activity, however, is only a means of safeguarding the Christian form of life, and it is this form of life, taken as a whole, that "corresponds" with reality. The core role of doctrine therefore lies

> in constituting a way of life, a way of being in the world, which itself corresponds to . . . the Ultimately Real. The same point may be made by means of J. L. Austin's notion of a "performatory" use of language: a religious utterance . . . acquires the propositional truth of ontological correspondence only insofar as it is a performance, an act or deed, which helps to create the correspondence.[10]

Hence, when a normally true doctrine is uttered in the wrong life setting, it is false. According to Lindbeck, the crusader who cries "Christ is Lord" while decapitating a Muslim is a liar.[11] The justification of our statements depends on their life context.

Finally, it is worth noting that there is a postliberal alternative to this grammatical way of understanding doctrine, to be found in the writings of Robert Jenson. For him doctrines are just very short stories. He understands the Trinity as "simultaneously a very compressed telling of the total narrative by which Scripture identifies God and a personal name for God so specified."[12] The Father, Son, and Holy Spirit are not therefore persons in the classical theological sense, but acts in a three-part play; acts that paradoxically are the actor. The acts are different from each other (Creation is not Redemption, etc.) but in all of them God is wholly given to us: each act is not just an expression of the divine, but Godself fully present.

POSTLIBERALISM: A RECOVERY OF CONFIDENCE?

Before considering the viability of this nexus of postliberal ideas, we need to affirm the great gains postliberalism has made. These gains concern five things: the status of modernity's dogmas; the place of apologetics; the context of faith; concreteness; and the corporate cultural dimension of religion. However, each of our affirmations requires a qualification.

The first gain is surely the deliverance from the three dogmas of modernity. Postliberalism purports to take us beyond a skeptically based foundationalism, the correspondence theory of truth, and a methodological,

10. Lindbeck, *Doctrine*, 84, cited in Murphy, *God*, 52–53.
11. Lindbeck, *Doctrine*, 64.
12. Jenson, *Systematic Theology 1*, 46.

deductive approach to theology. However, while Lindbeck explicitly rejects the notion of a direct correspondence between propositions of faith and religious "facts," and the postliberals generally reject rationalist foundationalism, we shall see below that they may only be replacing it with a fideist foundationalism.

Secondly, in contrast with the liberal Protestant tradition from Schleiermacher onwards, postliberals no longer regard the apologetic task as definitive for theology. Modernist skepticism ceases to be the judge before which theology must give account. It recedes into being just another important dialogue partner for a theology that is allowed to define its terms and develop its own tradition in the way that is appropriate to it. Parts of that tradition—the miracles and the stories that appear in all religions, and the resurrection and doctrines like the incarnation and the Trinity in Christianity specifically—do not have to be sacrificed just because they do not appear "rational" by modern standards. Religion returns to confidence in its own resources, and allows itself to expand and develop in its own way before engaging with secular critique; so that when it does engage, a more equal and constructive dialogue ensues. However, the move from giving apologetics a defining place to giving it no place is questionable from our point of view.

Thirdly, the verbal content of faith is restored to the context that gives it meaning. Theology is rightly seen as a secondary academic task in relation to the primary role of the day-to-day practice of the religions. Theology and the study of religion, especially comparative religion in the nineteenth and early twentieth century often appeared to reduce religions to "worldviews" or collections of propositions about the world that could be compared and contrasted. This was a neat way of simplifying the academic task, but did scant justice to the religions themselves. The postliberals are very clear that religion is a whole form of life, comprising stories, rituals, ethical judgments, and spiritual practices, as well as what Buddhists pejoratively term "views." Moreover, even the views can only be properly understood when interpreted in the light of the other factors, nor are the other factors encrypted views that need to be translated into propositional form. All this understanding has added a richness and a care to the study of religions and the doing of theology, and in many ways it has not yet penetrated far enough. Yet there remains a sense in which religions do sometimes evoke and sometimes baldly state "worldviews" that may be contested. When Buddhists say all is subject to impermanence and suffering, or St. Paul writes that "all have sinned, and fallen short of the glory of God" (Rom 3:23), we are being invited not just to understand, but to agree and respond appropriately.

Fourthly, and paradoxically, through being re-engaged with their living context, the stories and rituals of faith shine out in their concrete particularity. Frei and his followers invite us to look at the stories as stories, for their own inherent patterns, rather than trying to discern some external context that might tell us the author's intention. The return to the living, breathing, unique, and particular Jesus Christ narrated in the Gospels, and the affirmation of the role of the storytelling imagination, is much to be welcomed. It is certainly true that one thing that makes religions different from (most) philosophies is the way arguments and proposals are placed in the mouths of founders—Abraham, Moses, Buddha, Confucius, Lao Tzu, Jesus, Mohammad, Guru Nanak, . . .—who have biographies. The beliefs therefore do not float in the abstract but witness to a process of transformation that the founder has undergone, which might transform the believer's story too. (Possibly Platonism has to be regarded as a religion on the basis of the role of Socrates' story; contrast Aristotelianism.) Nevertheless, the beliefs are there, and they are beliefs about reality; they do not simply seep into our lives because of their meaning, but call us to make a judgment as to truth. It is this judgment, and the ensuing commitment, that transforms us.

Finally, the context that postliberalism restores is a social, corporate culture. The core question for religion moves from the modern individualist question of what can *I* know for sure, to the broader question of what wisdom is embodied in *our* tradition of story and practice. We can no longer regard religion in the modern way, as primarily a matter of personal stance, or as (in the words of Alfred North Whitehead) "what a man does with his solitariness." For postliberals, notably Lindbeck, religion like any other language game is *essentially* corporate, since meanings exist for individuals only because they first have meaning in the language people share. Moreover, it is as a people's whole way of life that, for Lindbeck, as noted, a religion corresponds with reality, or fails to. On the other hand, there is a problem here: Who is to make the judgment as to whether a religion so corresponds? If it has to be an individual who makes the judgment, do we not return, after all, to the importance of individual judgment and commitment? But if the judgment itself is corporate, and made by all those who adhere to the religion, is there not, at best, a circularity, and at worst—in the very notion of a judgment made by no particular person—a muddle?

And there's the rub for postliberalism. Whereas the understanding of meaning works from the corporate to the individual, judgment regarding truth works the other way. By making story and grammar the center of religion and theology, postliberalism puts some previously neglected aspects of them back where they belong, but at the price, perhaps, of limiting them in other ways. Taking up some of the queries above, but in a different order, the following four sections will ask whether:

1. story and grammar fail to do justice to the actual content of the Bible, Christian theology, religion generally, and even life itself;

2. even the story element requires a metaphysical reading, and if religious texts are to become religiously significant for us, it is via a metaphysical reading and a personal act of judgment;

3. if this is lacking, stories become single-focused melodramas rather than dialogical theatre, while theology consists in abstract self-referential expression rather than a depiction;

4. and what results is a new kind of foundationalism.

1) IS IT ALL STORY AND GRAMMAR?

Is the Bible best considered as story? Is theology the grammar that enables us to read and write religion correctly? Is life itself best considered as a story? These are the questions for this section, and most of the focus will be on the first.

Narrative theology is ambiguous. It could be claiming that the Bible consists of a number of stories, and exegesis is the skill of reading and critically analyzing those stories as the stories they are. Or it could be saying that the Bible is *a* story, or indeed *the one and only* story of salvation. That is a much bolder claim.

If the first is meant, then clearly are a lot of stories in the Bible, and exegesis will clearly be helped if we read them as stories and do not try to force them into some other mold. Nevertheless there is also clearly a lot of the Bible that is not storylike. The psalms and the wisdom literature generally do not consist of stories; and though they refer to stories, the prophetic writings do not consist of stories. In the New Testament, though the Gospels present the story of Jesus, and he in turn tells stories called parables, he also teaches more didactically; and though the Acts of the Apostles could be called a story, or the continuation of Luke's Gospel story, the epistles of Paul are letters, not stories. Moreover, simply calling the elements that are not something else "story" could blind us to the very different kinds of story we find, for example, in the Genesis myths, the histories of the Judges and Kings, the parables of Jesus, and the apocalyptic scenarios in Daniel and Revelation. Narrative theology therefore both claims too much (since probably the greater part of the Bible is not actually storylike) and offers too little (since it merges together all sorts of different kinds of genre as "story").

On the other hand, if narrative theology claims that the Bible as a whole is to be read as a story, or *the* story, then there is a danger that "the salvation story" becomes another procrustean bed. Typology—reading Old Testament stories as presenting allegorically the story of Christ—then displaces the particular living content of those stories. The rich tapestry of the scriptures risks being amputated and flattened into a long version of the Christian creed. Jewish theologians like Michael Goldberg are then justified in complaining that a text capable of a variety of interpretations has been appropriated by Christians demanding exclusive rights over the interpretation.[13] Similar challenges might come from liberationist quarters, where the attempt is made to recover voices that have been submerged by the grand Christian metanarrative. Nicholas Lash has argued that an exclusive focus on the story element of scripture can lead us to ignore oppressive ideological content.[14]

Moreover, the Jewish scholar Rabbi Jonathan Sacks argues that the Hebrew Bible is *inherently* self-subversive. Repeatedly we find in its pages "a *subversion* of myth, a consistent frustration of narrative expectation."[15] The story of Isaac and Ishmael, for example, whose interpretation has divided the three Abrahamic faiths, could be read as affirming Isaac as the true inheritor of the promises to Abraham. But Sacks shows how in the text the sympathy given to Hagar and her son Ishmael, and many other subtle features, subvert this simple interpretation. Neither Isaac nor Ishmael emerges as the hero of the story.[16] The same self-subversion applies, according to Sacks, to other stories in the Pentateuch depicting "sibling rivalry":[17] Jacob and Esau, and Joseph and his brothers. In all these cases what we expect of a good plot—either a heroic vindication or a tragic humiliation—is undermined, and our desire to identify with one of the characters is subverted. If there is a salvation history in the Bible, it lies not in the main lines of its narrative, but in this self-subverting tendency itself, which Réné Girard has also noted in the Bible. Sacks finds in this tendency "the rejection of rejection." In this vein Christians might read the narratives of the resurrection as the rejection of the rejection of the crucified God.

In view of these arguments, it might be possible to dispense with the creedal superstructure and yet find a unity in the Bible, allowing it to speak in its own terms. We might, for example, follow Jack Miles in reading scripture simply as "God's biography," that is, as a work of literature that tells the story and so portrays the character of someone called "God" much as

13. Goldberg, *God, Action and Narrative*, 46.

14. Lash, "Ideology, Metaphor and Analogy."

15. Sacks, *Not in God's Name*, 115.

16. Ibid., ch. 6.

17. Ibid., chs. 7 and 8.

Shakespeare's *Hamlet* and *King Lear* tell the story of their main characters.[18] The result might be illuminating in the way features emerge about "God" that are markedly different from those that theology has traditionally ascribed to him. God then emerges as a vulnerable character easily moved to envy and anger, loving in a possessive way, capable of greatness, but also pettiness; indeed, not unlike King Lear and the many other characters in Western fiction whom, Miles argues, were modeled on him.

The radical difference between such a reading and traditional "salvation history" approaches like those of Barth and Frei is that the faith commitment of the latter includes more than just the telling of the biblical story. It involves—as Barth would certainly agree—a commitment to the church and its particular way of reading the Bible. But that returns us to the question of whose book the Bible is, and what might give the church exclusive interpretive rights? Or should we after all concede that the Bible—even when taken as a whole edited book—is readable as more than one story, without any grounds for judging one way better than another except for those grounds that are internal to the interpreting faiths themselves?

That quandary applies equally to the notion of theology as the grammar that tells us what inferences we are and are not allowed to make in our Bible reading. It may be the case that *for Christians*, one is allowed to infer from a statement that Jesus Christ did or suffered something, that *God* did or suffered it. But such a rule could hardly apply for a Jewish, Muslim, or agnostic reading. Likewise, one might preserve belief in God's infinite love and mercy by means of a rule that descriptions in the Pentateuch of God commanding genocide should be treated allegorically—for example, as commanding us to wipe out our sins and leave no remainder. But whether we or our faith community is *right* to reapply these rules to the texts depends on what the truth is about God: whether God is, in the first place, incarnate in Christ, who is one person, both divine and human; and whether God is all-loving or capable of genocidal wishes. Such truths, if truths they are, are arrived at by other grounds than reading the texts. There is no direct interillumination between the biblical stories and our lives that necessitates one set of grammatical rules rather than another.

And that is not only because the Bible offers more than one story; so do our lives. An early precursor of narrative theology, Richard Niebuhr, argued that our lives are best understood as stories, while Stephen Crites argues for "the narrative quality of experience"; Alistair MacIntyre has argued that stories crucially enable us to develop ideas of the virtues, while Martha Nussbaum holds that our emotions are generated by, and in turn impose, a

18. Miles, *God: A Biography.*

narrative structure to life.[19] These theorists vary as to how far they see life, experience, and emotion as inherently storylike, and how far we impose a narrative structure that could have been different. But all regard the narrative structure as essential. Maybe we could tell a different story of our lives, but we cannot tell no story at all without rendering our lives meaningless.

At this point powerful questions would be placed by Buddhism. In insight (*vipassana*) mediation the aim is precisely to deconstruct the narratives that we habitually impose on experience, and to embrace experience itself without making it the story of an "I" doing or suffering something. To see our life as a story, in this view, is to see it in terms of good, bad, and indifferent, and this inevitably leads to a craving and suffering from which we need to free ourselves. Perhaps Buddhism accomplishes in meditative practice what the Bible does within its own narrative: the deconstruction of the kinds of story we like to tell.

And even if we reject that Buddhist account, and affirm that life *is* a story, the question remains, which *kind* of story? As Christopher Booker reminds us, there are several kinds of plot. He lists seven: overcoming the monster, rags to riches, voyage and return, the quest, comedy, tragedy, and rebirth.[20] The list may not be definitive, but it is easy to see that our own lives could be told in terms of several of these plots, with perhaps different ones prevailing at different times; and also that the plot we habitually choose tends to shape our lives in a self-fulfilling prophecy. We all know people who are always identifying hostile "monsters" to slay; others who are always making fun of themselves and other people; others again who prance about with an air of tragedy. Again, it seems clear that the canon of scripture is not designed to tell one kind of story at the expense of another. The four Gospels themselves arguably present Christ as respectively monster-slayer (Matthew), tragicomic figure (Mark), rags-to-riches hero (Luke), and the voyage and return of the Word of God (John).

Meanwhile, a significant move has been made in fairly recent theology towards recovering the role of liturgy as the place where theology and scripture come alive for the average participant. For liturgical theologians like the Orthodox Alexander Schmemann[21] and the Roman Catholic Aidan Kavanagh,[22] the liturgy is "primary theology" while academic theology is a second-order reflection on it. At first sight this might seem to confirm the role of story and the notion of theology as second-order grammar. But that

19. Cf. their chapters in Hauerwas, *Why Narrative?*
20. Booker, *Seven Basic Plots.*
21. Schmemann, *Introduction to Liturgical Theology.*
22. Kavanagh, *Liturgical Theology.*

would represent a simplification. In practice liturgy is rarely constructed so as to tell the story of salvation. The Christian liturgical year moves, with scant regard for biographical order, from the second coming (Advent) through the birth of Christ, his appearance to the gentiles, to his baptism, then back to his presentation in the temple, then in a forward leap to his transfiguration, through sundry signs in John's Gospel, to the one storylike part of the church year, through Palm Sunday, Holy Week, Easter, Ascension, and Pentecost. Finally in "ordinary time" it backtracks to a telling of Jesus story through one of the Gospels (which one varies in a three-year cycle) and finally culminates in Christ the King, all this interspersed with various festivals of Mary and the Saints.[23]

Each Eucharist includes, admittedly, two key narratives—that recited by everyone in the Creed, and that (reiterating parts of the former) proclaimed by the priest in the Eucharistic Prayer, relating mainly the Last Supper, death, and resurrection of Christ. But these narratives are set in a wider structure that is not narrative so much as a drama in which people interact with their redeeming God. In the Easter Vigil liturgy, finally, we find a series of readings like a telling of the whole salvation story, but the story is told as a series of stories that form typological interilluminations, all pointing to a redemption that takes us beyond narrative into another such participatory drama. And this combination of the use and the transcendence of narrative is not unique to Christianity. The Buddhist calendar is structured around the full moon days which celebrate at once the birth, enlightenment, and *parinirvana* (departure and going-beyond) of the Buddha, not as a narrative sequence, but all at once.

A multi-story Bible, then, interacts with our multi-story lives, through a multi-story liturgy; and likewise with the texts, lives, and liturgies of at least some other believers. If the church offers a grammar that narrows down the range on both sides to a happy-ending salvation metanarrative, perhaps interfaith dialogue with those who may tell similar stories through different scriptures, or (as in the case of the Christian Old Testament and the Hebrew Bible) different stories through the same scriptures, may help us overcome that temptation and restore the richness of our texts and lives. But then there remains the question, given all this richness of text and life, is it nevertheless possible to speak of a *reality* that the texts and our lives are related to? Narrative theology, with its avoidance of metaphysics—that is, considerations of underlying reality—cannot answer that question. But I shall respond that not only is it possible, but necessary and unavoidable, because when we tell stories, we already invoke a kind of metaphysics.

---

23. Cf. Thompson, *Spirituality in Season.*

2) THE METAPHYSICS OF STORIES AND GRAMMARS

In a classic work of great importance for narrative theology,[24] Erich Auerbach contrasts two texts: the description of Odysseus' scar in Book 19 of the Odyssey, and the story of Abraham and the near sacrifice of Isaac in Genesis 22. The former offers a rich, detailed account of the origin of the scar in a hunting incident with a boar in Odysseus' childhood. No stone is left unturned in Homer's leisurely explanation; we have as much detail in the story as we could wish. A world is presented that is all "foreground," sensuous, and rationally interconnected. By contrast the biblical story is sparse, with an immense amount unstated in the background, or left ambiguous, haunting us with things not commented on. What did Sarah and Isaac feel about the situation? When Abraham declares that God himself will provide the lamb for the sacrifice, is he just sheltering Isaac from the truth, or does he have a premonition of what will in fact happen? Summing up the differences, Auerbach writes:

> The two styles, in their opposition, represent basic types: on the one hand fully externalized description, uniform illumination, uninterrupted connection, free expression, all events in the foreground, displaying unmistakable meanings, few elements of historical development and of psychological perspective; on the other hand, certain parts brought into high relief, others left obscure, abruptness, suggestive influence of the unexpressed, "background" quality, multiplicity of meanings and the need for interpretation, universal-historical claims, development of the concept of the historically becoming, and preoccupation with the problematic.[25]

It is the open texture and unanswered question of the biblical passage—typical of so much of the Bible—that has spawned traditions of interpretation of the Abraham story in the form of further stories and commentaries, from Jewish midrash, through the connection with Christ's death and resurrection in Hebrews 11:17–19, and Kierkegaard's famous rendition in *Fear and Trembling*, to Wilfrid Owen's haunting war poem, in which Abraham refuses God's bidding to sacrifice the ram of pride, "but slew his son, / And half the seed of Europe, one by one."[26] By contrast Homer has been re-sung and quoted many times, but has not spawned the same kind of dialogue.

24. Auerbach, *Mimesis*, ch. 1.
25. Ibid., 23.
26. Owen, *Parable of the Old Man and the Young*.

My fundamental point here is that these different ways of storytelling betoken different metaphysics. Homer's detailed description foreshadows the classical Greek metaphysics of presence. It evokes a world where everything has a very solid and definable essence, is very directly experienced, and invites explanation. The Abraham story and other biblical stories suggest a metaphysics of transcendence, full of ineluctable mystery, in which existence questions us as much as we question it, and which places events much more surely in a setting that is the one in which we ourselves live and retell the story. Such stories are the beginning of a dialogue that invites us in. The Homeric story by contrast, for all its vividness as a causal account, presents a world that is complete in itself, everything seen synoptically at once from nowhere in particular, bearing no definable relation to the world in which we live. The very intensity of the imagery derives from the fact that the scar is mythical, and has to be "made real" by the poet's attention to detail, while the Abraham story reposes in a tradition that assumes its fundamental veracity, so that paradoxically the detail can be left safely to the imagination. The synoptic character of the Homeric text—to use the contrast explored by Jean Luc Marion (see chapter 8)—is closer to the metaphysics of the idol, which enables us to see the gods and draw them into our framework and our concerns, than that of the icon, through which Christ seems to see us and draw us into his perspective.

The contrast might have been further developed by introducing a third kind of story like that of the Buddha or Lao Tzu that would suggest a different kind of metaphysics again. But the core point is that stories are always already metaphysical in the way they structure themselves and the way they approach us and invite us to read and retell them. It is through metaphysics (in the sense of a way of approaching and negotiating with reality through words) that the stories reach us and touch our imagination and commitment. The converse is also true: that metaphysical systems are fundamentally storylike, being ways of telling the story of reality. To read the Bible as a story or stories is, for example, among other things, to read it as telling of the divine action, and to treat God as an agent with a life, and as one who might address us too. The Bible story demands a metaphysics in our reading of it, though that metaphysics is not something we deduce from scripture, let alone encounter explicitly stated in scripture, but something we experience as immanent in the way the Bible tells its story.

And there is a metaphysics implicit in our grammar. It will not do simply to regard, say, the Chalcedonian understanding of Christ as grammatical and not metaphysical. It may be true, as noted, that the heart of the doctrine is a grammar that allows us to say, for example, that God suffered and died on the cross in Christ without saying the Father or the divine nature suffered and died. But the question that arises, and is obvious to any non-Christian, is why should we allow these grammatical rules to apply, and not others? Crudely, is it in fact true—or even meaningful—to say that God suffered and died in Christ, and is there really something about God that enables him to suffer and die in person without the divine nature, the being of God, suffering and being destroyed? These are metaphysical questions about God and incarnation. involving claims about reality (that is, metaphysical claims), and when Jews, Muslims, Buddhists, atheists, and just about every kind of non-Christian disputes them, finding them either meaningless or offensive, they are not merely being confused or naive about points of grammar—as if they should not get so upset but simply be content to have different grammars for their own "languages." They are offering— importantly, interestingly, substantially, and metaphysically debatably—different understandings of Jesus Christ and God.

For if metaphysics arises from grammar, different grammars imply different metaphysics. If we wish to speak grammatically, we cannot then avoid metaphysics. We only have a choice between what philosopher P. F. Strawson called "descriptive" and "revisionary" metaphysics.[27] The former simply describes the way people use languages and notices the metaphysical implications of their using words the way they do. The latter—which includes the metaphysical systems of the Greeks Plato and Plotinus, the Indians Nagarjuna and Śankara, the Germans Kant and Schopenhauer, the English Berkeley and Whitehead, to mention but a few—seeks to expose mistakes in our ordinary metaphysics and to propose better ways of speaking that relate more truly to reality.

Descriptive metaphysics, for example, might ascribe the prevalence in all known languages of a similar grammar—with subjects, objects, and verbs, and adjectival and adverbial qualifiers—to the fact that we actually do live in a world of interacting substances with qualities. The success of narrating it that way implies a metaphysics, that is, a structure in reality itself. Meanwhile subtle differences in this narration—including how we narrate the structure itself, how we understand and explain substances, actions, and qualities—makes for differences in our metaphysics. We all start with a conventional, implicit metaphysics, derived from our culture's narratives, and descriptive metaphysics serves merely to explicate that.

However, if the narrative of our faith or philosophy is at variance with this conventional narrative, we either have to challenge and transform the latter, or subdue the faith narrative to fit the conventional one. The rise of the Yogacara and Madhyamaka schools in Buddhism witnesses

27. Strawson, *Individuals*, 9–11.

to a whole-hearted use of contemporary concepts to widen the Buddhist teachings on impermanence and no-soul into an entire metaphysical narrative, while arguably the patristic theologians did the same with Hellenistic culture for the Christian teachings. So while descriptive metaphysics—for example, an expounding of worldviews implicit in the sacred texts—will often be necessary to theology, when this worldview is at variance with contemporary assumptions, revisionary metaphysics will sometimes be necessary too.

3) THEATRE, MELODRAMA, OR DIALOGUE?

Story, therefore, is by no means a category that should be opposed to metaphysics, and narrative theology should not spurn ontology. For though there is a metaphysics implicit in religious texts, theology itself can impose an alternative falsifying metaphysics that leads us to read it, so to speak, in the wrong register. This is what happens, Murphy argues, when narrative theology turns the biblical story into melodrama, treating theatre as if it were film; and I would add, changing the analogy to the visual arts, when it encourages us to read the verbal icon of scripture as if it were abstract art: Rublev, we might say, as if he were Chagall.

Murphy has urged that narrative theology reads the biblical story as melodrama or as a movie, rather than a drama in which we encounter God. In live theatre the central actor is present among us, evoking our response by his living engagement with the text, which speaks to us through him. But in a movie the hero is actually absent, merely conjured up by the play of images on the screen; he is not over against us but rather, we imagine ourselves as him, as we experience the feelings evoked by the images. Melodrama meanwhile offers us spectacle without substance, the focus being on a series of spectacles rather than the unfolding of underlying character. In just the same way narrative theology, by rejecting metaphysical concerns about the nature and identity of God, and seeking God in the pure biblical play of images, can offer only something like film or melodrama, and never the dialogue in which God is found present. Quoting Wilhelmson and Brett, Murphy writes,

> like movies, [narrative theology] presents "the doing of an image, not the image of a doing." . . . It does not obey the curves of the narrative of salvation history. In order adequately to respond to the images of this revealed history, one needs to know or understand this image, but also to respond to it in love.[28]

28. Murphy, *God Is Not a Story*, 23.

Thus Frei sees the resurrection in terms of the identity of Christ shining through the imagery of the text, rather than as a dramatic encounter with the really existent Jesus.

> Narrative theology . . . thinks of Christ as an identity rather than as an existent. . . . Frei is imagining Mary Magdalene or the other apostles reading meaning off the resurrected Christ with an immediacy similar to that in which he himself, as a theological New Critic, extracted meaning from a text. No such writings as Frei had before him existed until several decades after Christ rose from the dead. Mary Magdalene did not meet up with a text, but with a person.[29]

In other words, rather than serving to bring us into a living encounter with the risen Christ following the model of Mary Magdalene's, narrative theology imposes on Mary and the other disciples in their encounter with him the model of a literary reading such as we have when we read the Bible and other texts. Christ becomes a melodramatic construction, presented to us in the text and its imagery much as the hero is constructed out of the imagery of a film. This melodramatic tendency is rooted in a "non-relational ideal of truth"[30]—something this book has criticized at many points. The Bible ceases to be read for what it seems obviously to be: a variety of stories, laws, poems, hymns, reflections, and other items telling of a rich and confusing plurality of living encounters: diverse literary items that have in common only the fact that they were gathered by particular communities (the Hebrew scribes, and latterly the church). Instead it is read as "a collective story told from no-where by no-one."[31] Once again this suggests film. In the process of filming, editing disappears behind a (literal!) screen of suggested objectivity, whereas in theatre, the makers of the drama and the audience are co-present in the act of making the performance. The modern desire for a universal and objective, subject-independent "view from nowhere" has imposed itself again.

This point might be strengthened by changing the analogy to the visual arts. Peter Fuller draws parallels between the rise of abstract art and that of Barthian theology at the same period in the twentieth century.[32] He affirms Ruskin's ideal of art as traditionally rooted in *theoria*, the contemplation of nature, as opposed to mere *aesthesis*, the titillation of the senses by modern works of art which Ruskin describes as "mere amusement, minis-

---

29. Ibid., 63.
30. Ibid., 80.
31. Ibid., 83.
32. Fuller, *Theoria.*

ters to morbid sensibilities, ticklers and fanners of the soul's sleep."[33] That certainly sounds like melodrama. Fuller draws parallels with the collapse of natural theology—which in the eighteenth and nineteenth centuries sought to rise from the contemplation of nature to that of God—under the weight of Barth's critique. This—we might extend the parallel—rendered theology effectively the self-expressive activity of the church, accountable to no notion of a shared objective world, but only to itself.

Now arguably there is a type of natural theology that needed to collapse. This is the type that attempt to find quasi-scientific evidence for God in the detailed workings of nature, much in the same way that one might find evidence for dinosaurs in the fossils. Arguably this process reduced God to the status of another cause working within the universe. But this type needs to be distinguished from the broader *theoria physike* or natural contemplation which rises from seeing the goodness and reality of creatures to affirming the eminent goodness and transcendent reality of the Creator.[34] While natural theology in the former sense developed only in the eighteenth century, *theoria physike* has roots in Plato and in mainstream Christian theologians such as Evagrius Ponticus, Augustine, Maximus the Confessor, and of course Thomas Aquinas. Barth rejects the analogy of being on which natural contemplation is based, and has nothing to say about the natural world disclosed by science, whereas for Ruskin art clearly represents a contemplation of nature parallel to that of science. Fuller's reference to natural theology may confuse the issue: it is not that theology can be scientific, but that science can be a pathway to contemplative theology. But he is surely right to argue that the loss of the contemplative perspective risks leading to a non-theological or antitheological art and an artless theology, both alike alienated from science.

Insofar as this has not happened, it may be because theology has not severed itself from the analogy of being as much as Barth and his successors might have liked, while art itself, however abstract, cannot avoid retaining reference to things in the world. Art may, as in Kandisky and in the surrealists, juxtapose such references in strikingly counterfactual ways, or as with the cubists, deliberately distort and re-form realities, but the references remain. Even in the whorls of a Jackson Pollock one cannot avoid sensing references to objects and energies, or wondering if the subatomic world of the particle accelerators has been anticipated! Art remains, not a photographic "representation" of the world (as it could attempt to be only after the Renaissance discovery of perspective), but a re-presentation, indeed

33. Cited in ibid., 45.
34. Cf. Wirzba, *Christian Theoria Physike.*

a re-making of the world (as so called "primitive" art has been ever since the first cave paintings and stone Venuses). It is in the remaking of *things* that the creative energy of the maker and her culture is manifest, as also is the thing itself, cast in a new light and co-revealed in the interillumination between art and object. Might theology likewise be a re-presentation, a re-making through re-telling, an activity whose truth does not lie in an accurate "representation" of the divine "object" or an objective revelation, but in the interilluminative dialogue between the one God and God's many religious remakings.

If we put Murphy and Fuller together, that might be the kind of dialogue that both are arguing for: the one through her urging that theology be live theatre rather than filmic melodrama, the other through his implicit plea that theology like art be a making with *theoria* at its heart.

4) FIDEIST FOUNDATIONALISM?

Central to Barth and to narrative theology, as stressed by Murphy, is the rejection of foundationalism. Barth vehemently spurned the notion that we first build by sound argument a secure philosophical or metaphysical (or even natural-theological) structure, then build what the Bible reveals upon it. For Barth and the narrative theologians, we start with the Bible, read in its own terms (so it is argued) as the story of salvation, and if philosophy and metaphysics have a place at all, it is to help faith to articulate itself within the church community. But does this move, reversing the relation between revealed faith and philosophical reasoning, overturn foundationalism, or does it merely change which is regarded as the foundation? That is Murphy's key challenge: "Neither reasoning about things nor believing in things is foundationalist per se; foundationalism comes into it when one reasons upon reason, or believes in one's believing."[35]

Murphy goes on to quote Schindler on the way Descartes built the principles of reasoning on the foundation of the self's self-consciousness, making right methodology a matter the self can know without knowing anything external to it. She points out that faith can be approached in the same manner, as a leap the individual or the believing community makes prior to, and creative of, the object believed in.

A difference needs to be noted here. If we ground our beliefs in reason we make them accountable to all other rational beings, who may mount rational arguments against what we have argued for. But if on the contrary we ground our rationality in faith, it is only the faith community, the community

---

35. Murphy, *God Is Not a Story*, 33.

of those who have made the same leap of faith, that is qualified to debate my arguments. Here part of the agenda of the faith-foundationalist becomes clear: to contain the debate within the church, and secure the latter from attack by "infidels" and also doubters within the fold. If rationalist foundationalism undermines church authority, fideist foundationalism restores it, making the believing church and its authorities an impregnable rock. But this impregnability has a cost. The appeal to a supposedly universal human reason is renounced; the truths of faith can only be shown to be true for the faithful, for those who build on the same foundation.

For many believers this might be a price worth paying. But Murphy argues that another price has also been paid. The universal appeal of God has been renounced. The God that remains is now the God *of . . .* Christians, Jews, Muslims, Hindus; the God of those who have made the same step, and tell the same story, of faith. However, "either that storytelling becomes the foundation upon which God stands, or else that story itself is the wider concept which contains the idea of God."[36]

So we have two possibilities. One is that our faith's story is foundational. In that case, God is a key part of this story, but ultimately God is no more than an idea erected on the basis of a fundamental story. In this case *"story is fundamentally God."* The other alternative is that the story that includes God is one story we can tell among many (or perhaps several stories, since the faith stories differ). In that case *"God is fundamentally a story"* (or more accurately, the Christian God is one story, the Muslim another, and so forth). In either case, story is the ultimate, truly foundational category; story is God.

A move that began in brave Reformation manner with an attempt to make God alone the foundation—kicking away all attempts to base faith on human reason and relying solely on faith in God—has ended by subjugating God to story. The truly fundamental category has become "story": the faith community is bound together—and segregated from the infidels and believers in other stories—by a common faith in the story and its central but ultimately fictional hero, God.

CONCLUSION

This chapter has welcomed the return of theology to attention to story, and the notion that story should hold a central place in the present-day articulation of faith, as it does in the sacred texts of all religions. It has affirmed the notion that reason should serve the articulation of religion and its stories,

36. Ibid., 93.

but should not be allowed to dissipate the imaginative density and specificity of religious stories, images, and rituals, in favor of supposedly more universally acceptable generalities. But it has noted many pitfalls in the attempt to make story—or even a combination of story, symbol, ritual, and other such elements opaque to reason—do all the theological work.

First, we have noted that the religions and religious texts do not consist solely of stories or the other "irrational" elements. Job and Ecclesiastes witness the presence of skeptical-rational elements in texts regarded by Jews and Christians as authoritative, and the same may obviously be said of many Hindu and Buddhist texts. Nor are our human lives, with which the sacred stories are said to interilluminate, unambiguously narrative in structure. Then it has noted that ways of telling stories—in scripture and elsewhere—themselves embody metaphysical commitments regarding the way the world is best read and understood, so that the understanding of narrative requires that we include non-narrative elements, like metaphysics, in theology. Thirdly, with the help of Murphy and Fuller it has argued that reducing religious texts to their story element does not enhance their concreteness and particularity, but rather produces the equivalent of filmic melodrama and abstract art, in which the drama of direct encounter is lost. And finally it has argued, with Murphy, that the emphasis on narrative does not overcome foundationalism but merely creates another, fideist or faith-based foundationalism, in which "story" becomes the category that grounds and even contains God.

Even if some of these arguments might be criticized, their cumulative weight is strong. They converge on a central flaw in the Barthian and narrative approaches to theology, namely that however powerful and meaningful stories—and symbols, metaphors, rituals, and the like—may be for the communities that share in them, that power and meaning cannot settle the question of truth: namely whether these wonderful stories actually relate to reality in more than the way good fiction does. To put it philosophically, the question of sense or meaning should not be identified with or allowed to displace the question of truth or reference. However convincing God may be as a character in the salvation story, that does not settle the question we need to ask: is this God real, and does he really save us?

Reality, as noted, *is* that referent that can have many senses, that object which can have many aspects; and which we find by turning (whether in solitary contemplation or dialogue with others) from aspect to aspect to see what patterns persist regardless, or change regularly, through them. By confining God to a particular set of stories, the narrative theologians reduce God to one aspect, or at best a single sequence of filmic snapshots, rather than a reality we can approach—or who approaches us—from many different angles. Because we humans are rendered powerless before the advance of the Barthian divine, which proceeds entirely on its own terms, God too is rendered powerless by being wholly identified with and confined to something that, however biblically vast, is essentially defined as just one line of approach, just one story of salvation. From being a theatrical subject of drama, engaging with and responding to his "audience," God has been reduced to Murphy's melodramatic sequence of moments: the stuff of collective dreams, rather than reality. We witness in the story of God something analogous to a sequence of photographs which seem to shift in perspective; but if we actually were to move our bodies around before and behind the screen to look at things from different angles, the illusion would vanish straight away.

What, after all, would assure us and those around us that the divine story-figure is more than just fictional? Not, of course, the discovery of some actual being that corresponded in all particulars with the fictional one our community had constructed! Put that way, the irrelevance of any simple correspondence theory of truth in theology becomes quite obvious. But is the only alternative a leap of faith, however "foundational"? What, after all, would we be putting our faith in? In the existence of the reality the story describes? In that case we would be relying on a rather naive correspondence theory after all. In the reliable authority of the community that tells the story, and its leaders? In that case my fundamental faith is in the church, not God as such.

There is another possibility, which many of the narrative theologians allude to. The theological story may be true because of a wider and deeper correspondence. It may be that the whole religious form of life is what corresponds with reality as a whole. My judgment of the truth of Christianity (or whichever faith) may be neither a mere cognitive noting that a certain reality exists, nor an ultimately social or political submission to a human magisterium. It may be primarily an *ethical* judgment. It may be a judgment that the community that believes this story does people good, or frees them from illusion, or gives them lives that correspond with how things really are.

Here we move to a whole body of theological understanding that has, as its focus, various kinds of liberation theology; and as a penumbra, a wide range of practical theologies that avert to the notion that orthodoxy—right belief—is grounded in orthopraxis, right practice. This is the subject of the next chapter.

CHAPTER 7

Doing Justice:
Liberation Theology

IN TERMS OF WORLD history, liberation and postliberal theologies belong to opposite contexts. Liberation theology arose in Latin America, spreading throughout the developing "South"; its seminal period was the optimistic, revolutionary 1960s and '70s, and it came to full strength in the '80s before being weakened by the collapse of communism and revolutionary hope generally. Postliberalism, on the other hand, arose in North America and the "North" generally, a generation later, as part of the reaction against "modern" secular hopes, in the 1980s and '90s. Nonetheless, these theologies share three of the four features listed at the outset of Part 2: the centrality of narrative; critique of the prevailing "liberal" forms of Western theology, or any theology shaped by rationalist metaphysics and the apologetic agenda; and the primacy of practice. In this sense narrative theology could be regarded as the protesting child of liberation theology.

That said, the difference in context and world-movement creates great differences in the outworking of these theologies. Firstly, in terms of the centrality of narrative, we noted that postliberal theology tends to see the Bible as one grand narrative of salvation, centered on Christ and his death and resurrection. Liberation theologies, on the other hand, tend to listen for many stories in the Bible, especially those that have been occluded by power interests that have helped to shape the biblical canon; and if any story is central, it is the story of the liberation from Egypt. Secondly, the postliberal critique of liberal theology arises from the debate with Western secularism and even atheism, where liberalism is seen as conceding too much; whereas liberation theology arose in areas where the struggle against Western oppression was much more significant than the debate with Western secular ideology. Finally, the kind of practice postliberalism focuses on tends to be the ecclesial practices that render Christianity distinct, including liturgy and worship; these are seen—in the virtue ethics that so often accompanies postliberal; theology—as translating into good ethical practice, by training people in the distinctive Christian virtues. Liberation theology on the other hand focuses on praxis in the Marxist sense of action informed by correct ideas leading to liberation, and this is something in which Christians can share with those of other faiths and none.

The previous chapter criticized postliberalism for making Christianity a self-contained and self-justifying language game, sealing it off from dialogue either with other faiths or with secularism, and hence, in our terms, from encounter with a reality outside itself. Liberation theology seems to correct these errors. It certainly claims to engage with reality more authentically than its alternatives. While postliberal theologies—for all their emphasis on concrete story content—seem to address an abstract humanity, or a theoretical individual, in need of salvation, liberation theology takes the ordinary historical and economic realities of people's lives much more seriously, defining both sin and salvation in terms of the dynamics of oppression and liberation. And (witness the writings of Paul Knitter, among many others) this understanding of concrete sociopolitical reality constitutes a basis for dialogue with other faiths, which can be seen as sharing in the same struggle for liberation. In the spawning ground of liberation theology in Latin America, dominated as it is by Roman Catholicism alongside smaller, often Pentecostal, groupings, little need was felt to engage in interreligious dialogue. But whenever liberation theology has moved to countries dominated by another religion, it has tended to seek alliance and common ground, as with Indian Dalit theology, Korean Minjung theology, and the like.[1]

At first sight it might then seem that in engaging with reality by way of dialogue—both with secular Marxism and with other religions—liberation theology represents the ideal to which this book moves. But this chapter will argue that this is not quite so. The first section will argue that liberation theology has conceded too much to secular Marxism in its analysis of reality, and too little in its vision of God, so that it falls short of true dialogue and a nuanced, dialogical engagement with reality. The following section will take up the issue raised here: if liberating practice is the litmus test for reality, by what criteria do we know when we are liberated, or that a particular action is "liberating"? Should we use secular criteria allegedly common to all reasonable people, or criteria internal to one of the faiths? Either case involves a

---

1. Cf. Küster, *Many Faces of Jesus.*

collapse into exclusivism, whether of a secular-based or a narrowly religious kind; so at this point issues raised in chapter 1 are revisited.

The central sections of the chapter present a crucial argument of the book, against the notion that secular represents a "neutral" public space in which diverse religions can meet in the pursuit of a common good. Global market capitalism, which seems for now to have won the day against socialist alternatives, is shown to constitute a *religious* kind of delusion, a false idolatry, and a diminution of intersubjective value and true dialogue. There are two points here. Firstly, secularism (whether socialist or capitalist), reared as it is in the cradle of capitalism, cannot fully express what it is that the market takes from us. Fully to express the failure of the market to do justice, we need to recover religion and faith from being minority options within the market; we need the religious categories like idolatry, spirituality, and sacrament, which critique and subvert the market, not as a purely material process, but as a quasi-religion. By allowing secularism to define the goalposts of "reality," before religion is permitted to start playing, liberation theology concedes the game before the contest begins. Liberation theology emerges as needing more intrafaith dialogue with the postliberal theologies discussed in the previous chapter, with their call to theology to arise from its prostration before the secular, and to be faithful first of all to its own God.

Secondly, and conversely, as a socially embodied set of economical practices, market capitalism cannot be overcome by mere ideals, whether secular or religious. Only fully embodied religious practices can provide forms of life capable of delivering the glory of human beings fully alive from the emasculating maws of the market leviathan. It is here that liberation theology concedes too little to secular Marxism. In keeping God out of the contest, so to speak, and failing to acknowledge the weight of the Marxist critique, the God of liberation theology is insufficiently "deconstructed," and insufficiently open therefore to dialogue with other religions, to allow glory to spill over into human liberation. Here liberation theology needs more intrafaith dialogue with the negative theologies discussed in the next chapter.

The penultimate section develops a notion of justice as co-flourishing, such that justice has both ethical and epistemological aspects. That is to say, it involves (interdependently) seeing beings (including oneself) for what they are and the hope of glory that they embody, and giving them (as ones like oneself) their due, in terms of what enables them to flourish. Then the final section explores what we mean by authentic flourishing and glory. These notions are both philosophical and religious; they are not anti-secular, but take us beyond any secular analysis of the common good.

Perhaps because of the politically engaged nature of liberation theology, this chapter will approach these questions in a more historical and less purely philosophical and theological way that the previous chapter. Such an approach seems all the more necessary because there are some who would see liberation theology, like the Marxism that partly inspires it, as a phenomenon of the past, no longer—in view of the alleged triumph of global capitalism on the one hand and growing skepticism in the Catholic magisterium on the other—to be taken seriously as a contemporary theology. More than is the case with other theologies, the claim of liberation theology to engage with reality is above all a claim to understand the forces at work in history, and the way a Christian theology can lead to a liberation realizable in history. So to evaluate its dialogical engagement with reality we have no choice but to question whether it has failed, and its hopes have proven false, in our time.

TOO MARXIST, OR NOT ENOUGH?

> Marxism, the Vatican asserts, is a reductivist form of social analysis; as such, it is intrinsically and so inseparably connected with a praxis of class hatred and struggle, which offends against Christian norms of charity, and with the denial of God and of the human person, which strikes at the core of Christian belief about God and the human. Liberation theologians, it concedes, propose to ally themselves only with Marxism as to an instrument of the "analysis" of the structures of oppression, . . . but in this they are multiply deceived. For Marxism is a totalising ideology of materialism and its "ideological principles come prior to the study of social reality." . . . They are inviting a theological cuckoo into the nest.[2]

Thus, Denys Turner sums up the critique of liberation theology expounded in the Vatican's *Instruction on Certain Aspects of the "Theology of Liberation"* (1984), better known as *Libertatis Nuntius*. But the criticism that liberation theology concedes too much to secular, atheistic Marxism to survive as a credible theology runs wider than the Vatican. It had already been made, more crudely and forcefully, by Edward Norman[3] and would be reiterated in 1990 in a much more complex and nuanced argument by Anglican theologian John Milbank, to the effect that Marxist and other social theory is far

2. Turner, *Marxism, Liberation and Negation*, 201–2.
3. Norman, *Christianity and World Order*.

from offering a neutral, "objective" analysis of our human situation, being anti-theological in its fundamental approach.[4]

We will return to Milbank's argument in the next section. Suffice it to say that the Vatican, the formerly Anglican (latterly Roman Catholic) priest, and the Anglican theologian agree that liberation theology erroneously attempts to use Marxism to provide a supposedly objective analysis of our oppressed situation and a correspondingly objective hope for a liberated future. Marxism is more of an ideological unity than that, and its atheism is integral to its analysis of history, not something that can be discretely ignored or laid on one side.

Turner agrees, but following Alistair Kee[5] he deduces the opposite: that far from embracing too much of Marxism, liberation theologians have embraced too little, too selectively.

> Insofar as liberation theologians have been prepared to acknowledge the force of Marx's critique of religion, they have done that too in an inconsistently selective fashion. For, as Kee points out, that critique of religion contains two inseparable but distinct elements, the first (and generally accepted by liberationists as legitimate) being the empirical, historical critique of the actual role of Christianity within society as normally reactionary, and the second (generally ignored by liberationists), the more radical and comprehensive critique of Christianity as involving in principle an "ideological reversal," involving a falsification therefore of the real relations of class and domination and a mystification.[6]

Marxism according to Kee and Turner regards Christianity, and indeed religion generally, not just as normally siding with the oppressors (an alliance that liberation theology coherently and rightly tries to reverse), but as essentially ideological and alienating. Marx developed the ideas of Ludwig Feuerbach, according to whom the idea of God represented an alienation of what was best in humanity, a projection of goodness and justice from the human world in which it could be achieved, to a divine realm in which it could only be contemplated and adored, but never realized. According to Feuerbach, we need to be atheists so that we can re-appropriate what was rightly ours, and instead of merely contemplating perfection from afar, realize it in our own history.

---

4. Milbank, *Theology and Social Theory*.

5. Kee, *Marx and Failure of Liberation Theology*.

6. Turner, *Marxism*, 204, referencing Kee, *Marx*, 41–68.

Now if Feuerbach was right and Marx were simply repeating him, then atheism would be written into the Marxist analysis of history, and the Vatican and the other critics would be right to caution Christians against the liberation theologians' use of Marxism. But Turner argues that Marx does not uncritically adopt Feuerbach. For Marx what is alienating is not the idea of God but the dualistic separation of God from humanity. Marx

> denies equally any theism which purports to identify a God in relations of opposition to the human and any atheism which can identify the human only through its negation of God. It is, therefore, in the radicalism of that atheism that Marx truly challenges the Christian theologian to construct a theology which is at once, and equally, post-theistical and therefore, post-atheistical, a theology which, being dispossessed of its language of affirmation, dispossesses the atheists of their language of denial; a theology therefore which joins hands with the radicalism of the *via negativa* . . .[7]

. . . and, we might add, the penetrating non-dualism of Hindu Advaita Vedanta, and Buddhist Madhyamaka with its fourfold negation. For Turner, rather than reject Marxism for its "atheistic" analysis, liberation theology needs to embrace its challenge to be theistic in a more mystical and negative way. Liberation theologians need to let Marxism help them do for their politically engaged theology what the mystics did in terms of their more private search for divine union. Marxism then emerges not as a blatantly secularizing analysis, but as already implicitly theological in the same paradoxical way as the mystics in their negations and affirmations. The Marxist goal lies not in the elimination of religion but in the cessation of the need for "the religious" as a separate sphere of practice, as our spirituality comes to be worked out and achieved through our economic creativity.

We will return to these hinted themes, but at this point it is worth commenting that liberation theology has perhaps both taken too much from Marxism and too little; and that this is typically what happens when our relation with "another religion" falls short of dialogue. Liberation theology has arguably tried to "use" Marxism for its analysis in the way that some Christians "use" Buddhism for meditation techniques. In so doing these Christians have taken from Buddhism too much, more than they are entitled to from their Christian perspective; but also too little, in that they have used part of Buddhism while avoiding true dialogue with the wider context of these its practices, namely precisely the *insight* in insight meditation. (As it happens, this insight is not unlike the Marxist insight; like it, it

7. Turner, *Marxism*, 212.

is often regarded as atheist, when in fact it is rather a non-dual rejection of both theist and atheist "God-talk.") In the same way, the liberationists take too much from Marxism while avoiding true dialogue with Marxism as a whole system. But the solution may not be—in either case—to stop taking such things, but rather to risk taking more, to listen to the critique of the Christian tradition that is actually posed, by Buddhism or Marxism. That, paradoxically, may be the way to a more authentic Christianity.

Liberation theology, Turner is saying, needs to be more apophatic, not only about God as such, but about God in history and the arrival of the kingdom. Early liberation theology seems from our twenty-first-century perspective, altogether too optimistic and affirmative about the imminent arrival of the revolution and through it, the kingdom of God. A greater apophatic sense of the elusive paradoxes of the kingdom and the recurrent absence of God from history might render theology better equipped, not only to deal with past challenges posed by the holocaust and continuing genocides, but also the challenge posed by the seeming "end of history" with the advent of global capitalism, as discussed below. Fundamentally this is the challenge of knowing what might be the signs of the kingdom, especially in times when there seem to be few. In other words, how will we know when we are liberated?

HOW WILL WE KNOW WHEN WE ARE LIBERATED?

And what are we to make of the concepts of "kingdom" and "liberation"? One of these concepts is rooted in the Bible and the messianic thought of the Synoptic Gospels, while the other (in this context) belongs to modern politics, and especially Marxist politics. Yet liberation theology uses them almost as synonyms. Is a biblical concept being adapted (or possibly hijacked) to express a fundamentally secular modern hope, or *vice versa*? So much in liberation theology stands or falls on finding the right understanding on this point, for what is in question is the "liberation" in liberation theology, and the rehabilitation of Jesus' preaching of the coming kingdom or reign of God (whose centrality in the Synoptic Gospels had become occluded by the Pauline and later emphasis on "salvation") stands at the heart of this theology.

Liberation theologians have often been adamant that secular language provides a totally adequate description of social reality, sufficient to inform good, liberative pastoral praxis.

> Theology is reflection, a critical attitude. Theology *follows*, it is the second stage. What Hegel used to say about philosophy can

likewise be applied to theology: it rises only at sundown. The
pastoral activity of the Church does not flow as a conclusion
from theological premises. Theology does not produce pastoral
activity; rather it reflects upon it.[8]

If this is the case, then pastoral activity seeking liberation is itself
something that does not *need* theology in order to identify and accomplish
its goals. We will all know what liberation means, from purely secular accounts like Marxism, and theology will simply assess the validity of our
praxis by reflecting on whether they produce effects that it does not take
theology to recognize.

This is evident in the "pastoral cycle," which was developed by liberation theologians such as Gustavo Gutiérrez, Juan-Luis Segundo, and Leon-
ardo Boff (though there were contemporaneous variants of the cycle as a
means of reflection in secular spheres.[9]) This cycle takes many forms, but all
of them start from experience, which is then analyzed in secular terms. Theology is only introduced at a subsequent stage of reflection, leading to action
as a final stage of praxis which then leads to more experience to be analyzed
in a further cycle. The insistence, *first* analyze, *then* reflect theologically,
precludes the possibility of reading experience, initially, in the light of one's
faith. Faith and theology then becomes reflective matters, distanced from
"pure" experience and its understanding and taking place on a relatively
remote, rational pedestal. It is as if the liberation theologians here accepted
the rationalistic role for theology which they elsewhere challenged.

It is on this matter that the pastoral cycle and its variations differ most
sharply from those cycles presented in this book, where one starts from
experience that is *already* charged, so to speak, by its interillumination with
theology; this interillumination needs *then* to be conceptualized, analyzed
and deconstructed by dialogue with both secular and other-religious models before becoming the basis for action.

The question of the priority of religious and secular accounts makes
for one of the sharpest of all the divergences between liberation theology
and postliberalism. For postliberalism the religions produce their own accounts of what they describe by various terms like liberation, salvation, and
nirvana. For postliberals, as for liberationists, praxis is primary, but the
significant practices for postliberals are the storytelling and ritual by which
the goal (whatever it is called) is identified and set before believers. There
is no reason to suppose that these goals for the different religions are all

8. Gutiérrez, *Theology of Liberation*, 55.
9. See Judith Thompson, *Theological Reflection*, 21–24.

ultimately the same[10] or indeed the same as what is identified as liberation by the "secular religion" of Marxism, or for that matter as the "end of history" defined by proponents of another great secular religion, free-market capitalism (see below). Theology, for postliberals as for liberationists, is a second-order reflection on a primary practice; but whereas for liberationists the practice defines itself in terms that are available to religion-independent secular description, for postliberals it defines itself in the religions' own terms. These are in part defined and refined by theology, so that theology is not merely a subsequent stage of reflection, but also an activity that helps define and inform the nature and goals of the practice itself.

On this point this book tends to side—with some qualifications—with the postliberals. The kingdom or reign of God in the Gospels is a far richer and more dialectically complex concept than any secular Utopia, despite— or perhaps because of—being presented in often crude, down-to-earth imagery. In Jesus' parables the kingdom of God is like . . . sown seed, growing corn, fermenting yeast, an angry landowner, an indebted slave, a wastrel son returning to his father, a pearl in a field, lightning flashing. . . . It is, as scholars have noted, fully realized, already here, whether we like it or not. Yet it is also yet to come, something to hope and plan for, or rather, something to drop all other plans for. Because of this rich, allusive elusiveness, the kingdom hope cannot desert Christians, whatever may happen to the world and them. By contrast, the rationalist secular utopias are far too much worked out in the mind, and hence inflexible; so they look as if they have already been defeated by events.

So to start with the biblical kingdom language, then try to unpack it rationally in terms of social policies (while retaining an appropriate Turnerian apophaticism regarding the ultimate "meaning" of God and God's reign), looks like a better option than to start with social analysis and tie the gospel talk to it. As one Christian socialist, John Milbank comments

> It should, in fact, be peculiarly the responsibility of Christian socialists at present, to demonstrate how socialism is grounded in Christianity, because it is impossible for anyone to accept any longer that socialism is simply the inevitable creed of all sane, rational human beings.[11]

Milbank is fascinating because he traces the uncritical adoption of Marxism by liberation theology to its acceptance of integralist principles promoted by the Vatican itself. Integralism denotes the understanding that

10. Cf. Heim, *Salvations.*

11. Milbank, *Theology and Social Theory*, 208.

in humankind grace and nature are inextricably intertwined, so that it is impossible to contrast a "natural" sphere—comprehensible by philosophy and natural and social science unaided by theology—with a "spiritual" or "supernatural" sphere requiring theology for its understanding. Milbank contrasts two versions of integralism, one pioneered by French thinkers like Henri de Lubac and Maurice Blondel, and the other by Germans like Karl Rahner: "whereas the French version 'supernaturalises the natural,' the German version 'naturalises the supernatural.'"[12] In other words, the French version argues that we need theology in order to understand human society and history, whereas the German develops a natural, philosophical understanding of the work of grace. Now in its rejection of any notion that the church should restrict itself to the supernatural, liberation theology represents a valid transfer of integralism to the social and political sphere. At the very heart of liberation theology is the conviction that whole of life is at once political and spiritual, and salvation cannot be worked out in a purely ecclesial and sacramental realm, but must embrace the political and economic aspects of human liberation.

So far so good, for Milbank; the error arises because liberation theology did for the corporate search for liberation what Rahner did for the individual search for God, namely affirm that the political and economic aspects of liberation can be understood by secular social and political science without any help from theology. Liberation theology simply invites Marxist social theory to take up the role which the quintessentially individualist philosophy of existentialism performed in the thought of Rahner: the role of providing the fundamental rational substructure on which the specifics of theology can be erected. But the whole weight of Milbank's very weighty *Theology and Social Theory* aimed to show how theology is necessary even for the creation of the substructure, and that the social sciences, though they purport to offer a purely rational, secular understanding, are already theological, in the sense of being anti-theological. Milbank traces the genealogy of social science in detail, in order to drive home this point.

But whether or not Milbank is right in detail, any theology that wishes to ground itself in practice faces a dilemma. If orthopraxis is understood to be the criterion for orthodoxy, and if good praxis is understood to be that which liberates, how do we define liberation and know when we have it? How will we know when we are liberated? How will we identify the kingdom when it comes; or more pertinently, in the present, distinguish actions that advance its coming from those that fend it off?

12. Ibid., 207.

If we privilege secular understandings of liberation, the first question that arises is, which account do we prefer: Marxist or liberal? Psychological or sociological? Or what? For notwithstanding broad-brush accounts of "secular reason," "liberalism," and so forth, secular accounts, especially in the area of the human sciences (psychology, sociology, politics, economics) are not monolithic, but plural, and far from offering consistent criteria. And the next question is, even if unified criteria could be achieved, and a consistent account of liberation could be developed that was acceptable across all secular cultures, would the religions be required to prostrate themselves before this account, and allow themselves to be judged and assessed before its tribunal? Or could a case not be made for urging that such an account was, in the terms of the monotheistic faiths, an idol, a construct of human hands set forth as the ultimate judge and as a worthy of all our allegiance; or in Hindu and Buddhist terms, one great delusion chaining us to samsara in our very pursuit of liberation? Would it not become all the more important for the religions to set before us their own alternative understandings of what we need to seek? Considerations in support of this will be advanced later on.

But if the religions avoid prostrating themselves before the secular idol, and people follow Milbank, Hauerwas, and others in seeking the criteria for liberation within their own faith traditions, then do those traditions not become freewheeling circles of self-justification? Christianity will then be justified in terms of the resurrection, salvation, and eternal life. But it has first defined and depicted these in its own unique way (which is not quite the same way as Judaism and Islam depict them); then it has claimed uniquely and supremely to offer them; and finally it is discovered by its adherents indeed to accomplish them. Buddhism meanwhile will be justified in terms of nirvana, which it also describes in its unique way (not quite the same as the Hindu way), claims uniquely to offer (for all the good other faiths may do to people on earlier reincarnational stages of the journey), and which, again, many if its adherents witness to accomplishing. Each religion accomplishes its own kind of liberation, in a circle of self-justification.

That is why our support of the postliberals on this issue of the priority of the religions' internal criteria needs strong qualification. But can we avoid postliberal circularity without performing the liberal and liberationist prostration before the secular idols? Only, I suggest, once again, by dialogue between the religions; and as suggested in the previous section, by treating relations with "the secular"—including secular Marxism and secular faith in the capitalist market—as interfaith dialogues. In dialogue we neither merely take ideas, insights, and practices from the other, nor merely justify ourselves in terms that are only relevant to us; nor conversely do we prostrate ourselves and allow the other's perspective to swallow us whole. Rather, we allow both the content and the criteria of our respective faiths to undergo modification in the light of the other, in a process—described especially in chapter 5—that teases us out of our self-justifying circles in a mutual modification of unpredictable outcome.

But that kind of interaction of subjective lives and worlds is under even more threat than ever from the process explored in the next section, which invites us all to a terminal prostration. That is why the struggle to do justice to one another involves us in a struggle to see beyond what looks like an all-encompassing, global horizon. The following two sections explain the nature of this horizon, which has the force of a global religion; which is the fundamental reason why a purely secular analysis cannot now see a way beyond it.

IS LIBERATION POSSIBLE
AFTER "THE END OF HISTORY"?

The question of how we know if we are liberated is, of course, not just an abstract epistemological one. It has a more poignant historical aspect. In a world where many things are designed to make us feel liberated, how can we distinguish "real" liberation? Has the path to liberation—in all the varied ways in which it has been understood—become not only unknowable but inconceivable because our minds and lives have themselves become transformed by global capitalism?

Since the 1980s a combination of political, economic, and ideological factors have conspired against the hope of liberation generally and liberation theology in particular. Politically, from seeming to master half the world in the form of the "communist bloc"—ranged menacingly against the capitalist West in a cold war, and winning decisive victories where the war was not so cold, as in Vietnam—communism has collapsed, with most former communist regimes, including Russia itself, adopting aspects of democratic practice. Economically even those nations, like China, which rejected this political road, have adopted market capitalism to a large extent, while other nations in the developing world, such as the G8 group, have come to see economic progress in terms of a freer global market. (Ironically it is now frequently the richer nations that protect themselves against this ever-fiercer competition by means of trade barriers and subsidies.) We have seen the arrival of the "global market" in which Indian and African farmers can (ideally) trade and agree prices directly with consumers in the West by means of mobile phones and publicity on the worldwide web.

This combination of political and economic developments has led to profound ideological shifts, some utopian, others apocalyptic. Among the utopians some have welcomed an "end of history";[13] a final withering away of the state and the historical clashes between states, and the inauguration of an endless peace in which we all live happily and prosperously as consumers and traders in the global market. From the eighteenth century onward Whigs and Liberals had argued that market forces are sufficient to generate equable relations between people, so that the strong arm of the state could safely be withdrawn, and people could be "left to get on with it" (*laissez faire*) because the "invisible hand" of market forces would ensure the best outcomes. Now, the Utopians argued, the final stage had come: globalization of market forces could be left to triumph over the nation state. Liberalism as the ideal of democratic politics combined with *laissez faire* economics and individual rights, could be seen to be triumphing over the ideologies of both authoritarian nationalism (fascism) and international socialism (communism).

For those on the left, including liberation theologians, the response was more apocalyptic. For them, globalization signified not the dawn but the end of hope; a choking of history at the capitalist phase, unable to deliver the ultimate socialism. While the utopians welcomed the general increase in prosperity brought about by globalization—which it was assumed would eventually "trickle down" to the poor—these apocalypticists noted the increase in the divide between rich and poor, both between and within nations, as well as the ecological devastation that globalization was wreaking. For the balance of power was shifting away from the national and local communities affected by environmental destruction, towards the multinational corporations and the shareholders they represented. These were interested only in profit, and wholly unaffected by the local effects of the industries involved.[14] On the left, the hope of global socialism receded in favor of a more fragmentary liberal concern for the rights of various groups, in a move masterfully criticized by Petrella.[15] In theology this shift was reflected in the tendency of a global liberation theology that prioritized the plight of the poor and the working classes to give way to black, feminist, gay, queer, womanist, and a multiplicity of other minority (or in the case of feminism, majority) group theologies. Such a multiplicity fitted well with postmodernism and its emphasis on local perspectives rather than global metanarratives. On the other hand, it was argued that postmodernism itself

13. Fukuyama, *The End of History*.
14. Cf Cavanaugh, *Being Consumed*, Ch.3.
15. Petrella, *Beyond Liberation Theology*.

represents "the cultural logic of late capitalism," namely global capitalism.[16] Postmodernism is "an inverted millenarianism in which premonitions of the future, catastrophic or redemptive, have been replaced by senses of the end of this or that (the end of ideology, art, or social class; the 'crisis' of Leninism, social democracy, or the welfare state, etc., etc.)."[17]

In postmodernism faiths and ideologies morph into consumer choices, perspectives, local stories, and the values of small special interest groups. However, the public ground that is thereby ceded does not, as is frequently alleged, become nothing, or simply "end." The postmodern *nihil* or absence of universal story masks the one grand super-narrative and super-praxis that now prevails, global capitalism, which generates the one kind of "objective" value that both effects and profits from the subjectivization of all others: market value.

THE RELIGION OF THE MARKET

In the face of global capitalism and the collapse of state-sponsored communism, liberation theology has failed to die, though it may have moved from its original hopeful innocence to a more stoic "refusal to cease suffering"[18] befitting a much longer and costlier struggle than initially envisaged. Indeed, the advocates of global capitalism face two kinds of vulnerability, one historical, the other general.

Historically, the withering of the state welcomed by the advocates has failed to arrive. Though in the '80s and '90s, there was a rolling back of the welfare state, the military and police have continued to tighten the state's grip. States have, on average, become smaller (both in terms of welfare provision, and geographically), but stronger, with ever more pervasive surveillance. The market, after all, needs a strongly protected infrastructure: a system that thrives on increasing desire, and needs to ensure that people look to market exchange rather than say theft or conquest to gain what they increasingly feel they want or need. Increased desire needs increased constraint (which arguably increases desire still more). What has arrived is not a benign "capitalism with a human face" but a "savage capitalism"[19] for which large tracts of the population of the third world become effectively redundant because they have little to trade, and little purchasing power. This

16. Jameson, *Postmodernism*.

17. Ibid., 1.

18. Bell, *Liberation Theology after the End of History*.

19. Hinkelammert, *Cultura de la Esperanza*, 25–38, discussed in Bell, *Liberation Theology*, 10–12.

development has been wittily described as "the coming out of capital, a new golden age of greed that dares to say its name,"[20] since greed is now seen as the motor driving progress toward the common good.

This historical point witnesses to the general problem that the advocates of the global market have in establishing the market as an overall benign force. Crucial to their case against controlled economies is the notion that the market is an "emergent," complex phenomenon that cannot be predicted, so cannot be controlled. But if market forces are essentially unpredictable (as their own argument requires, and as actual history, with the recent banking crises, shows to be the case in fact) then how can we be so sure they will (eventually) work out in everyone's best interest? John Rawls classically argued that if we could choose what kind of society we would be born into, but did not know who we would be, rich or poor, within it, it would always be rational to choose a relatively egalitarian welfare state in which we would know we would not be overwhelmingly rich, but would not be destitute either.[21] If society governed by global capitalism cannot be guaranteed to bring relative prosperity for all in the here and now, it is irrational in Rawls' terms to prefer it. Yet this is the world we now live in.

The market as such is not, of course, inherently an enemy; indeed local markets and town centers where market economies prevail are often better places to be than the drab streets run by state controlled economies. And it is probably rightly argued that without the economic mechanism of the market, economies cannot develop beyond the degree of complexity that prevailed in the 1960s, after which the centralized command economies of the communist bloc began to stagnate. What needs to be contested is the ideology or religion of the market that sees a free market unconstrained by redistribution as a sure and necessary way to prosperity for all. Here the advocates are in a double bind, because on the one hand they have to argue that the market is complex and unpredictable—so that it allows for innovation in a way that controlled economies do not—and, on the other hand, there is something inevitably benevolent about its workings. Just as Marxists argued that there was a deterministic force in history making the socialist utopia the inevitable outcome of history, so the advocates of the market invoke some mysterious refinement of Smith's invisible hand. Some invoke chaos theory and the emergence of spontaneous order, in economics as in science.[22] But chaos theory is a two-edged sword precisely because it is *non*-deterministic, and cannot predict whether the order that emerges will

20. Massumi, *User's Guide to Capitalism*, 131.

21. Rawls, *Theory of Justice.*

22. Pre-eminently Friedrich Hayek in, e.g., *Pretence of Knowledge.*

be good for everyone, or otherwise. Others, like Fukuyama, invoke Hegelian theory to argue (questionably) that democratic society, coupled indissolubly with the free market, satisfies our fundamental desire for recognition, since nobody is excluded, all being equally affirmed.

But it is clear that belief in the enriching power of the market involves a faith that goes beyond the facts. Indeed, Jung Mo Sung argues that this belief has all the key features of a religion.[23] It offers a secular form of *paradise* through economic progress. It thereby ascribes *magical powers* to a human institution and activity: the power to bring (economic) salvation is ascribed to the market economy. Then to explain the failure of utopia to arrive as the theory dictates it should, it invokes its own version of *original sin*, namely Hayek's "pretence of knowledge" as to how markets can be controlled, leading governments to tamper with them in the supposed interests of welfare. And emerging from this there is the need for *sacrifice*: the poor who suffer in the present from the operations of the market must (involuntarily) offer their poverty as a sacrifice in the cause of the long-term prosperity that the market will bring about.

To this religious tetrad—paradise, magic, original sin, and sacrifice— we might add a fifth typically religious factor: the *faith* in the market, whose salvific power like God's is beyond rational demonstration. And regarding sacrifice we might note a further sacrifice we all have to make to market forces, whether or not we are poor: namely the constraint on our desires. As Bell shows convincingly, capitalism is like an Edenic snake with infinite undulations, twisting us to desire most those things the market can provide. Our pleasure in things that are free, like sex, play, and exercise, need constraining or directing towards marketable forms (pornography, toys—ever more toys—and the gym). Capitalism, as Weber classically noted, has benefited from a kind of Puritanism; it is just that with late, global capitalism, the Puritanism of restraint and abstinence has been replaced by a curious Puritanism of greed and indulgence, a "technology of desire" in which desires and wants are identified, and our natural instincts are limited and "sacrificed" to the worship of the commodity.[24]

If this is the case, then the market is not just an economic stage that will, according to the inevitable laws of history, as Marxists have argued, succumb via revolution to a more benign socialism. The market has the force of a religion, a religion that paradoxically makes us see the realities that matter in a secular, religionless way. That is why secularism, as the child of market capitalism, cannot see our way beyond the market. As we shall

23. Sung, *Desire, Market and Religion*, 12–22.
24. Bell, *Liberation Theology*, 19ff.

see in due course, only authentic, dialogical religion can overcome the religion of the market, and the religions as commodities competing on the market. But before we can argue that, we need to take the present argument a stage further, turning from the religion of the market (that is the religion that bases its hopes in the market) to the notion of the market as in itself a religion—a form of idolatry.

THE MARKET AS RELIGION

Many have noted how religion is marketing itself ever more as a commodity with a great feel-good factor.[25] But the converse is equally true: the doubtless related fact that the acquisition of goods on the market is becoming more and more of a religion. Advertisements increasingly emphasize the spiritual benefits of products, using words referring to spirituality, awesomeness, transcendence, and the mystical. Shopping, for many, has become the family's primary activity on Sundays and other "days of [consumer] obligation," undertaken in costly buildings that ever more closely resemble lavish temples. These can inspire great awe and pride, as in the case of seventy-year-old illiterate Bangladeshi farmer Abdus Salmad who saw the crystal dome of the 80 million dollar Bashundara City Shopping Center as proof of how much his country had improved.[26] Salmad was valuing the market not in a secular, utilitarian way—the goods on sale could never be his or benefit him personally—but in a quasi-religious, contemplative way, through his awe and wonder regarding the goods in themselves, and perhaps a kind of vicarious joy akin to the way the medieval peasantry might delight in the glories of the liturgy, without normally sharing in Holy Communion themselves.

These reflections take us in the opposite direction from the utopian religion of the market just considered, according to which the market is seen as a kind of ultimate dialogue in which free, rational, and egalitarian relations come to prevail over the ideologies of the religions and socialism. In reality market exchange is as unlike dialogue as can be.

In a dialogue, say, about a painting, each person attempts to communicate their subjective impression of the quality of the painting and what it means to them. The other person will typically utter responses that take on board the other's impression but offering their own "take" on the painting. The subjective impressions and meanings matter to the participants; they

25. Heelas, *Spiritual Revolution*.

26. Sung in Althaus-Reid, *Another Possible World*, 71–72, citing journalist David Rohde.

motivate the dialogue in two ways. One motive is the movement towards intersubjectivity and perhaps an objective evaluation of the painting; and the other is that, even in the absence of that convergence, the dialogue provides insight into the mind of the other, or how things are for them regarding the painting, thus securing a greater intimacy, and also the expansion of the mind of each by means of sharing alternative possible ways of seeing. The dialogue enhances both subjectivity and objectivity.

In an act of buying and selling—let us again use the example of the painting—something very different happens. After some verbal exchanges, typically one person will hand over to the other some "token": some metal coins, or a piece of paper with some writing on it including his own name, or a piece of plastic. The other will hand over to him the painting itself. The token is in no way a "response" to the painting; it is a completely different order of entity, though it is the act of exchange that makes the pieces of metal, paper, or plastic into tokens, or more precisely, "money," while the painting now becomes a "commodity," that is, an item with a quantitative (rather than qualitative) value defined by the tokens. The subjective meaning and value that leads the one person to buy the painting is of no concern to the seller. It matters nothing to him whether he is going to hang it very tastefully, or tastelessly, on his wall, or put it in his collection in his garage to sell on at a better price, or dispose of the picture in order to use the frame for a picture of his own. What the seller wants is the tokens, which he can use to exchange for commodities more desired by him. The movement is no longer via the exchange of subjective value and towards both intimacy and objectivity. Rather, subjective value becomes a purely private and essentially irrelevant matter. (To counteract this depersonalizing aspect of course buyers and sellers often engage in dialogue about subjects easy to agree on, like the weather, so that subjective impressions are affirmed.) What emerges is another, quantifiable value that the parties do not organically co-create but conventionally agree upon. This value continues to "haunt" both money and commodity. The commodity somehow embodies the price that was paid for it, while money becomes a physical embodiment of the value of the commodities it might purchase. In advanced capitalism the trust in the market system itself may come to outstrip any real monetary back-up and exist in a kind of fantasy land of its own making, as in the times leading up to the recent banking crises.

Long ago Karl Marx noted something religious about this embodiment of value in capital and commodity.

> To find an analogy, we must find recourse to the mist-enveloped
> regions of the religious world. In that world the productions of

the human brain appear as independent beings endowed with life, and entering into relations both with one another and with the human race. So it is in the world of commodities and the products of men's hands . . . .[27]

Marx is discussing what he called the "fetishism of commodities." Commodities are things thought to bear a certain value. Though this value is determined by market forces (i.e., by the role the object plays in the exchange ritual as just described), we think of the objects themselves as possessing value, just as the ritual object for the tribesman, the "fetish" possesses divine power. Value is something immanent in the precious objects of a wealthy middle-class drawing room, such that sometimes the works of art and craft are no longer seen as creations embodying the subjectivity of their makers, but rather "commodities" important for their price tag and the status they confer on their owner.

The market therefore involves us in a kind of religion. But this religion is not an authentic glorification of the Maker, but rather an adoration of something that comes about through our own human activity of commodity exchange. In terms of the monotheistic faiths it therefore constitutes a worship of our own creations, idolatry. Though it seems so neutral, impartial, and inevitable, capitalism commits us to an idolatrous rival religion that privatizes our subjective value and replaces it with a supposedly objective market value that is negotiated, supposedly between equals.

And in this process the authentic religions come to seem inauthentic. The rich intersubjective domains conjured up by the material manifestations of our religion—temples and churches, rites and sacraments—become a kind of historical relic marking what once made life meaningful for many, but can now be at best the means for private experiences of beauty, awe, and transcendence, and all too often, occasions for entertainment and encounter with odd forms of difference. In the secular city of late capitalism, the cities of faith seem quaint and false by comparison with the "true religion" of the market. They represent the trespass of something that ought to be subjective onto the objective political domain. But in this process there is in fact a reality whose possible advent is being denied or suppressed: namely the possible emergence of intersubjective reality: the transformation of the objective, political and economic conditions of life into something meaningful, participatory, and celebratory to everybody, albeit in many different ways.

Now the fetishism of commodities is a concept of the early Marx. If the commodity represents a false kind of religion, Marx's criticism of it might

27. Marx, *Capital*, Vol 1.1.1.4, 77.

have led to a rehabilitation of authentic religion as a means of overcoming the market and its false values. But in Marx the religious dimension here simply adds to the critique of capitalism, being one way of emphasizing how irrational and ridiculous it is. The later Marx continued in this anti-religious trajectory. But the reverse trajectory remains (as Turner noted) a logical possibility, one that this book will pursue.

There is something deceptive as well as idolatrous in the market exchange.[28] The market is valued by its advocates for the supposed freedom and equality it generates; for according to some (including Fukuyama) it is the only economic system that is compatible with democracy. And on the face of it, the market exchange looks like the paradigm of a relation that is both equal and free. The partners of the exchange are equally free to buy and sell or not, and the price is agreed and not forced on either party. But this freedom and equality pertains only if the partners are free and equal in other respects. Suppose the buyer already has a mansion with hundreds of other paintings in his collection; he does not particularly like this painting but if he can get a cheap price he knows he'll be able to sell it on at great profit. And suppose the seller has lost his job and his family is facing starvation, and selling this, his only valuable possession, is the only way he can get money to buy food. In this case the seller will be desperate and the buyer will be able to settle for the low price he wants.

> Normal language is full of ideology, words that say one thing and effect another. The primary Marxist example is the way an exchange of work for a wage "says" that the two people are freely agreeing to a contract as equals. What the exchange effects may be a situation of dire exploitation by the employer of the worker, who may be compelled by poverty to accept the meagre wage she apparently freely contracts into, which is always less than the value, in other senses, of what she makes or does. Not only that, but the misrepresentation of the effect by the sign actually helps effect and perpetuate the inequality, because if people saw the inequality for what it was, they would condemn it. . . . So we can define an ideology as a sign or set of signs that effect the evil they falsely signify, and moreover, effect or perpetuate the evil by means of the false signification.[29]

Therein lies the inequality and compulsion involved in the market. It is the rich and the powerful who can set the terms to which the parties "freely" agree. It is well known how in many countries those with land are able to

28. Cf. Cavanaugh, *Being Consumed*, ch. 1.
29. Thompson, *Sacraments*, 167.

set the price for the peasants who rent it, and when famine impoverishes the latter, they will agree to whatever rents and loans the landlords decree, in order simply to be able to go on growing food and stay alive. The market system is inherently unstable. Those with just slightly more wealth will have slightly more power to set the terms of exchange, enabling them to become steadily more wealthy at the expense of the poor, who become ever more poor until they reach destitution.

At that point, having nothing to exchange, they become redundant as far as the economy is concerned. Indeed, on a global scale large parts of Africa and large segments of the urban poor have become economically redundant. Their disappearance would make scant difference to the world economy, and indeed such people are often "disappeared" because their existence, as people inclined to resort to crime as the only means of sustenance, gives them a negative value as far as the economy is concerned. A careful look at the news will show that a terrorist attack in, say, Paris is given hugely more coverage than say one in Palestine, and one in Palestine more than one in Nigeria, which will merit little more than a single short article. Meanwhile, the hundreds of thousands perishing in wars in other parts of Africa like the Congo often receive no coverage at all. This is not just a matter of geographical distance; the factor that determines how much news about people matters to us is—chillingly—correlated with something like their economic significance for us.

The market—at least, the market allowed to rule and not counteracted by perpetual redistribution to restore the initial equality—is therefore not just a neutral religion, but a dangerously deceptive one, namely an ideology. Ideology (in the Marxist sense) presents a benign humanitarian face, but this benevolence on the level of signs enables effects that are the opposite of benign. An ideology involves a mystification, a "false consciousness," whereby people come to be dominated by their relations instead of being masters of them, precisely because those relations are hidden from them, disguised as a different sort of relation. In the case of the market, the free and equal exchange on the level of signs (money and commodities) enables conditions of inequality and oppression to prevail on the real level on which people live and work and accumulate wealth, or alternatively suffer, starve, and die.

The market, then, fails to do justice in two ways. It fails to do justice to everyone, and to reality itself, by forestalling the process so central to this book, whereby subjective values and qualities intermesh in dialogue as they move towards greater intimacy and objectivity. The market renders our values private and essentially irrelevant, while giving a false objectivity to the commodity and the quantitative value it represents. But in particular it fails to do justice to the poor, presenting as free, equal, and democratic, relations that impoverish many and render them marginal and irrelevant.

The market is not going to disappear. The neoliberals are right in this at least: that the market provides a very efficient *means* to the end of organizing supply and demand. Planned economies cannot match this efficiency beyond a certain level of complexity, and after that level is reached—approximately in the 1950s for Russia and the 1990s for China—tend to stagnate unless, as in the case of China, elements of the market economy are introduced within an overall centralized and totalitarian politic. It is also true that the global market sets the scene for a greater interaction between different cultures and their stories, provided they are allowed to interilluminate as equals. (In the market the danger is always that one culture will become commodified, its rituals and narratives becoming "spectator sport" for the more powerful, consumer culture.) Michael Doyle is also *broadly* right in his assertion that democracies have never waged wars against each other.[30] In free-market democracies the (relatively) win-win game of trade comes to replace the win-lose "game" of territorial acquisition and political expansion, while (relative) freedom of information makes wars harder for democracies to wage, since it is less easy to shield their populations from knowing the effects of war.

The advocates of the market are not incorrect to argue for these positive features. Their mistake has been to idolize the market as if it were an end in itself, or an "end to history," automatically securing (eventually) all the justice we need. What is needed is not to replace the market but to surpass it and deprive it of its quasi-religious fascination.

In the same way, the arrival of market economies has not (*pace* the neoliberals) seen the vanishing of the state and the centralized hierarchies that preceded it. On the contrary, the state has become all the more necessary as (ideally) the one means of correcting the instabilities and redressing the inequalities generated by the market. (In practice of course it has often represented a "savage" capitalism, safeguarding the rich against the potential violence of the marginalized and impoverished.) What one hopes for is to deprive the state of the fascination it once held, and still holds in nationalistic and religious fascist settings. These last, which are on the increase, represent the defenses of savage capitalism against both the potential aggression of the dispossessed, and the undermining of local traditions and values by globalization. One hopes that this defended state can be surpassed in a new global and international economy that is only just beginning to

---

30. Doyle, *Kant, Liberal Legacies, and Foreign Affairs* (but also note https://en.wikipedia.org/wiki/List_of_wars_between_democracies).

arrive. (In reality, we are actually still a long way from achieving international trade, let alone a corresponding movement of labor, that is anything like free from national barriers.) The future we hope for is surely one in which the market and the state serve as correctives to each other, ensuring neither has unchecked power, but both are used as means to securing an intersubjective intimacy in which justice is done to each and all.

JUSTICE AS CO-FLOURISHING

Global capitalism is an economic phenomenon, and part of what will help us overcome its negative effects concerns economic policy, which lies beyond the scope of this book. But we have also argued that it is a materially embodied religious phenomenon. Firstly, as a *religious* phenomenon, its transformation into something better has a religious dimension. This section will focus on three aspects of this religious dimension: intrinsic value, the affirmation of subjectivities, and peaceful convergence. And secondly, the very fact that global capitalism is a *materially embodied*, economic phenomenon, means that even the religious dimension of its transformation and overcoming needs to be equally material, equally rooted in actual human relations. So the final section of this chapter will develop an account of this material and practical dimension of religion, with a particular focus on the worship that gives glory to God and affirms and releases the glory in creation. The reader may be relieved that we are returning to the main theme of this chapter: liberation theology and its need to release itself from the secular embrace; to invoke religious notions of idolatry, spirituality, and sacrament; to engage more fully with the sacramental and liturgical dimensions of our liberation; and generally, so to speak, to allow God more fully to enter the fray, both as the source and the object of critique and deconstruction.

Firstly, regarding intrinsic value: we have noted how the market relativizes all values, reducing all values to exchange value, value as a commodity that may be exchanged for other commodities; how those who have nothing to offer on the market are, as noted, effectively "redundant" non-persons, and the economically insignificant are not newsworthy. But the concept of doing justice to others implies that they have, simply by being, a claim on us irrespective of the goods I might get from them. The suffering of others seems somehow to speak, even shout: to "cry out" to me. The liberation theologians refer so often to "the cry of the oppressed" that it has become a cliché, but in doing so they refer back to biblical precedents: the blood of murdered Abel which, God says, "cries out to me from the ground" (Gen 4:10) and the cry of the Israelites in Egypt, whom God hears and promises to deliver (Exod 3:7). The suffering of people, even after their death, has an imperative quality, commanding action from us and from God.

Chapter 3 developed the idea of creation as dialogue. To be is to be spoken and to speak: to be already, from one's foundation, in dialogue with God and other beings.

> The heavens are telling the glory of God;
>   and the firmament proclaims his handiwork.
> Day to day pours forth speech,
>   and night to night declares knowledge.
> There is no speech, nor are there words;
>   their voice is not heard;
> yet their voice goes out through all the earth,
>   and their words to the end of the world. (Ps 19:1–4)

Such descriptions are often seen as opposed to modern scientific understandings, but in fact cohere well. The truth in the "myth" of the selfish gene is that each being contains something that "wants" to propagate copies of itself as much as possible. That "want" is expressed in the tendency to develop a biological structure that is fit for preserving and propagating the gene. In the much older but fundamentally similar language of Aristotle all living beings seek *eudaimonia,* a term which literally refers to good spirits, and is often translated as "flourishing" or in a more recent idiom, "well-being." Maximus the Confessor writes in similar vein of the unique *logos,* the word or pattern of being whereby each creature is created to mirror the eternal *Logos,* the pattern of the universe that is incarnate in Christ.[31] And in genetic terms each living being, including every human one, breathes and feeds in order to grow into a good, fit example of the creature its genes are telling it to be.

There is something intrinsically beautiful about a creature that is healthy and flourishing. Likewise we find beauty in the song by which a bird secures the territory it needs for its flourishing, and to secure the mates it needs for its propagation. Though we now "know" that the bird's song is not sung simply for the joy of sheer being, the song does represent the bird's claim on being, its wanting to flourish; and flourishing is something we (and why not the birds?) subjectively experience through happiness and joy. Rather than see concepts of beauty and joy as anthropomorphic projections, is it not more reasonable to see joy and beauty as the experience, in our own subjectivity, of that which a much wider range of sentient beings experience when they are maximally flourishing? Conversely creatures that are sick or undernourished or crippled, or have otherwise failed to achieve well-being,

---

31. Cf. Wirzba, *Christian Theoria Physike,* 221.

elicit an equally immediate response. Sometimes there is a recoil from ugliness, pain, and suffering. On the other hand, if we are able to identify with the creature, we may feel a direct compassion for it, and perhaps anger with the causes of the impoverishment.

Taking up the discussion of grammatical moods in chapter 5, we can now see how we need to broaden our understanding of being beyond indicative description to cover all the grammatical moods. To be is not just to be a describable fact, but to change the range of possibilities. Being is a question poised, an imperative summons, and a cry of hope or perhaps despair.

If we considered things only from the point of view of making an indicative description, issues of justice in the ethical sense would be outside our view. Our intent would be only justice in the ontological sense: we would be concerned only that our descriptions did justice to their subject. But if, as this book argues, the whole range of moods is relevant to what a subject is, ethical and descriptive justice cannot be separated. We need to do justice to the hopes for what the subject might become, and the questions it poses, and the imperative demands it makes on our behavior. We do justice to a starving child, for example, not by simply giving a description of her appearance and perhaps the causes of her situation, but also by responding to her need to be fed, and registering the questions she poses to the system that allows her to starve. These ethical and descriptive demands for justice belong together. We cannot do ethical justice in the sense of ensuring the children are fed without doing descriptive justice to their objective situation now, including its causes; and we cannot fully appreciate their objective situation while being in denial about the ethical demands it makes.

The increasing descriptive knowledge of how wild nature works—through some excellent television series, and the growth of ecology as a science—is surely one factor making people more concerned to do justice to wildlife in the ethical sense. The ethical demand for justice is not an inference from doing descriptive justice, but intrinsically connected and immediate. Doing justice to the reality of the natural world goes hand in hand with doing justice to what it needs to flourish.

If this intrinsic link holds true, there is an objective basis for justice. There will be about every being that to which we need to do justice. Value will no longer be a conventional "market value" we agree on. On the contrary, we will have grounds for saying that in many cases the market fails to do justice to people and indeed to the wider range of creatures in the environment. For the concept of flourishing and its denial applies much more widely than the human, though only in the human will we humans subjectively feel and understand what it entails. The cry of the human whose flourishing is denied or constricted will always sound more clearly in our human ears, leading to a greater requirement to do justice.

Secondly, regarding the affirmation of subjectivity: such an account reaffirms what individuals find subjectively meaningful. To the intrinsic value of each being, as just described, there corresponds its own valuing. People are valuable and valued as valuers, as sources of meaning that may through dialogue become mine. We want to do justice to what it is like to be such and such a person: to how they experience the world. Things in the world then become much more than mere commodities with a quantitative value attached; they become valuable in all sorts of ways for different people and different sentient beings, and these kinds of valuing are something to which we will need to do justice. Things that are too abundant or available to be commodified may be the things we value most, because we need them most for our flourishing: rainfall and water, the light and warmth of the sun, the free joy of sex.

Finally, regarding the convergence of subjectivities. The notions of value and justice just developed confront a problem. Not all flourishings are compatible. The flourishing of people, for example, is not compatible with the flourishing of the smallpox virus, and host of other viruses and bacteria. For us humans that problem is easily decidable; as humans we know what it is like for humans to flourish and we do not know what it is like for bacteria to flourish, but as bacteria are objectively much simpler in structure than we are, we can infer that their flourishing is not as fine and valuable as human flourishing. But conflicts can exist between groups of humans too. The flourishing of a group of nomads who want the land for their flocks will obviously conflict with a group of agriculturalists who want to till it. Both may conflict with a group of industrialists who want to mine it for minerals, or perhaps state authorities claiming to represent "the national interest," who wish to build a nuclear power station in the area. We hear of such conflicts frequently, and they are often resolved by the use of market forces: the right to use is bought by the wealthier and more influential group.

In this context it becomes clear what justice means, at least in principle. It means the state of affairs that promotes the greatest flourishing of the greatest number. The definition, of course, adapts the old utilitarian definition, replacing subjective "happiness" with "flourishing." How to evaluate, let alone achieve that goal is another matter. Advocates of the market look to it as a way of arbitrating efficiently between conflicting interests, but we have seen that it does not necessarily do so equably, and that even when it does so it empties the world of subjective reasons for valuing, and so takes away what actually promotes the flourishing of all of us. No doubt justice will be best achieved through an untidy mixture of means: a state to make the laws that in principle allow for maximal flourishing, independent law courts to arbitrate between claims, and markets operating in parallel with a state committed to redistribution of wealth and provision for those who have intrinsic worth but no market worth, so as to limit the negative effects of the market economy.

But these measures are not the concern of this book; rather, we are interested in what might sustain the belief that there are some steps we can take that make for justice in the sense of co-flourishing just defined. For this to happen we need to be able to evaluate degrees of flourishing, so that we can to some degree know when we are succeeding. And we need some reasons to believe that we are not *inevitably* rivals competing for individual flourishing, but rather, some societies are more just than others in the sense of making flourishing a win-win rather than win-lose situation, such that we can aim to create those sorts of society. It is precisely these possibilities— the measurability of flourishing and the possibility of mutual co-operation in flourishing—that the market utopians tend to deny.[32] Market value and economic progress are then left as the only measures of a society's "success." These things can indeed be measured, but their relation to what really matters for the flourishing of beings is obscure, to say the least.

Regarding measurability, flourishing has an objective, observable aspect as well as the subjective aspect that is (usually) registered as happiness. Happiness is what it feels like to flourish, and we can only judge our happiness for ourselves. That is why the utilitarian criterion does not work: we cannot tell whether x's happiness outweighs y's sadness, so as to perform the calculus of what makes for the greatest happiness of the greatest number. But we all know what it looks like to flourish, and can tell a flourishing plant or ecosystem or human being from a languishing one. We may not be able to measure it, of course, but the awareness of one another's flourishing may be sufficient for us to arrive at consensus. Surveying the cultures of the world, though none can be singled out as the best, *some* are palpably better to live in than others.

Regarding convergence, Christian theology has traditionally spoken of "the common good" as if there were one identifiable thing that is good for all beings. However, such a "good" will either be identifiable only within a religious system (in Christianity, for example, it consists in the vision of God) or it will be some pallid "highest common factor" all can agree on. But a third alternative is to speak of the mutual inclusion of our different ways of flourishing. This means two things: firstly, that I *cannot* truly flourish in isolation, at another's expense. Compassion is one of the qualities we can

32. Cf. Cavanaugh, *Being Consumed*, ch. 1, Section 4.

expect to develop in the process of coming to flourish as a human being; the more I flourish, the more sufferings and injustices done to others make me unhappy. The other's flourishing is included in my own, and vice versa. And secondly, taking up the suggestion at the end of chapter 1, though we have different religious (and secular) ways of defining flourishing, dialogue enables us to include the other's understanding of it as an enrichment to our own, and our own as fulfilling the other's, *and vice versa*. So our understandings of what it is to flourish do not so much converge on a common good, as open out to a horizon of mutual inclusion.

So much for the need of a dialogue-based religious understanding to overcome the distortion of values involved in global capitalism. We now turn to consider the other sense in which religion is needed, as a set of social practices capable of embodying and communicating values alternative to those of global capitalism. But this in turn, arguably, requires that liberation theology needs paradoxically both to worship and to deconstruct God more, and in a sense, thereby to allow God more fully to enter the fray.

GLORY AND THE HUMAN FULLY ALIVE

For theists, "God" names the aforementioned horizon of mutual inclusion. God is the ultimate source of valuing that guarantees the value of each being as not ultimately conflicting with others' values, because each is valued as an indispensable part of a whole creation that God makes, knows, and loves. All things are believed to co-inhere in the mind of God, so that conflicts of interests in the here and now can only be apparent, not something we can only fight over, or even barter over, but as challenging each of us to a change in our valuing to do justice to the other's valuing; to find, against all apparent odds, the point of the opening of our values to God.

In the terms of the market, this cannot happen; true liberation cannot appear. Because the causes of injustice are tied up within the capitalist story of free and equal relations, the emergence of liberation within capitalism will require a new and different language, and new and different signs that are more transparently aligned with the effects of freedom and equality. Liberation will require what I have called metacausality[33] or emergence in the scientific sense. Just as life, emerging from its material origins, cannot be described fully in physical terms, and yet does not require us to invoke some extra "spiritual" cause, so liberation, within the market system, needs to invoke terms that do not make sense within that system, yet does not have to evoke some direct divine or supernatural intervention. If liberation

33. Thompson, "Creation, Dependent Arising," 56ff.

is defined in terms of the market it will become (as it often does) just another commodity; if it is defined in wholly supernatural terms, it will not be something people can bring about for themselves; the people will be disempowered, given a merely passive relation to liberation. If emergent, then liberation becomes a matter of divine grace, but (as Blondel perceived) not *external* grace.

Liberation, therefore, cannot simply come about by changing our beliefs and attitudes. It will not be something we can accomplish simply through our own secular powers of reason, or by changing our individual attitudes or spirituality. It will require, as Bell notes, forms of practice and ways of living that are at least as embodied as those of the market system itself. As the market involves a "technology of desire," so "Christian resistance to capitalism is contingent upon Christianity's enactment as a counter ensemble of technologies of desire."[34] Christianity must be "reclaimed as a fully material or embodied reality . . . whose practices—such as baptism, catechesis, Eucharist, discipline, prayer and discipleship—do not merely mediate 'ideas' and 'values' but rather transform the material circumstances of Christian (and more generally, human) existence."[35]

In this sense the sacraments constitute a "language of the kingdom."[36] They represent an alternative to ideology, a radical reversal of Feuerbach's alienation.[37] Whereas in alienation values are drained from the material and human world and projected onto an alien world of the spiritual and divine (or into the world of "awesome" commodities), in the sacraments the latter is introjected into material bread and wine shared in the human feast. A Tibetan nun once pointed out to me that it is hard for us humans to see ourselves straightforwardly as the wonders we are. We need the movement of "alienation" in which our beauty is realized through the imagination of some other perfectly beautiful being. This is what the Tibetans do in *puja* when they visualize and worship the deities. But the act of worship always concludes with the "dissolving" of the deity. The imagined divinity is brought into the heart and there dissolved, so that his or her beauty is realized in us. In the Eucharist God could be said to be broken in bread and poured out in wine, dissolved into us, reversing our alienation. At the same time we are dissolved into God. We, the "consumers" of bread and wine, are, as Augustine insisted, consumed into the body of Christ.[38] Without the

34. Bell, *Liberation Theology*, 86.

35. Ibid., 85–86.

36. McCabe, *The New Creation*.

37. Thompson, *The Sacraments*, 167–68.

38. Cf. Cavanaugh, *Being Consumed*, ch. 4, section 2.

movement of alienation involved in the imagination of God, this movement of reintegration and realization might not be possible. In the next chapter we will explore yet more radical ways of reading this "dissolving" of God.

It will still be possible to view the world as a cacophony of sounds each screaming to prevail over the others. But even to do that would be to ignore, on the one hand, that we are all variations on a single genetic theme, made of the same organic stuff, and on the other, that we inhabit an ecological whole as *interdependent* rivals. We can take the view that the song of the bird is *nothing but* a scream to rivals to clear off its territory; or that the starving African child is *nothing but* a failure in a struggle to survive that we flourishing fat Westerners have won. But such a view ignores a lot (not least, that to be fat and rich is not necessarily to flourish). It is also possible to hear the world as a symphony in which the song of the bird, the bodily beauty of the athlete, the intellectual beauty of the scientists' theories, and the cry of the hungry, are all part of a symphony that both celebrates existing flourishing, calling us to natural contemplation, and reaches forward to greater flourishing yet to be achieved, calling us to action for justice.

But to hear it that way is to do justice to God. In the psalms, God's coming in justice coincides with the joyful flourishing of all beings:

> Let the heavens be glad, and let the earth rejoice;
> let the sea roar, and all that fills it;
> let the field exult, and everything in it.
> Then shall all the trees of the forest sing for joy
> before the LORD; for he is coming,
> for he is coming to judge the earth. (Ps 96:11–13a)

The beauty of beings, their inmost goodness as described above, valued and valuing, gives rise to a sense of the glory of which heaven and earth are full (Isa 6). Doing justice to one another is only ultimately possible if we do justice to God as the ultimate valuer of ourselves and the other, one who can act as go-between and enable us to entrust ourselves to the adventure of intersubjective intimacy without fearing that it will lead to loss of our own cherished identity. And the only way we can do justice to a God who creates all and values all equally is to worship God with our whole selves. Glory should then be "the first passion of theology."[39] At the end of the next chapter the demand to do justice to one another and to God will form the basis of a kind of ontological proof.

It is true that worship and sacraments, like everything else, can be captured and become a thinly veiled idolatry of consumerism (as in the "prosperity gospel") or the nation (which has often been seen—blasphemously—as

39. Rivera, *Glory, the First Passion.*

the defender of God). But authentic worship displaces God's glory from the seats of power, and as noted with the Eucharist, relocates it in the places of weakness and vulnerability. Worship needs to be judged not only on whether it is beautiful (though aesthetic criteria are no less important in theology than in science) but on whether it is leading to greater justice. Isaiah and the other prophets are clear on that: liturgical beauty without justice is inglorious, even blasphemous; something the liberation theologians have always been at pains to emphasize. Liberation theologians rightly use Irenaeus' saying, "the glory of God is a human being fully alive" (*Gloria Dei est vivens homo*),[40] to show the intrinsic link between the glorification of God and human flourishing.

But these theologians do not often quote what immediately follows: ". . . and the life of a human being consists in beholding God." If worship and doxology need to be judged by whether they lead to greater justice, the converse holds true also: justice can only be affirmed as justice if it is leading to worship, or the vision of God, or its equivalent in the different religions. The joy of seeing a human or any other sentient being "fully alive," if authentic, immediately lifts the heart in a felt need to ascribe or celebrate the glory. At this point, if God does not exist, we need to invent God. And conversely, the experience of ascribing glory to God in worship, if authentic, transforms our vision of human and other sentient beings, such that we desire to bring them to greater fullness. And at this point, if beings did not exist to be brought to glory, God would need to create them, as of course God has.

That is a point concerning which liberation theology needs more intrafaith dialogue with the postliberals discussed in the previous chapter, with their emphasis on worship as the place where the Christian virtues are learnt. If orthodoxy is translated properly as "right glorification" then to set it in opposition to orthopraxis would be misguided. Worship is itself a kind of praxis, often the most distinctive and challenging kind of praxis a religion undertakes. If questions of justice and liberation must be the basis of our assessment of theologies for truth—as indeed they must—they need to be rooted into this doxological perspective which alone enables us to tell that we have found liberation, that is, the setting free of ourselves alongside everyone and everything in creation to give its own glory to God.

And it is at this point, paradoxically, we need to note that the demand for orthodoxy in the sense of right glorification is far from being a demand that we have a perfectly satisfactory picture of who God is; a picture to which beings simply conform or submit. Here we need to welcome the kind

40. Irenaeus, *Against Heresies*, Book 4, 20:7.

of Marxist theological deconstruction that Turner describes. For right worship is worship of the right God. The thrust toward right glorification demands that we destroy all idols, including the mental idols that anaesthetize the demand for justice and right action by persuading us that we have in our theology attained a fully satisfactory worldview. Turner is right to argue that liberation theology has not taken negative theology seriously enough, and has become content with a God and a kingdom that are too easy to identify with events in history, and conversely as we have noted, too easy to lose hope in when those events fail to materialize. So as well as dialoguing with the postliberals of the previous chapter, liberation theologians need to dialogue with the theologies discussed in the next.

CHAPTER 8

God above Being:
Is Ontotheology a Sin?

THE PROPOSALS OF THE previous chapter about doing justice to God as the horizon of the flourishing of beings could be interpreted in two alternative ways. They could be read as involving a return to a new variant of natural theology, or a new variation of Kant. These alternatives look incompatible, as well as being somewhat unfashionable, though not without advocates.

I could be arguing that to do justice to people and other sentient beings, we need to have the idea of God as the point of convergence of their respective claims. Otherwise those claims will remain competitive, if not violent, and no final good will come about. God then does not exist in the empirical sense in which creatures exist, but God is an idea that we need to have in order to do justice to creatures' reality. Though he exists as an idea, it is an idea more fundamentally real (for Kant, as ultimately an idealist) than their merely empirical reality. On the other hand, I could be arguing that to do justice to the reality of people and other sentient beings, we need to do justice to the reality of God. The argument shifts from the necessity of God as an idea to the participation of beings in the supreme reality of God. Something in the being of beings points us to the being of God. Though it is not, as in classic natural theology, the *design* of creatures that points to the Designer, our argument could be termed a variant of natural theology in the broad sense of the *theoria physike* to be found in patristic writers such as Maximus, and the analogy of being, associated chiefly with Aquinas, between creatures and Creator. And recently Rowan Williams has entered a plea for the revival of a kind of natural theology.[1] In most of these writers it is both the completeness or beauty of creatures and their incompleteness

1. Williams, *Edge of Words*, ch.1.

174

and their lack—what I have referred to as their cry—that indicates, points, and thrusts towards that which is complete in beauty: pure act.

It would seem that the Kantian and natural theological modes of interpretation cannot both be right. After all, was Kant not the one who defeated natural theology and indeed any kind of metaphysical theology, that is, any kind of argument that started with beings in the world and deduced a Creator or ultimate Being? But two hesitations suggest themselves here. One is that Kant was, in his own fashion, as a self-styled transcendental idealist, metaphysical. His argument also runs from the world (this time, the possibility of morality in the world) to the necessity of conceiving of God as real. The other is that my concept of "doing justice"—as noted at the end of the preceding chapter—combines ethical and metaphysical dimensions. To do justice to another is to do the right thing for them, but also to acknowledge and take on board their different reality. The rival interpretations may involve a prizing apart of notions that belong together. If the dimensions of justice are held together the divergence between the two interpretations may disappear. In that case it might be possible to be both Kantian and Thomist, both hostile and friendly to natural theology, at once.

This chapter will begin with a brief examination, not of Kant himself, but of strands of more contemporary theology that orient themselves primarily in relation to Kant and natural theology. Mostly they side with Kant against the natural theologians, but some take Kant one step further and understand "God" just as a good idea.

I shall lay on one side a noble, mainly Anglo-Saxon tradition of atheistic theology—or "atheology"—as we find it, for example, in Thomas Altizer and Don Cupitt. For it is arguable (but too complex to argue here) that though they reject a metaphysical God, such accounts are "ontotheological" in this very rejection. The rejection forces them to build an alternative metaphysics that replaces God. In the name of trying to rid us of the metaphysical God, their thought represents the triumph of metaphysics over God. In case of Altizer, the metaphysical rendering of Christianity by Hegel triumphs over the freedom of God to "make all things new." The God who (in some real sense) dies on the cross and pours himself out into humanity at Pentecost is henceforward totally identified—as with Hegel—with the unfolding of human history.[2] In the case of Cupitt we witness a fascinating theological journey that culminates in the "strange return" of a highly metaphysical (but not on that account to be ignored) Trinity of God, Man, and Language.[3] Challenging as these theologians are in themselves, they are

2. Cf., for "early" Altizer, *Gospel of Christian Atheism*, and for "late," *Genesis of God*.
3. Cupitt, *Theology's Strange Return*.

in a sense eccentric and outside of the theological mainstream, with less to contribute to the argument of this book.

The chapter will focus instead on the more nuanced tradition that has roots in modern Jewish thinkers, like Martin Buber and Emmanuel Levinas. The discussion will focus on two theologians: Jean-Luc Marion, who was heavily influenced by Buber and Levinas, and the eco-feminist Grace Jantzen. These two thinkers have the benefit (for our argument) of representing very different ways of being anti-metaphysical without being atheological. Between them they represent an opposition to metaphysics that would be shared, if less intensely, by most of the postliberals and liberationists discussed above; something that could not be said for the atheologians. They mount an immense challenge to the kind of view this book is trying to develop. The remainder of the chapter responds by presenting arguments that take on board their critique, and try to show a way of being both Kantian and naturally theological.

OPPOSITE WAYS OF OPPOSING METAPHYSICS: MARION AND ECO-FEMINISM

The desire to avoid construing God as a metaphysical idol is an underlying motive of many theologies. But there are two contrasting ways of avoiding such idolatry, one emphasizing God's transcendence of all being, and the other emphasizing God's immanence in everything that is. Both move God beyond any idol we can locate and any concept we can grasp, but as it were in opposite directions. Paradigms of these cases are, respectively, the negative theology of Jean-Luc Marion and the eco-feminist theology of Grace Jantzen.

The negative or apophatic tradition Marion claims as his pedigree has a long history. Pseudo-Dionysius the Areopagite (whom I shall henceforward refer to in medieval fashion as Denys) regarded God as so far beyond concepts that we could strictly ascribe neither being nor non-being to God; God was *hyperousios* ("superessential" in Latin), meaning beyond or above being. A tradition probably beginning with Gregory of Nyssa and continuing through his Irish translator John Scotus Eriugena (and including Hegel and Altizer) identified God with the "nothing" out of which the world was made. According to Eriugena God "neither was nor shall be nor has become nor shall become nor indeed is."[4]

But Marion was also heavily influenced by more recent, mainly Jewish, thinking, flowing from Martin Buber and his seminal distinction between

---

4. John, *Periphyseon*, 3 (628B).

the "I-it" relation we have with objects in the world, and the "I-thou" encounter with God and our fellow human persons. Metaphysics, on this view, tries to reduce God to an "it" we can theorize about in the third person without ever having to encounter. Buber also influenced the Jewish philosopher Emmanuel Levinas, who argued that ethical demands have a priority that cannot be inferred from any vision of how things are. The ethical therefore has priority over the ontological; goodness is "otherwise than being," but for different reasons than those which led the negative theologians to place God above being; both however influenced Marion.

Buber's famous distinction seems to lie behind Marion's distinction between the icon and the idol. According to Marion, the idol, which seeks by art to bring the god within the range of the visible by reflecting him in stone or paint, contrasts with the icon, which brings us within the gaze of the invisible God, which we ourselves begin to mirror. "If man, by his gaze, renders the idol possible, in reverent contemplation of the icon, on the contrary, the gaze of the invisible, in person, aims at man."[5] Idols, for Marion, seek to fix the god and pin him in our perspective, placing him as it were in our power. The word "idol," we note, derives from the Greek *eidolon,* whose root is from the verb *eido,* to see (literally, or in the sense of understanding, as in "I see that"). An idol is essentially a seen-thing or phantom. "Icon" derives from *eikon,* image or likeness, derived from *eiko,* to be like, and used theologically when humans are declared to be in the image of God.

In Orthodox theology, icons do not seek to place the *nature* of the historical Jesus before our eyes, but rather invoke the divine *person* who relates to us in the face of Jesus and the saints. We note that John of Damascus, Theodore the Studite, and others defended the icons on the grounds that the icon of Christ represents neither the divine nature, nor the historical human Jesus (whose looks are, after all, unknown!). Rather, it conveys the divine person of the Word that was incarnate in him.[6] This explains the way icons pare away the bodily and fleshly nature of Christ or the saint, and emphasize the face—the almost caricatured persona—and especially the eyes and their gaze. Rather than depicting them and bringing them bodily into the gaze of the worshipper—as an idol does—icons serve to bring the worshipper into the personal gaze, judging and loving, of Christ and the saints. Icons do not bring God into our horizons, but allow God to open our limited perspectives up to his divine perspective

Marion argues that concepts can be idols. This happens when we construct theological and metaphysical systems, grand narratives of being (or

5. Marion, *God without Being,* 19.
6. Cf. Lossky, *Vision of God,* 111–12, and Ouspensky, *Theology of the Icon,* 153ff.

"ontotheologies"—see next section) of which God is a part. Marion's grasp of the mystical tradition and of the Orthodox understanding of the distinction between idols and icons is subtle and profound. But if God addresses us from beyond being it remains the case that God addresses us through being, just as in the icon God addresses us through the physicality of wood and paint. If concepts can be idols, can they not also be icons? While metaphysical systems may involve an attempt to render God an object in our intellectual gaze, can they not be doing with concepts what the icon painter does with paint, namely filling in the detail in order to make the whole more transparent to what lies beyond it? More on this in the next section.

Grace Jantzen is equally concerned to avoid idolatry, but would see, both in the subordination of God to metaphysics, and in the removal of God from being and the cosmos, a typically patriarchal form of idolatry that needs to re-learn how to befriend the physical, the emotional, the feminine, and the earth. She argues that

> a whole new creative possibility is opened for theology when a holistic model of human personhood is explored. If human personhood and particularly the relationship between the mental and the physical in human persons is still to provide an analogy for the relationship between God and the world . . . the analogy will no longer point towards a God existing independently of the world and interacting with it like a majesty from on high, because we can no longer think of our souls, the analogate, as being essentially different from our bodies and ruling over them. Rather, the relationship between God and the world will be much more intimate.[7]

Jantzen's use the mind-body relationship as an analogy for that between God and the world is not new. It is to be found in Thomas Aquinas, in the thirteenth century, and in Maximus the Confessor, in the seventh century, who suggested that

> God in Trinity might be *through all and in all things* (Eph 4:6), contemplated as the whole reality proportionately in each individual creature . . . and in the universe altogether, just as the soul naturally indwells both the whole of the body and each individual part.[8]

Jantzen combines this ancient tradition with a more recent, "ecofeminist," holistic understanding, to argue that God and the world are like a

---

7. Jantzen, *God's World, God's Body*, 9.

8. Maximus, *Cosmic Mystery of Christ*, 101.

mind-body whole. God is no longer disembodied; God has a body and it is the world, or the totality of being.

An obvious counterargument would be that such a position under-mines the transcendence of God and creates a pantheistic fusion of God and the world: so it is "ontotheological" with a vengeance. But Jantzen argues that such an interpretation would deny the transcendence of persons, that is, of the soul-body unity itself.

> If God is personal and human persons are our best available model for an understanding of what God is like, then recon-sidering the relationship between personhood and embodiment in human persons may help us to understand how God could be embodied in the universe. This approach is all the more promising because a particular use of transcendence which has attracted considerable attention in recent years is the idea of the transcendence of persons. Although we are frail, finite creatures, a part of the world of nature and produced by natural evolution-ary processes, reeds within the tidal beds of endless flux, we are still, to use Pascal's phrase, "thinking reeds." Personal conscious-ness, which emerges through physical and biological processes, nevertheless seeks intelligibility and meaning in those very pro-cesses, and in that sense transcends them.[9]

Janzten thus uses the notion of emergence—the way thoughts and feelings transcend the processes that embody them—as an analogy for the divine transcendence.

Though at first sight Jantzen's arguments pull away from ontotheology in the opposite direction from Marion, both thinkers use the decisive no-tion of the personal. In Marion the personal defines the divine address of the icon and distinguishes it from the attempted representation of divine nature that defines the idol; in Jantzen the personal defines the transcendent aspect of the soul-body unity and offers a way of affirming transcendence without disembodiment. In terms of the tension with which this chapter opened, Marion carries to the extreme Kant's rejection of metaphysical the-ology, while Jantzen offers us a radical kind of natural theology in which the transcendent God does not just explain aspects of the cosmos, but is wholly embodied in it. What this book seeks is not some middle position, but in a sense a combination of both extremes.

9. Jantzen, *God's World*, 124–25.

WHAT IS WRONG WITH ONTOTHEOLOGY?

Though varied, the accounts described in the previous sections converge on a rejection of what has come to be called "ontotheology." The term was used by Kant to mean "ontological theologies" or theologies based on metaphysical reasoning: roughly equivalent to "natural theology" as so far discussed. It was, however, popularized by Martin Heidegger to mean, in effect, theological ontology, that is, metaphysics that makes claims about ultimate or absolute reality and hence, explicitly or implicitly, about God. It is debatable whether Heidegger was himself a paradigm ontotheologian, speaking about Being in a way similar to theological talk of God. Nevertheless, as Marylin Adams remarks in a seminal critique, "in some circles, 'the ontotheological error' is a buzz-word, a dismissive pejorative hurled at philosophical theologians who say that God falls under the concept 'being.'"[10] She goes on to ask "what exactly is the ontotheological error? and why is it an error?" In this section I shall argue that, while some forms of ontotheology or metaphysically based theology are vulnerable to some of the criticisms advanced against it, not all ontotheology is suspect. Then in the rest of the chapter I shall suggest ways of advancing an ontothelogical God—that is, a God who can be said to "'be" or "really exist"—that escapes the criticisms, and may form the basis of a dialogue-based, realistic theology.

Most of the criticisms have an ethical dimension: ontotheology is seen as involving the sin of idolatry, either because it involves an excessive pride, inflating the power of human reason, and encouraging us to an idolatrous worship of our own (intellectual) creation, or conversely because it reduces God to an object of thought, making God an idol, a being or thing alongside others within our worldview. The following summarizes and then criticizes the main arguments concerning ontotheology, or philosophical or metaphysically based theology. It will be obvious that the distinctions between these arguments are often subtle, and they generally overlap in any one author's discourse.

Human Pride and Idolatry

1. *Ontotheology prunes God to a procrustean bed.* We have noted the criticism in connection with narrative theology, namely that if we fist build a metaphysical or philosophical vision of how things are, and then construct a theology on that foundation, the philosophical account may limit the theological. Theological revelation may be cut down to fit the metaphysical

10. Adams, *Ontotheological Error*, 1.

questions we are asking, rather than allowing revelation to open up new questions for us to answer. Revelation will be "hole shaped," tailored to fit the "gaps" we have identified in our scientific and/or metaphysical understanding. Certainly this can be the case, and perhaps is the case, both in crude understandings of natural theology and in more sophisticated totalizing accounts like those of Spinoza, Hegel, and the German idealists against which Karl Barth contended. However, it is not obvious that it *has* to be the case. Surely metaphysics can be an attempt to tell the story of being in the light of the story of Christ or some other revelation, asking, "If such and such is the true revelation of God, what must it mean to *exist*?" Rather than create an ontological "hole" into which God must fit, metaphysics may involve a transformation of our understanding of being and beings into a "hole" large enough to accommodate God.

In Strawson's terms (see chapter 6), we could say that "descriptive" metaphysics designed to explicate the metaphysics implicit in scriptural texts is always appropriate, but unlikely to give rise to an "ontotheology." But a "revisionary" metaphysics will often also be an appropriate theological activity, as when we seek to effect a dialogue between our own metaphysical assumptions and those of the text, in the process perhaps creating new ontological concepts (as when, for example, in this chapter we consider the nature of the icon or the personal). And this is much more likely to involve ontotheology. What the critics of ontotheology rightly criticize, surely, is imposing an *a priori* metaphysical understanding on the texts and traditions of faith.

Significantly, after considering the Buddhist practice of insight meditation (*vipassana*) as reaching beyond what can be said, and a hollowing out of the solidity of being into *sunyata* or emptiness, Rowan Williams invites us to consider "the whole enterprise of a reconfigured natural theology as a *method*, perhaps even a skill. Natural theology is a practice—or at least outlines possible practices which bring us to the point at which we run out of things to say . . . but recognize that this running out is not an ending."[11] Before the arrival of natural theology as we understand it, we have seen how theologians such as Maximus the Confessor, Peter Lombard, and Bonaventure advocated a practice of natural contemplation that allowed the creation to open us up to the Creator, urging people

> to begin by contemplating God in and through the material
> world; then to turn inwards to contemplate God in the essential
> workings of their own minds; then to turn attention upwards to
> contemplate God first as Being supremely simple and yet within

11. Williams, *Edge of Words*, 16–17.

all things, and then as Goodness self-diffusing itself into a Trinity of persons.[12]

In short, though ontotheology may serve to tie God to a rationalistic understanding of what actually exists and what can and cannot be, in the Christian tradition it has often served as a contemplative practice of reaching through reason about beings to what transcends them, opening philosophy to "more things in heaven and earth" than it would otherwise dream of.[13]

2. *It proudly goes beyond what we can claim to know.* We noted the critique of metaphysics—in relation to the skepticism of Kant, and we could also have mentioned Hume in this connection, and the (later) positivists and linguistic philosophers—regarding whether rational thought can resolve issues that go beyond empirical evidence. Theologically ontotheology can be criticized for parallel reasons, as an instance of human pride. It can be defined as "a project of rendering the whole of being intelligible in accordance with the principle of reason."[14] "The onto-theological gesture . . . consists in positing . . . God as an excuse for making the claim that we can occupy a divine perspective on the world . . . in the pride that refuses to accept the limits of human knowledge . . . ."[15] To be sure, some ontotheologies (Aristotle, Spinoza, and Hegel spring to mind) have looked like attempts to map out a God's-eye view of what the world, or even all possible worlds, must in principle be like. But can the ontotheological enterprise not be a more modest reaching out towards such a vision humbly aware of the inevitability of failure? As the next chapter will clarify, ontotheologies can actually lead us to negative theologies.

Moreover, insofar as the criticism of pride is valid, it counts not only against metaphysically based theologies, but equally—and perhaps more— against narrative and fideist accounts that spurn metaphysics and purport to rely on revelation alone. A theology based on human reason is vulnerable to human reason arguing against it, whereas revelation, as the word of God, brooks no such contradiction. And revelation itself is a metaphysical concept, based on notions of the hidden and the disclosed, and the idea that the transcendent can make itself known to us in special miraculous ways. Kant and the others cited were certainly as skeptical about that idea as about metaphysics as such.

12. Adams, *Ontotheological Error*, 21.
13. Shakespeare, *Hamlet* 1.5.167–68.
14. Westphal, cited in Caputo and Scanlon, *God the Gift*, 154.
15. Westphal in ibid., 149–50.

Finally, it has often been argued that the notion that reason cannot reach beyond the empirical is itself a metaphysical idea involving a precise definition and delimitation of what we mean by reason, and what broad kinds of thing can and cannot in principle exist. Now there is a sense in which, to live well in the world of beings, we cannot avoid ontological commitment, or some broad account of the world we are in. We all therefore have to take the risk of speculating and being wrong. The path to rationality is surely the humble path of being in dialogue with those of different commitments, rather than proudly fixed on our own account, whether we base our account on the event(s) of revelation or the impossibility of such events. The choices are: to be irrationally atheist; to be irrationally a believer in some exclusively special revelation; to be ontotheological in the proud sense of claiming to have proven by reason a worldview that includes God, or else claims to be itself an all-inclusive God's-eye view; or to be ontotheological in the sense of wanting to do justice to being, knowing how difficult it is to do so merely from our own standpoint, and hence to be in dialogue with others who have participation in and knowledge of what it is to be. This latter, far from being proud, seems the humblest approach.

3. *It encourages worship of a human construct.* Traditionally—in the Old Testament and the Qur'an for example—idolatry denoted the worship of a physical object one has made. But it is natural to extend the notion to cover worship of an intellectual object one has conceived in one's mind. Ontotheology is viewed in this way, as committing us to the worship of a humanly constructed vision or set of ideas, which displaces encounter with what transcends not only physicality but *all* human concepts. However, all worship involves some *use* of physical things, words, and concepts. Even the absence of any visual symbols in a Muslim, Puritan, or Quaker act of worship involves a strict and careful use of the physical setting so as precisely to avoid any potentially idolatrous distractions. And of course there is always the reading and exposition of sacred texts, and often singing or chanting; and unless these activities are to be completely rote-based, some exercise of concept-formation will be involved. Even the silence of the Quaker meeting is punctuated with verbal and conceptual expression. If the mere use of matter and conceptuality is in itself idolatrous, *all* worship is idolatrous. But it is more reasonable to hold that it is the use of such things that may or may not be idolatrous. If the material or conceptual object is adored and worshipped as divine, or in place of the divine, or as completely defining the divine, such that it draws to itself the total allegiance that should only be given to God, then clearly idolatry is involved. But to use matter and concept to raise our minds and hearts to that which transcends us and them

is surely not so. If a metaphysician presents her system as replacing or better defining God and rendering traditional patterns of worship obsolescent or redundant, idolatry is certainly involved. But if her arguments are presented as establishing the transcendence of God and God's worthiness of worship, or otherwise opening our intellects to that which lies beyond intellect, then her "ontotheology" is the reverse of idolatrous.

God as an Idol

So though there probably are idolatrous kinds of ontotheology or metaphysical theology, there would seem to be nothing inherent in the consideration of being in the light of theology and vice versa that implicates us in idolatry, or in excessive pride about human reason. Nevertheless, it could be argued that ontotheology offers us a God who is in some sense an idol, or something less than the true and living God encountered in our traditions. There are two ways in which this is argued, one crude, one subtle. We shall consider both in what follows.

4. *It treats God as a being*, making us idolatrously worship a being as if it were God. This is quite often argued, the point being that God becomes one of the entities delineated in the metaphysical system. The real God is then the system, to which God is subject; even if the system posits God as the supreme, most perfect or otherwise best of all the beings there are, God remains just one of them. It becomes possible to count God in as one of the elements described by the philosopher, and related by the philosopher to the other beings. Or in the Marxist terms adopted by liberation theologians, God becomes "fetishized" or "reified," given a false substantiality or objectivity, which gives authority or even inevitability to the social order supposedly based on God. Such a God can be adored and served, but underwrites "how things are" rather than inspiring change or legitimating the cry of the oppressed. As Marion argued, the system enables us to have God in our sights, as part of a satisfyingly complete vision that we sit back and admire. God is not allowed to step out of such a system and address us. Marion, as we have seen, argues that the true God who addresses us must be beyond such a vision of being, "above being" as pseudo-Dionysius and the Christian apophatic tradition, as well as the pagan Plotinus, affirm.

However, Adams notes that Augustine rejected the idea that God is superessential. "Augustine God . . . is not beyond being: God is Being itself. . . . Augustine denies that God is beyond being. But it doesn't follow that sees God as a being alongside others."[16] Augustine took this view, according to Adams, because unlike Plotinus he wanted to take on board the biblical revelation, which describes God as personal, as having a mind and intentions, and as loving us and desiring to engage with us as persons. To be such, God must be a being in the sense of a unity of memory, love, and will. But this does not make God "just another being" and hence, if worshipped, an idol. "Augustine's reintegration of platonizing philosophical frameworks identifies transcendent Goodness with Being Itself, and insists that personality, intelligent voluntary agency, is the heart of reality."[17] Even Marion—I would argue—must accept that God is "being," or "real," in this sense, if God is to address us with coherent justice and integrating love from beyond the world of beings that we know. Icons require careful concept-laden use of matter like wood and paint, just as idols do; what makes the difference between icon and idol is not materiality or conceptuality as such but the way matter or concepts are used.

Moreover, the sense of being in the judging and loving gaze of another person, which for Marion differentiates the icon from the idol and offers the authentic sense of God, involves *both* seeing *and* being seen. It is not as if the other's gaze takes her out of our sights. The paradox of the interpersonal face-to-face encounter is that I do see the other's face (and body), but see it as the face of a person for whom my own face (and body) are likewise an item in their gaze. The face is crucial here.[18] If I see only the body of the other without the face, I see only a piece of matter, not a person who sees me. And a body and face that are both shrouded, or a face that is reduced just to the seeing eye (as in the case of those sinister "eye of God" motifs found in some Orthodox churches) gives rise not to an interpersonal exchange, but rather to an eerie, dehumanizing sense of being seen without seeing who is doing the seeing; in short, being spied on. If God's gaze is experienced in this way, and all sense in which we can see God through creation and/or incarnation is denied, then God's gaze becomes eerie and dehumanizing, making God the ultimate Spy in the Sky. Marion's fulsome rejection of the idol as the seen-ness of the deity risks doing this to God, as does anti-metaphysical theology in general.

There is, of course, a vast difference between our interpersonal exchange with other human persons, and with God. It is not so much that we cannot in principle "see God." *Pace* Marion, theology affirms that we will see God, and though in Western theology the full vision of God is usually

16. Adams, *Ontotheological Error*, 4.
17. Ibid., 5.
18. Cf. Pattison, *Saving Face*, and Ford, *Self and Salvation*.

deferred till after death, in the Orthodox tradition St. Gregory Palamas affirmed its possibility in this life. It is rather that we cannot see God either in the way we see other human persons, or in the way God sees us. However much we may empathize with other people, we always see them "from the outside," through their bodies and faces. Not that we merely "infer" what they are thinking and feeling; research has shown that when we empathize, the same brain circuits are activated in us as are involved in the other person's experience. But that does not make us feel what they are feeling, or think what they are thinking, or know exactly what it is like to be them in their situation. People's thoughts and feelings remain their own, they do not become ours. In that sense, and also of course because they can hide what they are thinking and feeling, other people remain opaque to us. But to God's omniscient gaze we are transparent. In the theistic traditions, God sees us, not from the outside, by looking at what our bodies are doing and our faces expressing, but directly. God experiences what we are thinking and feels what it is like to be us (though, of course, God knows these are *our* thoughts and feelings, and does not think them as God's own thoughts). As Anna put it, "People can only love outside, and can only kiss outside, but Mister God can love you right inside, and Mister God can kiss you right inside."[19]

The icon reflects this inward loving and seeing. Whereas the idol is usually a three-dimensional representation located in our own space, symbolically placing the god in our external visual perspective, the icon is a two-dimensional representation, of a stylized, non-literal kind, employing, a special inverted perspective that as it were locates the divine or saintly person within us. Arguably the biblical narrative differs from, say, the Homeric, as Auerbach noted (see chapter 6), in likewise presenting a sparse, stylized, rather than a saturated, lifelike description, drawing us toward an inwardly involving meaning.

These thoughts, which differentiate the idol from the icon, and consider what is involved in personal relationship with God, are metaphysical thoughts. Metaphysics may be used either to frame an idolatrous vision or bring us face to face with the living God. It is, of course, very tempting to step from belief in God as personal to belief in God as just another being like us persons, only infinitely greater in power, love, and wisdom. But it is possible to avoid that step if we identify God not as *a* person but the personal ground and meaning of all being, evident through beings without being identifiable with any particular manifestation of being, however great.

19. Fynn, *Mister God*, 41.

5. *It considers God in terms of being.* Against the preceding suggestions, it is argued by some, notably the Radical Orthodox group centered on John Milbank, that to describe God univocally in terms of being at all is a step too far. Milbank's arguments are based on a dispute between the Dominican Thomas Aquinas and the Franciscan Duns Scotus, as to whether, when we speak of God as being or existing, this is meant univocally, that is, in the same sense as that in which people and chairs and rhinos are said to exist, or whether God is, or exists, in an analogical way. The dispute may seem arcane, but for Milbank much depends on it, for on his view it is the belief that God exists in the same sense as us that leads to ontotheology.[20] In particular, he argues that it has led to later attempts in natural theology to infer the existence of God in the same empirical way as that in which we infer the existence of natural things, and then to the atheistic reaction that since God cannot be so inferred, God cannot exist.

Milbank argues that therefore Aquinas' view is to be preferred. God does not exist in exactly the same sense as we or chairs do, but in an analogical sense. In other words, when we apply the concept of being to God, we have to stretch it beyond its everyday sense, just as we do when we apply a concept like "wisdom." But there is a problem here. The notion of analogy in Aquinas is based (partly) on the idea that God's existence explains the existence of creatures. To explain our qualities, God must have those same qualities in an eminent degree, such that our qualities like wisdom provide an analogy for the infinite (eminent) wisdom of God, while God's wisdom explains such wisdom as we may possess. But if God's existence is itself analogical to ours, we seem to be basing an analogy (regarding wisdom) on a further analogy (regarding existence). We are forced to ask what analogy this analogy in turn is based on, so risking a regress of analogies in our attempt to explain.[21] Aquinas would have responded that the fundamental difference between our wisdom and that of God is that our wisdom is a potential we can realize more or less (we can, of course, be very stupid), whereas in God the act of existing is wholly fused with God's essential qualities like being wise. We are, as Aquinas put it, composites of potency and act, whereas in God there can be no potency that is not actualized. God cannot fail to exist or be wise, and God cannot grow any wiser than the infinite wisdom he already realizes. That makes his wisdom and his existence very different from our own.

Different, yes. But it is probably a matter of definition whether one describes such a difference in existence as analogical. After all, what it is

---

20. Milbank, *Theology and Social Theory*, 302ff.
21. Cf. Thompson, *Holy Ground*, 253.

for a chair to exist is not the same as what it is for a human being, or the number 2, or the United Kingdom, to exist. The meaning of existence, like most terms, varies according to its subject, and furthermore it varies in a metaphysical way, according to the ontology we ascribe to human person, inanimate objects, numbers, and nation states respectively. But when Duns Scotus affirms univocity between our existence and God's he should not, according to Adams, be construed as saying that God's existence is ontologically the *same* as ours, or that of numbers. To understand him in this way

> confuses the issue of conceptual subordination (the essentially harmless notion of God's falling under the abstract universal concept "being") with ontological dependence (the metaphysical absurdity of God's ontologically depending on being-in-general) and/or act-potency composition (which Scotus and Aquinas agree is not to be found in God).[22]

Milbank is surely right to counsel against thinking of God as existing in exactly the same way as we do, let alone numbers or nations or chairs. But these things do not exist in the same way as each other anyway. Whether one wishes to capture the difference between God's existence and ours in the language of analogy will probably depend on the detail's of one's understanding of analogy. Not as much depends on that particular difference between Scotus and Aquinas as the Radical Orthodox would have us believe. It remains the case that to believe that God is as real as we are, or more so—whether or not that constitutes "ontotheology"—is not an error or a sin, but essential to Christian belief in a transcendent God.

In conclusion, regarding the first set of criticisms (1–3), it would seem that ontotheology, or metaphysical approaches to God, can limit God to a human conceptuality, can be proudly idolatrous, and can involve us in worshipping a conceptual idol. However, it is not the metaphysics that makes the difference, but how it is used; what practices it is attached to. The missing part of the argument so far is a positive description of what might make the difference, and how a non-idolatrous, liberating ontotheology might be constructed.

This part of the argument becomes all the clearer in relation to the second pair of charges (4–5): that ontotheology reduces God to *a* being, and that it thinks of God in "being" terms. In response to the first we suggested—following the common ground in Jantzen and Marion—that the notion of God as personal might deliver us from thinking of God as *a* being.

---

22. Adams, *Ontotheological Error*, 15.

That is not an obvious truth, and in the next section we explore more fully what the notion of personal means, in terms of the theology of the person of Christ and the philosophy of dialogue. In response to the second, subtler point, it was suggested that to think of God as literally (rather than just analogically) existing, or real, is not necessarily to subject God to prior notions of existence or being. But more needs to be said if we are to offer an ontotheology that takes us beyond the limitations described by Milbank and the like: an ontotheology that does justice to both God and beings. So the two sections that follow enlarge on possible ways of thinking of God/being in terms of grammar in general, and then grammatical mood in particular, suggesting that to each kind of metaphysics belongs a certain kind of narrative plot. Some of these are seen to be more idolatrous and others more personal and dialogical. The conclusion argues that there are indeed ways of affirming of God both immanence in being and transcendence of being: so that we can after all uphold both Kant (and Marion) and natural contemplation (and Jantzen).

CREATION, INCARNATION, AND THE PERSONAL GOD

Altizer's atheology can be understood as projecting the doctrine of the atonement—the death and resurrection of Christ—onto the understanding of creation as a whole, so that creation itself is seen as a self-emptying dying of God to "rise" in the world. Jantzen can be said to do the same with the doctrine of incarnation, seeing the incarnational embodiment of God as applying not just to Jesus Christ but to the whole cosmos. It would not be un-Barthian in intent (though probably it would in substance) to suggest that the mysteries of the relations between God and being are best resolved, for Christians, by examining the person and work of Jesus Christ.

First consider the logic of creation out of nothing. The doctrine was first developed by the early second century gnostic Basilides, and adopted by orthodox Christians as a way of engaging with Greek philosophical speculation about cosmic origins.[23] Irenaeus and others from the second century onward favored it as a way of countering the dualistic heresies of Manicheans and gnostics. But how does it do so? Precisely by dispensing with the idea of "being" that is common to God and the world. If God and the world are ultimately different beings, a God-world dualism as in Manicheanism holds true, while if they are one and the same being, pantheism results. In either case they share the "being" of which they are the same or

23. May, *Creatio ex Nihilo.*

different instances. But if being itself is the creation of God, God cannot be said either to share being with the world or to be or have a different being.[24] (That, perhaps, is the sense in which Milbank's Aquinas is right, over against Milbank's Scotus.)

But how is this to be explained? Marion and Jantzen have already provided a clue in the way both focus on the notion of the personal or the I-thou relation. We noted Adams' suggestion that for Augustine "personality, intelligent voluntary agency, is the heart of reality." For Marion the personal is epitomized in the gaze from beyond being that addresses us in the icon. Yet Jantzen warns us against interpreting this "beyond" in terms of a metaphysical otherness. If we take the human person as the whole being, the unity which is so often divided into body and soul, then the notion that being itself is personal can be equated with the idea that something transcendent of being (but not another being) addresses us through being.

Now the Athanasian Creed (I here refer to the version used currently in the Church of England) affirms of Christ:

> Although he is both divine and human, he is not two beings but one Christ; one, not by turning God into flesh, but by taking humanity into God; truly one, not by mixing humanity with Godhead, but by being one person; for as mind and body form one human being, so the one Christ is both divine and human.

The significant point for us is that it is denied that in Christ God and humanity are either "two distinct beings" or one "mixed" divine-cum-human being. The means of Christ's unity is neither separation nor fusion, but his *personhood*. And our mind-body unity provides an analogy for the unity of God and humanity in the one person of Christ.

What I am suggesting is that what the incarnation says about the personal unity (without fusion) of God and humanity in Christ provides a profound analogy for the personal unity of God and being (without fusion) in the creation, as affirmed by Jantzen. The concept of a person, unlike that of a soul, is not of something separate from the body, yet the person transcends the body; it is the body as manifesting agency (which as we have seen is a kind of dialogue with things) and entering into a fuller I-thou dialogue with other persons. The person is not another being alongside bodily being, but bodily being in its dialogical aspect, which transcends mere physicality.

To conceive of God as personal in this way does not involve a step beyond "ontotheology" in the broader sense of metaphysical theology. To invoke the personal is not to reject metaphysics but to offer a metaphysical

---

24. Cf. Thompson, *Buddhist Christianity*, 253–54.

account that does not chain or subordinate our understanding of God to an understanding of being and beings, but which does establish rich possible connections between God and beings, working primarily from God to beings, but secondarily the other way around, as analogies (see next chapter) always do.

The analogy of God as personal underpins the dialogical reading of the creation narrative offered in chapter 3, which in a benevolent foundationless circle in turn undergirds our present christologically based understanding of creation. To describe God as personal is to ascribe to God something analogous to our own life as human persons. It is to affirm that there is something it is like to be God, and this something expresses itself in creation, but cannot be fully known from creation; just as with other persons, there is something it is like to be them, and this something expresses itself in their every action, yet I will never know fully what it is like to be that person. In this sense the personal is not a type of being, but being conceived in a certain way, as self-revealing, and at the same time as hidden; and both hidden and revealed because relating and communicating.

Now analogies (see next chapter) imply unlikeness as well as likeness. There are two significant theological disanalogies between the personhood of God and that of human beings. A person is a being in relation in two ways: internally to itself, through thought and feeling, and externally to other beings and other persons, through dialogue and communication. These relations inform one another, though it is hard to assign priority to the internal or the external relationship. But for God—as will become clearer in the next section—nothing is external, nor are there pre-existing internal distinctions "within" God. And this is precisely because God is not *a* being happening to engage in relation and dialogue, but relationship and dialogue as founding being, just as described in our exegesis of Genesis. The personal dimension of God—as creating, knowing, loving—emerges from this relational aspect; as noted in chapter 3, according to Thomas Aquinas the persons *are* the relations. The quasi-external God-world relations of creation emerge seamlessly, in Genesis, from the quasi-internal divine relations "before" the creation. The begetting of the Word begets creation, and the breathing of the Spirit inspires and fulfills creation in God. The "internal" and "external" divine relations (or what theologians call the immanent and economic Trinity) are, as theologian Karl Rahner affirmed, one and the same (which is why we have to speak of "quasi-internal," etc.).

If this is grasped, then perhaps the divergence between the personal faiths of Western monotheism and the non-dual beliefs of Advaita Vedanta and Mahayana Buddhism becomes a matter of emphasis rather than sheer contradiction. We can affirm with the former that God is personal while agreeing with the latter that the Ultimate is non-dual, and certainly not "a person," which would mean a being among beings. God is personhood, pure making-knowing-loving, without a boundary or outside, and therefore without the internal complexity that characterizes human persons. Both personalists and non-dualists can be regarded as affirming something absolutely essential regarding the Ultimate; though very hard to clarify conceptually, this is perhaps something we can grasp on a feeling level. When we love someone intensely, we love them in and for their difference from ourselves, but not as wholly alien to us; rather as forming, with us, one non-dual reality, vulnerable to rupture. In God this personal but non-dual distinctness of us all becomes invulnerable.

And that makes for the other significant disanalogy when we speak of God as personal: the difference between our relation to our bodies and actions, and God's relation to them. In our own case our bodies are givens; we do not create them but rather they arise from causal processes over which we have only marginal control. We can slim and exercise and grow lean and muscular, or we can eat too well and grow larger, but that is about it. Our actions are performed through our bodies, and we need our bodies in order to act, but our bodies are not themselves actions, or vice versa. But in the case of God there can *ultimately* be no causal process that creates the world other than the action of God. God's action creates the world as his self-expression or body. And this involves a Trinitarian process.

Taking up the Trinitarian suggestions gleaned from Panikkar in chapter 3 we could say that the Father denotes the divine person in the sense of the source of agency. This source, as in human persons, is transcendent in the sense of being irreducible to the nature that belongs to the person—we see the actions, never the agent. But this transcendence is not unknowability or dark otherness. As Karl Barth affirmed, there is in God no dark side analogous to the other side (not always, of course, dark) of the moon, which is always turned away from us; his actions, and paradigmatically the act of incarnation, communicate God to us without reserve. The transcendence (as with human persons) lies in there always being something more to be known and loved, as Gregory of Nyssa affirmed; the hiddenness lies in the fact that revelation has not just a past but a boundless future.

The Son or Word then represents the divine person in the sense of embodiment or self-communication. Christ is the person who communicates the divine nature to us, in the cosmos as a whole, but yet more fully in the incarnation in Christ. If in Christ human and divine being are united in this communicative person, then we could say that we find in Christ that of which there is always something more to be known, simultaneously in terms of God, and in terms of the human Jesus.

In this scenario, what is the Holy Spirit, if not that person which is *energeia*, energy or in-working, immanent in all beings, and pre-eminently in inspired humans, traditionally epitomized in the *fiat* or "Let it be!" of Mary. The Spirit offers the returning "Yes" and "Abba!" to God's self-communication in creation and Christ, completing the dialogue; so that it is in us that the action, knowledge, and love of God becomes completed in doxology. If God is dialogue, then though complete in Godself as Trinity, regarding the creation the dialogue that is God is incomplete until this completing doxological response comes forth from beings inspired by the Spirit.

To say this is to speak "ontotheologically." We are speaking theologically, in terms of the Trinity, of course, but we are expounding it in terms that derive from our experience of beings, including human persons. But what choice do we have, unless we wish to leave the Trinity as a barren dogma or unsolvable theological puzzle? If we wish to take up Marion's and Jantzen's critique of some kinds of metaphysics we need to speak in some other kind. It seems obvious that the above descriptions do not reduce God to an individual being, but follow through the claim, following Adams, that "personality, intelligent voluntary agency, is the heart of reality."

GOD/BEING: GRAMMAR

But though we are not construing God as a being, are we still committing an ontotheological sin in conceiving of God in terms that relate to being and beings? The slash (/) in the titles of this section and the next stands for the fact that what should go here is precisely what is being explored. We do not wish to preempt the discussion by using a conjunction here, or some other part of speech. Rather, we seek to widen the discussion of how we should relate God and being or beings to a very general level. There are different ways of "parsing" God and being, that is, different ways of asserting how the world of beings, and especially the human, stands in relation to God (though even putting it that way suggests a particular answer to our question, namely that God and the world are separate things standing in relation to each other).

Put in this way, the question then becomes much subtler than whether "to be or not to be . . . ontotheological." We shall see that the different ways offer quite different kinds of ontotheology, some more theologically acceptable than others. Each grammatical way, we note, has a parallel analogy with a way of relating mind and body and conceiving of the person, as discussed in the previous section. Here are some of the main ways that are significant for our purposes:

- *Animism* makes beings into *proper nouns* standing as the subjects of what goes on. River flows, Bear prowls, Rain falls, Forest sheds her leaves. Each activity is seen as a spontaneous, personal free act, self-explanatory in just the way our own free acts seem to be. If we want the rain to fall—for those who believe in this perspective—we do not try to cause her to do so; we try to persuade her. Modern scientific views that see the ultimate explanation of the universe in terms of a huge number of self-generating or self-created fields of force can arguably be regarded as animistic in this sense; but I mean this as a comment, not a criticism. Such an account is thoroughgoingly ontotheological if, and only if, the proper nouns are taken to represent divinities. In this case, of course, it is a polytheistic ontotheology, of interest perhaps to poets, but not to Christian theologians. However, animism offers a reasonable way to consider the mind-body relation: that I am a spiritual entity denoted by my proper name, and that my body and my actions manifest this spiritual entity, is a natural way of thinking. Philosophically it translates into a kind of idealism: mind is the real thing, while the physical is relegated to the realm of appearances. It is seeing the whole of nature in this idealistic, person-expressive way that these days seems contrary to all that science tells us (though if Chalmers is right, nature may well express the prototypes of personhood and consciousness).

- *Pantheism* makes beings into *adjectives* describing the one divine substance. The river, the bear, the rainfall, the forest are all qualities of God. Thus Aristotle regarded God as the ultimate substance of the world; in his terminology this meant the subject of which all beings are the predicates. If creatures are God's attributes, we can see from them very clearly what God is like, since we can simply use them directly to describe him, in a way that makes God one with nature. That is why Spinoza—the most coherent modern Western exponent of this view—speaks of *Deus sive natura*, "God, or nature," which is the one eternal substance of all things, and of all beings as "modes" of God's attributes of thought and extension. Hegel, who saw history as the unfolding of the divine logic, represents a subtler form of pantheism, and arguably the German Romantic idealists of the nineteenth century (against whom Karl Barth so strongly revolted) all seem to represent forms of pantheism. Pantheism, in which God and being are straightforwardly identified, would seem to constitute the strongest possible case of ontotheology. In terms of the body-mind relationship, the analogous account would be the identification of body and soul, with the physical body and its activity regarded as an "epiphenomenon" of the mind, that is, as constituted of qualities that attend mental phenomena but have no independent substance of their own. (This, of course, reverses the currently more popular kinds of epiphenomenalism, for which mental events are insubstantial qualities that attend the substantial physical events.)

- *Classical theism* regards beings as *common nouns* in the objective case. God is the subject who in various ways relates to them as object. Verbs like "creates," "loves," and "knows" clearly and definitively distinguish between beings in the world, as objects, and God, as the subject, even if they also form the link between beings and God. In sentences like "God created the world," "God loves the world," etc. God is one thing, the world another; together they make two things. This represents a classical understanding that is very popular, perhaps even constituting the norm of the way Western theists conceive of God. In terms of body and mind the analogous account is mind-body dualism: mind and body are separate entities conjoined by various causal relations, whereby mind and body cause events in each other. (Here the analogy with God and world breaks down in that events in the world are not traditionally said to cause events in God, though in modern process theology this is possible.) Rather, God is said to know things in the world eternally. This understanding creates a different kind of ontotheology from the preceding; God is separate from the world of beings, but God and the world as a whole are distinct instances of being. (Scotus, according to Milbank, would agree, but not Aquinas.)

- *Buddhism* regards beings as *verbs*, denoting happenings. These happenings are joined in a web of karmic or causal relationships, but according to the doctrine of dependent-co-arising there is no ultimate cause of the events. Rather, events form an interdependent whole that is empty (*sunya*) of any single ultimate self-existent being as their cause. Hence, they are, as it were, verbs without nouns to be their subject or object. We ourselves, though we can genuinely cause better karma for ourselves, are not ultimately self-existent egos, but are ourselves bundles of caused and causing activity. We and the world of objects are insubstantial ripples on a sea of emptiness. This emptiness, however, is not negative; it has the positive quality that good actions improve the karma of the agent and speed her on the way to nirvana, in which the cravings for solidity in self and object is extinguished to leave the bliss of the flux. So the karmic order of the world is referred to as *dharmakaya*, the body of the law, the most refined of the three "bodies" of the Buddha. Such an understanding, evidently, is different from any Christian view, yet, as we shall see, the best Christian view begins from an acceptance of it.

- *Thomism*—the thought pattern initiated by St. Thomas Aquinas—effectively regards beings as *verbs* in the sense that they are the actions of the divine subject. To be created by God is nothing other than to be caused by God, to have God as the source of one's being. "The createdness of creatures is simply their relatedness to their Creator as source of their being; and the active creating of them is God's action, identical with his substance."[25] Timothy McDermott interprets this as saying that God is the doing of all being: "The being of the world is the doing of some agent (let us call it God). . . . God exists as the doing of all being, the existence that acts in all existence . . . ."[26]

The Thomist position falls between pantheism and classical theism as we have defined them. (There are, of course, those for whom Thomism *is* classical theism; my interpretation of Aquinas gives us a "radical Thomism," which is admittedly not the only possible understanding.) Beings are not so close to God as to be his (necessary) attributes, nor so distant as to be merely the (contingent) objects of his creativity. They *are* his creativity, his activity; they are the effects that prove that God exists. They flow from him, not as inseparable, necessary qualities, but as his contingent, freely chosen acts.

But though they are not identical with God, they are not extra beings alongside God, such that God forms one among a totality of beings, which in one sense would then surpass him. Classical theism (and Milbank's Scotus) always tended to suggest just this: God's being related to creatures as noun to noun; God became another being alongside them, albeit separated off by the act of creation as the supremely active Subject, while they are denigrated as passive objects. But for Thomas, according to McDermott (in an interpretation Milbank would agree with),

> God exists (as is proved by the existence of his effects), but he does not *share* existence in the way everything else does, he is not a member of the genus *thing*—he is no thing, though not nothing. He is his own existence: not even the existence that other things share, but the doing of that existence.[27]

In Thomism we cannot, as in pantheism, simply use creatures straightforwardly as adjectives to describe God, or as qualities that belong to God.

25. Thomas, *Summa Theologiae*, 86 (8:45.1).
26. Ibid., xxx and xxxii.
27. Ibid., xxxiii.

But creatures, as God's actions, do speak of his being in a forceful way which allows an analogy of being. Creatures are God's loving activity, as well as the object of the love, and one can argue from the quality of the love to what the lover must be like. The problem of how the transcendent God can relate to the world is overcome if things in the world are not conceived of as objects requiring some relation to God, but are his activity; yet this is achieved without pantheistically merging God and the world. Theism as expounded, for example, by Ockham and Calvin, by contrast, does not allow of any argument from what God's objects are like to what God is. Creatures are simply the object of God's love, and one cannot tell from the beloved what the lover is like. And the problem of God's relation to creatures remains.

Such a view is different from Buddhism in that the verbs that (ideally) describe beings in the world do not just describe happenings but actions. That is why the view implies, and depends on, the notion of a divine agent, whereas the Buddhist view does not. But as far as description of the world goes, Thomism and Buddhism agree that the reality, or beings, are best described in terms of actions. In Buddhism we ought to parse the world in terms of verbs without a subject; in radical Thomism we should do so in terms of sentences like "God worlds." In Buddhism there are no real substances; in Thomas there are real substances, but their reality is not self-defined or self-existent, nor are they attributes of a world-substance; they are contingent upon God's existence, not substances in their own right. That is why I suggested that the Buddhist understanding of the cosmos is the necessary precursor of the best Christian understanding.

Whereas the other accounts of God/being tie God to being (except, of course, the Buddhist account, which is non-theological), in the Thomist account God is intimately connected with beings as his actions or makings. Yet as actions he is free to do them or not; he is not harnessed to the way beings are, and can do new things. Hence, Thomas was one of the first theologians clearly to affirm the newness of creation, and the possibility of newness within creation. Yet God is not cut adrift from beings to become an unknowable "wholly other." Rather, God is being in its personal aspect, which is both immanent and transcendent. For the mind-body analogy related to radical Thomism is the view that we are mind-body unities or persons. A person's actions are not constrained by her nature, but they do express that nature, such that something about her can be known from the actions she does. And likewise for God in his actions, which are the beings of the world. Persons are not something lurking behind our actions; we are thoroughly immanent in our bodies and actions without being identical with them, and thoroughly transcendent of them without being "something other" than them.

GOD/BEING: MOOD AND PLOT

If beings are, in our theological "grammar," verbs, the question that inevitably raises itself is what is the grammatical mood of these verbs? This is a significant issue because arguably ontotheology becomes problematic precisely when it is versed entirely in the indicative, that is, in descriptions of what is the case. If that is so, then maybe we can make ontotheology liberative by liberating it from he dominion of the indicative mood.

Most forms of metaphysics and ontology of course have been so versed, as descriptions of how things are or what it is to be real. Because of this, the metaphysics frames a worldview. Two disastrous consequences follow. As both the narrative theologians and Marion have noted, God is then placed in the frame, along with all the other "beings." And as the liberation theologians have noted, "I" am outside the frame, as the onlooker contemplating with satisfaction this nice picture of God and the other beings. I can do so from my armchair, without feeling any need for or even any possibility of entering the picture to change it.

However, chapter 5 introduced the notion that the different grammatical moods are equally relevant to an account of God and beings. This question relates to the grammatical issues discussed in the previous section. When we see God and beings primarily in terms of nouns and adjectives, it is hard to move beyond the sheer indicative predication that attaches the latter to the former. But once we see beings as essentially verbal, and God as the subject, then the mood of the verb becomes inherent in the way we construe reality. The indicative mood continues to be relevant, but equally relevant are the subjunctive, which considers what would follow from alternative actions, and suggests potentials yet to be realized; the interrogative, which shows us being as questionable, always already in dialogue, responding to search; the imperative, demanding that we do justice to it; the optative and jussive, crying out for greater fullness of being; and we might add, the deontological, containing a necessity (moral or causal) that cannot be otherwise. If being is activity and agency, then these aspects, which are curiosities if the world is seen as a solid sum of things and their qualities, become part of a whole dynamic account of reality as coming-to-be, failing-to-be, interacting, and causing-to-be.

Consider even a very simple object like a sheet of paper. If I describe it in the indicative as an object with a certain size, shape, and color, made of such and such substances, it remains somehow inert. But as soon as I interact with the sheet of paper the whole range of moods becomes applicable. I can interrogate it, imagine what it might become—perhaps any number of origami shapes, or a letter, or a paper aeroplane—and what it could not become—like a viable chair—and begin to wish what it might be for me, and then "command" or force it to become one of these things. In the process, I argue, we literally and metaphorically get to grips with what the paper is, by placing it in the world of hopes and questions we actually feel we inhabit. Such a many-mooded account expresses what it is actually like to exist, which the purely indicative picture fails to capture.

Chapter 6 introduced the seven basic plots described by Booker, and suggested that stories always imply a metaphysic, and all metaphysics imply a kind of story. So it might be worth taking our thought about moods further, speculating about the way Booker's plots major on different moods, and express different potential metaphysics.

Overcoming the monster tells us of being as demanding: the *imperative* command in us and all beings to assert ourselves over all that threatens to diminish us; the demand that justice be done.

Rags to Riches tells us of being as hoping and hopeful: the *optative* expressed in the cry of the poor, in hope of greater justice and abundance.

The Quest tells us of being as puzzle and mystery: the *interrogative* aspect of being, the question each being poses, the way each thing is a mystery demanding answers.

Voyage and Return tells of being as delightful illusion and the dream of adventure, referring us to the *subjunctive* and the conditional "what if . . . ." This moves us from the thickness of being to the land of dreams in which new possibilities are envisaged, and perhaps realized, perhaps dispersed, as we come home to reality.

Comedy tells of being as "just so": it seems to focus on the *indicative*, the awkward peculiarity of reality that defeats our proud abstractions—and makes us laugh.

Tragedy tells us of being as necessity. It relates to the *jussive* "must," which can denote moral necessity, or causal necessity, or both. In tragedy an unavoidable necessity works itself out, but this may be the blind necessity of fate or the moral, karmic necessity stemming from the faults in the hero's character.

Rebirth tells of being as emergent—not merely changing, but bringing forth new orders of relationship that demand new description. No "mood" corresponds with this, but arguably the *future perfect tense* does so, as it speaks of what things are now in terms of what they shall have been, that is, how they will be seen from the point of view of the newness that is emerging.

In practice, though metaphysics and theology alike tend to present themselves in indicative mode, some kind of mood-laden plot nearly always lurks beneath the surface, giving the theory its compelling force. Materialist reductionism is often narrated either in comic form—ridiculing and bringing down to earth our lofty pretensions—or tragic—heroic man with his flawed delusions of grandeur pitted against the merciless necessity with which the cosmos is winding down to heat death. Idealist metaphysics has often taken the form of the myth of being's voyage from and return to its home in God. The "many worlds" hypothesis renders the subjunctive, indicative, and jussive indistinguishable: whatever might be is and must be, so that all the worlds to which we might voyage in our imaginations are, tantalizingly, real worlds, but we ourselves cannot reach them. In liberation theology the optative mood and the rags-to-riches story of Moses and the Israelites becomes determinative. Liberal theology by contrast constitutes an interrogative quest, while in Barthian and much patristic theology the imperative voice predominates, and Christ by his bloody death overcomes the monsters of sin and death.

When ontotheology narrows down this range of moods, presenting itself in the indicative mood as the one true metanarrative, the mistake is not in the metaphysics, but in the retreat into the indicative and the claim to be definitive. There are two ways that distinctively avoid this temptation to prioritize the indicative. Buddhism "equalizes" the moods, by making them all imaginary, denying that the indicative is any less imaginary than the other moods. Just as the other moods result from projecting our desires and hopes upon objects, making them enter our story, and in the process subordinating our own story to these desires and hopes, so the indicative represents a false crystallization of the flux of things into solid graspable entities. Buddhism seeks to release us from these stories and projections, and bring us back to the flux of the "actual" prior to all moods.

The obvious alternative way to equalize the moods is to regard them all as pertaining to the real, but in different ways. The indicative relates to the real by presenting or describing it, but the interrogative does so by seeking deeper into it, and the imperative by commands to transform it. The challenge for metaphysics and theology will then be to weave together a rich tapestry of stories relating to different moods, so bringing our different subjectivities together in a metanarrative that does justice to our different actualities, and releases action that increases justice for all of us. This process will need to be an interfaith project

There are no obvious reasons why such a project will prove impossible. We note that it is only in certain moods that contradiction can occur—principally the indicative, jussive, and imperative moods. And because of the different modes of relation to reality, contradiction will mean different things: for example, in the case of the imperative mood, this will involve a practical contradiction between the practicalities of doing x and y, for example standing and sitting. Contradictions therefore will not in general be able to occur between utterances in different moods—for example, a question cannot contradict a statement or a hope. Our interwoven meta-story might prove possible provided no particular story insists on being regarded as the definitive indicative description. And indeed, probably most of us who are not religious exclusivists probably do construct our understanding of the world in something like the tapestry process, weaving "reality" together not only out of the texts and liturgies of our own religion, but out of novels and poems and newspaper articles we have read, what trusted friends and teachers have told us or lived by, and our own life story. Some threads will be more important for us than others, less easy to break or unpick, but there may not be a thread on which all the others depend.

There is a third and subtler approach which combines these two, which has a Buddhist "focus" and a wider Christian or interfaith penumbra. At times we will meditate, and strip all the stories away from our lives in order to focus on the ineffable actual, the flux of activity that we cannot name without stopping it from being what it truly is. At other times our minds will expand to the penumbra provided by our tapestry of stories engaging with the actual through all the moods.

AN ARGUMENT FOR GOD BASED ON JUSTICE

This chapter examined the case made by several authors for following Kant in rejecting, in our theology, arguments based on how or what reality or being is. We saw how Marion and Jantzen rejected "ontotheological" speculation. The following section examined the types of argument generally presented against "ontotheology." However, these arguments were seen to resort to some kind of metaphysical argument even in their rejection of metaphysics. So the arguments cannot hold against the theological use of metaphysics or ontology as such, but only against certain rigid and reifying kinds of metaphysics. A personalist metaphysics was seen to avoid the pitfalls of other kinds of ontotheology. Various understandings of the relation between God and being were then considered, to show that a "verbal" account of being as God's action could provide the basis of a non-idolatrous understanding of God as personal, and like all persons, embodied yet transcendent. A practice was advocated, involving at its core a "Buddhist" return from story to actuality, but as a penumbra, weaving a broad rich tapestry of stories involving all the plots and moods.

So to return to our initial question, are we proposing God as a Kantian idea necessary to bring peoples' subjective stories to converge, or as the reality in which we all participate, which actually enables this convergence? The answer is both. With my "Buddhist" focus I am suggesting an apophatic stripping away of all the gods and all the stories, to leave the naked actuality of the flux that can be experienced but never spoken. But with the penumbra I am suggesting a recklessly kataphatic celebration of all the stories.

It was noted above that "'doing justice' combines ethical and metaphysical dimensions. To do justice to another is to do the right thing for them, but also to acknowledge and take on board their different reality." In that case the (imperative) command of God to do justice to one another must not be merely an external decree, but call upon and assist a real convergence of our various (present, indicative) needs and abilities in a (future hoped for, optative) common good. A mere ideal of God might be a consoling delusion of possible harmony flying in the face of reality; but the ideal we have in mind by definition involves a thrust towards real harmony. It has to run, as Stanley Hauerwas memorably put it, "with the grain of the universe."[28] The optative future hope is not separable from the present possibility of becoming actuality. The realizability of the ideal commits us unashamedly to a metaphysics of becoming, capable of setting people free to flourish more fully as the beings they are, in the God whose act their being is.

Our argument rests not on the bare idea of God but on the necessary goodness of God, that is, what is needed if God is to transform our lives for the better. In particular, I argue that the work of bringing our subjectivities together to converge in reality could not be carried out by a mere idea within any of our conceptual or religious frameworks. Any such idea would have to belong to one tradition, and the convergence would then arise from a triumph of one of the traditions over the others, rather than from reality itself. This tradition would not then be doing justice to the others, but assuming its own priority. If it is just the idea of the Trinity that brings us together, for example, then our convergence represents merely the triumph of a Christian idea. An injustice is done to other faiths. But if it is that which the Trinity names—for Christians—that is really bringing us together, then there is a transcendent guarantee for all faiths that justice is being done. But in that case what we name as Trinity (and other traditions name differently, and which in our convergence and further dialogue we may find other ways of naming) is really at work, transforming all of our understandings. But something cannot be at work, accomplishing real change, unless it exists. So what we call God must really exist.

It is in this sense that a variant of what is often called the ontological argument is valid. Our idea of God makes sense only if God is really able to transform us. Therefore, if the idea of God does make sense, God is really

28. Hauerwas, *With the Grain of the Universe*.

able to transform us. But if God can transform us, God must be at least as real as we are. With all the apophatic qualifications of not existing as a being among other beings, but as the agent whose actions beings are, if "God" makes sense, God must exist. Atheists who deny that "God" makes sense may have a case. But those (for example, Richard Dawkins) who are very clear about what "God" means yet deny that God exists cannot be right.

We note that in the forms of the ontological argument that really are "ontological" the need for God to exists rests on the idea of God. God is defined as a necessary being, who therefore necessarily exists; or as the perfect being conceivable, who must therefore include the "perfection" of existing. Kant justly criticized such arguments on the ground that, basically, we cannot define an idea into existence. But Marion argues[29] that in the first form in which it appears in Anselm, the argument is neither called "ontological," nor is it so. Kant's refutation therefore misses the point. In this argument Anselm defines God as that than which nothing greater can be conceived, and Marion argues that such a concept is itself beyond rational conception, and represents a good we can desire but cannot locate among the beings in our conceptual sights. Our version of the argument, though different, likewise relies on placing God beyond the sights of any particular religious or metaphysical system. In that sense it is not an ontological argument, though it employs ontotheological categories.

I offer this argument tentatively because it shows that ontotheology and issues of justice can work together. But more importantly for this book, it bases the reality of God on the necessity for God *not* to be a concept in any one faith, but rather to be what justice-doing dialogue between them adumbrates.

The next chapter will follow up the inevitably abstract and sometimes difficult discussions of this chapter with some proposals for what theology, and in particular interfaith theology, needs to be like if it is to reflect the apophatic-cum-kataphatic process just described, and so do justice to God and beings. This will enable us to draw together the threads from previous chapters, and in particular shed new light on the fourfold process described in chapter 5.

29. Marion, *Ontological Argument.*

CHAPTER 9

Beyond the Desert :
Interreligious Illumination

> In every way, something has been lost, irremediably lost; imme-
> diacy of belief. But if we can no longer live the great symbolisms
> of the sacred in accordance with the original belief in them, we
> can . . . aim at a second naïveté in and through criticism. In
> short, it is through *interpreting* that we can *hear* again.[1]

As Paul Ricoeur argues that the critical study of sacred texts tends to
create a distance between us and the texts. From the naivety of childhood,
when we live ourselves into the biblical stories with an innocent belief in
the reality of the world there described, we move to what Buber might have
called and "I-it," quasi-scientific study in which the text is taken apart and
analyzed by various critical methods. Ricoeur states in this passage his belief
that we cannot return to the original innocence as if none of the criticism
mattered, but also that "beyond the desert of criticism, we wish to be called
again."[2] He states his hope for a "second naivety": that after criticism has
done its work we will be able once again to live ourselves into the texts to
sustain belief in and relationship with God.

This chapter will reaffirm that hope, but by a longer route than Ricoeur
envisages, involving not only dialogue with the critical tools and perspectives of the Enlightenment, but dialogue with other faith perspectives too;
so that transformative encounter with another faith, though it renders impossible our original simplicity of belief, can restore the innocence of our
belief and perhaps an even greater simplicity. The basic strategy will be to
use the ontological perspective established in the previous chapter—which

1. Ricoeur, *Symbolism of Evil*, 351.
2. Ibid., 349, cited in Jansons, *Second Naïveté*, 1.

affirms a trinitarian Reality with an apophatic focus and kataphatic penumbra—to enhance and confirm the fourfold strategy for dialogue outlined in chapter 5. Thereby I hope to show how what that chapter offers is more than a method for dialogue; it also represents a pathway to encounter with the realities proclaimed by religious belief systems. Thus, interreligious encounter and the religious realism we arrive at in the second naivety are intricately interconnected.

I shall first outline what becomes of the four stages outlined in chapter 5 when enlarged by the considerations of chapter 8: they become four hermeneutical approaches that may be pictured, following chapter 5, as the four vertices of a square. I will then show that these ways converge in the sense that any pair of them (and there are six possible pairs) make sense as a valid religious or theological pathway of dialogue. The conclusion (which concludes both this chapter and the book) will take this further, showing how these pathways form part of a broader pattern that forms a sound basis for religious knowing through dialogue.

FOUR HERMENEUTICS:
LITERALISM, ANALOGY, CRITIQUE, AND
METAPHOR

The four "hermeneutics" sketched in Table 2 involve different hermeneutical approaches to the understanding of our and other people's sacred texts. They involve different ways of understanding and carrying out our religion, different priorities in encounter with others generally, and different kinds of metaphysics or understanding of reality. I shall first discuss them as phases in the history of ideas, but later we shall see how at the fourth phase they all begin to work together as stages in a single process of theological development.

Table 2: Four Phases of Hermeneutics

Phase	Herme-neutic of Text	Hermeneu-tic of Other	Religion	Inter-faith	Meta-physics
1. First Naivety, ancient	Literal	Body: full presence without sense of otherness	Mythol-ogy and idolatry	Exclusivism	Naive realism: things are what they seem
2. Metaphysics, classical to modern	Analogical	Face, expressing/concealing soul	Classical onto-theology	Inclusivism	Reality underly-ing appear-ance or illusion
3. Critique and deconstruc-tion: modern to postmodern	Critical	Priority of language and culture	Negative theol-ogy, God beyond being	Pluralism	Relativ-ism and affirma-tion of appear-ance
4. Second na-ivety, beyond postmodern	Meta-phorical	Person in dialogue	God personal, embodied yet tran-scendent; icons	Interaction	Intersub-jective, dialogical

Let us look more closely at what the table means.

1. Ricoeur's *"first naivety"* prevailed in early times and still applies to the understanding of children and of "simple believers" from all faiths. It is a way not to be regarded as crude or unsophisticated, since children can be intelligent and perceptive and mythology is often full of a richness and subtlety that is opaque to the other ways of under-standing. But stories in the texts are regarded as literally true; for example, the demons Jesus exorcised in the Gospels are regarded as objectively existing and literally possessing and being expelled from

them. Metaphysically, naive realism holds; things are what they seem, and the secondary qualities like "green" and "bitter" really do inhere in the green or bitter object. Likewise, people are generally trusted to be what they appear to us to be, with no devious hidden depths behind what their bodies present. (That is why, for a small child to hide, it seems sufficient to cloak his eyes so that the person he is hiding from no longer appears.) The gods of our myths appear to us in our space, in the idols, and in our time, in the storytelling and ritual. For that reason, perhaps it would be more accurate to say that story and history, or literal and symbolic, are not distinguished. The stories mother reads carry authority for the child because mother is trusted; the myths of the tribe are trusted because the elders who pass them down have authority. Neither the child nor the tribe member has the critical apparatus necessary to discern "what really happened." The introduction, "Once upon a time" or "In those days"—or in the case of Orthodox liturgy, "*Today* . . . Christ is baptized . . . crucified . . . risen . . ."—is sufficient to establish the essential veracity of a story that has direct relevance to present life, without the mediation of historical considerations regarding what might have actually taken place when and where. In interfaith terms, exclusivism will tend to result, not in a strident sense but because it is the stories of one's own people, told by the people's trusted authorities, that engage with the people's life; other stories are not so much false as irrelevant and without authority.

2. The *metaphysical* phase arrives with the speculations that marked the "axial age"; the period when people moved from localities where their myths and rituals could be taken for granted, to the larger cities and states where these could easily be lost in a mix of cultures. The world of innocence began to shift and break and people began to look for truths and ideals that could be trusted always and everywhere. The naive identity of appearance and reality was therefore severed, giving rise to the notion of a more solid world—of atoms or ideas or divinity—persisting behind the flux of appearance, which came to be regarded as often, perhaps always, illusory. The stories in the texts now become allegories and analogies, standing for something more perfect and dependable than themselves: a metaphysical or ethical reality that is more important than the story that presents it to the imagination. For example, evil spirits now become identified with moral vices that need to be driven out of our souls. In this perspective inclusivism becomes possible, because the religion interprets its stories in the light of a wider perspective that may (or may not) embrace others from

other religions. Likewise, the person becomes not a solid body but a face, a visual representation of something hidden, the soul, which may communicate through the face or hide itself. In terms of religion "ontotheology" has arrived, and with it a focus on ethical demands. The ritual requirements laid down in the naive phase are seen as sometimes expressing moral values, but sometimes obscuring them and so needing to be criticized (by the prophets, for example, or the Buddha or Christ) in the name of the ethical imperative. There is gain here in the discovery, beyond local rituals, of universal ethical considerations, and the rise of philosophy, mathematics, and (eventually) science. But there is also a loss of immediacy, a tendency to deprecate the physical, particular, and temporary, and an absentminded tendency to get lost in lofty speculations. We are now familiar with the lament for this loss in narrative theology, which perhaps fails to appreciate the gains.

3. The *critical* phase arises when this doubt and critique concerning ritual and the temporal world begins to be applied to the eternal moral and metaphysical laws also. With global empires and global capitalism and trade, it becomes apparent that even these are the constructs of particular societies. Such critique represents a persistent undercurrent in the modern era, and becomes dominant in the relativism of the postmodern period, about which much has already been said in this book. Philosophically the result is a deprecation of the kinds of eternal "reality" esteemed in the metaphysical phase, and a corresponding re-valuing of the particular and transient: the "surfaces" of Lyotard, the "return of the secondary" celebrated by Cupitt (2010), and the "virtual" of Beaudoin's "virtual faith" (1998). In terms of the sacred texts, a host of critical methods are now applied that relativize the texts in terms of the culture in which they were produced, or more radically, in deconstruction, in terms of their own self-contradictions and silences. To continue with our evil spirit example, whereas the metaphysical hermeneutic attempted to "save the truth" of the relevant passages in the face of the difficulty of believing in literal demons, by making them allegories of ethical verities like the vices, a critical hermeneutic tries to expose the untruth, seeing the evil spirits as products of political repression or ideological distortion. The truth apprehended is not the truth in the text but the truth of the cultural situation behind the text which explains the production of the text. The other person, meanwhile, is no longer either a present embodiment nor a meaningful face, but a construct of her society's "language": no longer are words primarily things we make to communicate meanings entertained in a

substantial soul; rather, it is language and communication that creates the illusion of the mind or soul. We do not make language, it makes us. In this context theology survives, if at all, by the jettisoning of the "ontotheology" of the previous era, and resorting to a starkly negative theology, if not an atheology. The relativism that relates a religion's texts to its cultures means that in interfaith terms pluralism is likely to prevail, each religion being potentially "true," but only for its culture (and perhaps ideologically "false" even for that).

4. The *"second naivety"* represents a step beyond postmodernism that returns us to aspects of the first naivety, but without (for Ricouer) abandoning the benefits of the critical phase, or (I would add) the metaphysical phase. What returns is a certain ability to place oneself imaginatively in the text and trust it to take you to real places and real engagement. Whereas the first naivety took the text literally, and the metaphysical way regards it allegorically and analogically, and the critical phase views it suspiciously, the key to the fourth phase is the power of metaphor to illuminate actualities, and return us to our experience—a power we will shortly explore. For example, whether demons literally exist or not, there is no need to take them at face value, or to allegorize them, or to deconstruct them and reconstruct them as psychological factors. What matters is to read ourselves imaginatively into the texts where Jesus exorcises the demons, so as to discover what his action on us and our negativities—however we understand them metaphysically—might be. In this context, the other is understood as a person, a body-mind unity whose thoughts and experience are thoroughly immanent and yet also transcendent, as described in the previous chapter. As argued there, this enables us to reappropriate theology; God is seen as personal too, but theology proceeds not via a literal, idol-based mythology and ritual, as in the first naivety, but in the fashion appropriate to the icon (indeed Orthodox theology has always regarded the Bible as the verbal icon of Christ). The stories and images of faith are valued not only because of a literal history they describe (though that factor drawn from the first naivety need not vanish altogether) but because they interilluminate with one another and with life, enabling transformative action and also a more interactive approach to the images of other faiths.

This optimistic notion of a second naivety is obviously more controversial than the other phases and approaches, which follow, broadly, patterns widely discussed in accounts of the relation between the premodern,

modern, and postmodern. It represents a further stage, beyond criticism without rejecting criticism, which many theologians might welcome. In it, the other phases are brought to life again, but in a new way, as parts of a single process. But is this actually possible? Certainly it is possible to retreat to a naive approach. It is true that the cultural barriers that enable each "tribe" to take its traditions as literal truth cannot easily be reinstated (though some tight knit societies like the Amish and some Muslim sects seem to manage this). But we have noted how types of narrative and postliberal theology attempt to replace them with philosophical barriers that encourage people to treat their own religion as a self-contained language game. What Ricoeur commends, however—as is clear from the opening quote—is not such a return to innocence but something that recognizes that the "immediacy of belief" involved in the first naivety is "irremediably lost," so we have no choice but to "aim at a second naïveté in and through criticism." So "it is through *interpreting* that we can *hear* again," which presumably means that the critical interpretations that seek to get behind the text to its causes can actually help establish that simple participation in which through the text we hear the Word of the Lord.

I will not pursue Ricoeur's account of how this is possible, because my own project is even more ambitious, since I wish to incorporate the metaphysical phase and hermeneutic as well as the critical in my "second naivety." So our question becomes: is it really possible to involve the other approaches in a "second naivety" that allows us to engage, through the religious texts, in reality and the hearing of the divine Word? And in particular for our purposes, will the kind of interactive approach between religions which this book has advocated so far be lost in a return to the exclusivism that seems essential to the first naivety?

My approach to answering this will be to break the question down. The first and biggest stage of the argument will investigate the fruitfulness of smaller combinations of pairs of our four pathways, and by showing that each approach is enriched by such combinations (which become methods and approaches, rather than simple hermeneutical phases) suggest that mutual enrichment involving all four approaches has a logic and a necessity of its own. The second stage will then relate the four approaches to the fourfold processes of theological development discussed in chapter 4 and the four modes of interfaith dialogue discussed in chapter 5. The final stage will argue that since the four approaches enrich one another, and since they can come together in a single process, a new "naivety" that brings the four phases together is indeed possible.

Regarding the first stage of the argument, then, there are six possible pair combinations, to be examined in the following six sections. (The use of the arrow symbol ↔ indicates that we are not here speaking just of adding approaches together, but of allowing the one to inform and develop into the other and vice versa.) For those who find geometry helpful in theology, Table 3 shows the structure to be borne in mind.

Table 3: Hermeneutical Pathways

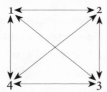

1 = Literal, First Naivety,

2 = Metaphysics

3 = Deconstruction

4 = Metaphor, Second Naivety

1↔2: MYTH, METAPHYSICS, AND TYPOLOGY

A great many religions combine mythology and metaphysics, and ritual and ethics. Hinduism obviously combines a vast array of myth, ritual, and often very down-to-earth *puja* with some of the most sophisticated metaphysical accounts known to humanity. In other religions, like Mahayana Buddhism and Catholic Christianity, a series of stories and rituals (some adapted from pre-existing folk cultures) coexist in a similar way with abstract metaphysical systems. This coexistence could even be taken as definitive of what it is to be a religion; for Nicholas Lash, a religion consists in story plus metaphysics, or metaphor plus analogy.[3]

This practical combination however does not guarantee that the combination makes sense: that the religions thus composed represent conceptual and lived unities rather than being one kind of mythological-cum-ritual thing for the "naive," and another metaphysical-cum-ethical animal for the more "sophisticated" classes. This is all the more problematic in that it is the essence of the metaphysical approach to see things in terms of appearance and reality, so the sophisticated are likely to understand themselves as being in harmony with the true essence of religion, while the lower, uneducated classes are making do with what is at best a simplification, and at worst a delusion.

Occasionally however this prioritization of metaphysics over story is reversed. Theravada Buddhism represents a rejection of the lofty metaphysics of the Mahayana in favor of a simple focus on the stories of the Buddha

3. Lash, *Ideology, Metaphor and Analogy.*

and his ethical teaching. And the lineage stretching from Karl Barth through Albert Ritschl to the narrative theologians notes (probably simplistically) that the church drew its metaphysics mainly from non-biblical Hellenistic sources; hence, they urged a return to the primacy of the biblical narrative.

The theologians of the patristic period would have defended their strategy of making use of Platonic and Neoplatonic metaphysics on the basis that it offered the best way of making the Judaeo-Christian God credible. (Jews like Philo followed the same strategy.) It might have been possible to interpret the Hebrew stories of God literally speaking to Abraham and Moses, stretching out his victorious right arm, speaking to his servant in thunder on the mountain, and sending fire upon earth, in terms of similar stories of the Greeks and Romans. YHWH would then have been a greater and more solitary version of Zeus, while Jesus might have been a holier Apollo (as indeed he is depicted in some of the earliest Christian art). The insight that this would have resulted in a severe distortion, and the move to invoke Greek metaphysics rather than its mythology, seems quite natural and spontaneous, involving, so far as we know, no debate or dissent or even decision at the time. Even to this day, those theologians who wish to expunge Greek metaphysics and return to "biblical" story do not (with the notable exception of Jack Miles) actually read the stories in the literal, anthropomorphic way, but in a way that takes the patristic move to Greek metaphysics largely for granted. Thus, Barth's Jesus is not the new Apollo but the sublimely metaphysical Chalcedonian Christ; only on that account has he the right to command humanity's total allegiance.

But the patristic move was subtler than it looks at first sight, for the theologians, and the Orthodox liturgies, adapted Greek metaphysics in a radical way. Platonic metaphysic centers around the notion (a typical variant of the metaphysical approach) that earthly things are degraded copies—types and shadows—of eternal forms. But in biblical and patristic thought material things and historical events are types of other material things and historical events. The Hebrew temple is a shadow of the tabernacle on the mountain, and both a shadow (cf. Heb 9) of Christ's atoning death on the cross. What results is not only a contemplation of eternal verities that leaves the shadowy earth behind, but also a powerful engagement with history. It is not that metaphysics as such is abandoned, but Platonic metaphysics is abandoned in favor of a historically and practically grounded—and also doxologically engaged—metaphysics. And this metaphysics not only projects us from the temporal to the eternal; it projects us back again into the temporal; it does not converge on the eternal but on the past historical or future historical (that is, eschatological). It is not just that the eternal ideas shed light and interpretability on earthly things; the earthly historical things *inter*interpret and interilluminate. Later, when we look at analogy and metaphor, this process will become clearer.

In all, in terms of religious practice and devotion the blend of story and metaphysics has much to commend it. The metaphysics saves us from idolatrous anthropomorphism—worship of a God imagined as a human being writ large—while the stories "embody" the metaphysics and the associated universal with a thicker description, easier for people to identify with and model their own lives upon than general abstractions.

2↔3: METAPHYSICS, ANALOGY, AND APOPHATICISM

In much of the debate about ontotheology, as noted in the context of Marion, negative or apophatic theology is seen as its major alternative. If God is not construed metaphysically, following Augustine and Aquinas, as identical with being itself, God must be, following Denys, *hyperousios*, beyond or above being. But there is something strange about this. Aquinas did not see Denys as a heretic or an opponent; rather, he saw himself as standing in the tradition of both Denys and Augustine. Metaphysics and apophaticism for all of these thinkers went hand in hand with each other and with a third term, the approach that Denys terms symbolic, and Aquinas analogical. The reasons for this are both semantic and devotional.

Denys' apophatic approach is set forth most clearly in his *Mystical Theology.*

> Neither can the reason attain to him, nor know him; neither is he darkness nor light, nor the false nor the true; nor can any affirmation or negation be applied to him . . . inasmuch as the all-perfect and unique Cause of all things transcends all affirmation, and the simple preeminence of his absolute nature is outside of every negation—free from every limitation and beyond them all.[4]

So his negative theology, importantly, negates all negations as well as all affirmations regarding God. And it does so on the basis that God is the Cause of all. In *Mystical Theology* Denys refers to two related works, since lost: *Theological Outlines*, which describes a kataphatic, affirmative theology, or *theoria physike*, based on the fact that all things must reflect something of the cause from which they arise, so the names that apply to creatures must apply in some supreme or "hyper" sense to God; and *Symbolic Theology*,

---

4. Denys, *Mystical Theology*, 209.

which describes the liturgy and other symbolic ways in which God's revelation in scripture and worship enables us to speak of God. The three modes of discourse about God all belong together and are grounded in God's creative and redemptive activity (though Denys says less about revelation and redemption than creation).

We note that a cause cannot explain a quality in an effect if it literally possesses that quality itself. Thus, it does not explain the redness of a rose to say that it consists of red particles, since redness (of the particles) then still needs explaining. The way we do explain the redness, in terms of atoms and particles and waves of light, invoke things that *categorically transcend* redness, being neither red nor non-red but of a totally different order from color. Yet paradoxically these things do have what-it-takes-to-explain-redness. And by virtue of that we can refer, metaphorically, to rays of red light; the light is not literally red, but it is the kind of wavelength that causes the experience of red in the eye and mind. In analogical manner God, to explain the qualities of things in the universe, must categorically transcend those qualities. God cannot have them literally, but God must have "what it takes to cause them." Classically he was said to have the qualities in an eminent way, or in the language of Denys, have them as hyperqualities, and by virtue of that, we can say of God that he has them analogically. And when what we want to explain is sheer being as such, God as the cause of being must not literally be, otherwise he fails to explain being; he must be *hyperousios*, as Denys put it, above being; God must categorically transcend the universe. God categorically transcends being: we cannot say literally that God is, or that he is not. But metaphorically, as the cause of being, we can say God is.

It is clear that apophaticism, kataphaticism, and symbolism belong together, and that the argument does not *only* place God "above being." Though it does do that, the reasons for doing so remain metaphysical or ontological—the logic of causality and creation—though they are also mystical and devotional. This is because Denys was not only concerned with the "downward" movement from God to creatures, but also the upward "ascent" of creatures to God. If the former represents an ever richer kataphatic outpouring of the divine energies, the latter represents an ever more austere stripping away of concepts until we are left with the bare union with Godself beyond all understanding. (This devotional aspect is perhaps more familiar in the work of the English interpreter of Denys who wrote the classic, *The Cloud of Unknowing*.) Moreover, in Denys both movements are bodied forth symbolically in the Divine Liturgy, which is where we encounter both movements most intensely.

Essentially the same structure of thought is to be found in Aquinas. What distinguished Aquinas from his predecessors was his use of

Aristotelian thought to refine our understanding of the third term, which Denys refers to as symbolic or metaphorical. Aquinas distinguished analogy from metaphor, a distinction we will build on in section 2↔4, below.

> When words are used analogically, one use is primary and helps define the others. It is because organisms can be called healthy in the first place that the word can be used secondarily of diets and complexions with reference to that first use. Words used metaphorically of God apply primarily to creatures and only secondarily to God, and this would be the case with non-metaphorical words too if they simply expressed God's causality. But, as we have seen, calling God good or wise doesn't simply mean that he causes wisdom or goodness in creatures, but that he himself possesses these perfections in a more excellent way.[5]

For Aquinas it is analogy rather than metaphor that applies to language about God. As the symbolic for Denys mediated between the affirmative and the negative, so for Aquinas the analogical allows us to say both that God is and is not (to return to the example used in chapter 8) wise. God *is* wise, but God *is not* wise in the limited sense in which we may be. Rather, as the cause of all wisdom, God must be wise in some "eminent" sense. God has a wisdom-making wisdom: analogical wisdom, or what Denys might call hyper-wisdom. In the order of meaning, we learn first what wisdom means when we hear the term applied to human beings, then apply it to God, but in the order of being, wisdom must exist first in God, and then in a more limited way in us.

In all this analysis Aquinas never loses sight of the dimension of mystical ascent to be found in the theology of Denys and his apophatic successors. In all these writers negative and metaphysically based theologies are interdependent. In Denys and Aquinas at least, negative theology is a kind of ontotheology: perhaps the most dialectically subtle kind there can be, since it offers metaphysical reasons for going beyond metaphysics, and finds language that reaches beyond what words can say.

1↔3: DISSOLVING THE DEITIES—FROM STORY TO ACTUALITY

One of the effects of biblical criticism is that the characters we naively loved, including God, disappear from our mind's sight, or vanish from our imaginative grasp. A familiar example might be what happens to the Christmas

---

5. Thomas, *Summa Theologiae* 32 (1:1.13.6).

story, which we have all naively loved from childhood onward, when we discover that two of the Gospels do not find it necessary to mention the birth of Jesus at all, while the other two that do, Matthew and Luke, offer quite different stories that are quite hard to reconcile. Moreover, these stories may be best explained in terms of the different theological priorities of Matthew and Luke. The crib, the shepherds, and the Magi appear to belong to different story worlds conjured up by different authors; and so their solid historical reality may dissolve before our eyes, "deconstructed" in a sea of doubt. The realization that many biblical stories deconstruct themselves (see the discussion of Sacks in chapter 6) may not mitigate our sense of loss.

Interfaith dialogue may have the same effect. Not only particular stories but whole ways of viewing the world, and interlocking metaphysical systems that we have taken for granted, can emerge as foundationless, because they conflict with other ways of storytelling and thinking that suddenly seem truer, or more reasonable, or to offer better ethical standards or a more challenging vision.

Do such experiences have to amount to irretrievable loss? In Tibetan Buddhist practice there is a way of making the dissolving of our vision and our deities positive. As well as meditation, such traditions encourage the practice of *puja*, worship, which is something rare in the Buddhist context. But it is worship with a twist, probably learnt from Tantric Hinduism. As I describe it here, after being imagined and invoked and worshipped, the deity is dissolved.

> The imagination is invited to focus on vivid figures such as . . . the five Dhyani (meditation) Buddhas, figures which in Tibetan art are characterised by their different colors and genders, by the objects they hold, or sit on, or which hover above their heads, and the compass direction from which they appear. Some have many arms; some are serene, and detached, some smiling and compassionate, others again wrathful. Devotees imagine these beings as they recite the detailed descriptions in their puja (worship), and they may be invoked with their specific mantra. . . . [But] as his mantra is said, the "deity" is "dissolved"—allowed imaginatively to disperse into thin air—and then visualised as a power emanating from the meditator himself, usually from the heart center.[6]

Here we find a corrective to idolatry very different from the negative injunctions of the Western monotheism; a third alternative, perhaps, to the icon and the idol. The worship of an imaginary idol is encouraged, but then

6. Thompson, *Buddhist Christianity*, 172–73.

the idol is destroyed to leave only the presence it has invoked within the believer. The deity emerges as a construct of the believer, though at the same time it is no less "real" than the believer, who is also, in Buddhist thought, only a transient bundle of sensations and imaginative constructions. Indeed, the deity could be regarded as gaining intensity as it moves from the visual imagination to the concentration of the heart center, becoming something the mediator can realize in herself.

There is a pathway here leading from what I have called the "penumbra" of story and ritual to the "focus" of actuality: the living, breathing, and imagining that is what is going on as the meditator sits. This is a move that traditional Christian faith has resisted, and even Nietzsche's Zarathustra found the death of God a matter for lament, while modern criticism and postmodern deconstruction have destroyed the old assurances only at an intellectual level. But Christian mystics like St. John of the Cross have found a spiritual purpose in the dark night of the soul: the time when the richness of the Christian story and imagery runs dry for us is, for him, a sign that we are drawing near to a more naked union with God. Is it possible to make the intellectual practices of criticism and deconstruction part of a deeper spiritual process of dissolving on the Tibetan pattern, in which what we imagine is not lost but actualized in our life and experience?

3↔4: MEDITATION: FROM DECONSTRUCTION TO ACTUALITY

To answer this we need to look at the three pathways that lead towards the second naivety of interilluminative actuality. What does this mean? "Interillumination" will be discussed in the next section. By "actuality" I mean, in the first instance, what meditation discovers. I distinguish "actuality" from "reality" because the latter term means actuality seen in the context of all the verbal moods: the event in the context of what might happen, or might have otherwise happened, and whether it had to happen, and what we hope to happen as a consequence, and why it happened, and so forth. Actuality emerges out of the stripping away of all these moods, including the indicative description of "what actually happened"—since this, too, for Buddhism and for meditation, is a construct of the mind. Actuality is by definition ineffable, indescribable; but it is not the ineffability of God or the Ultimate, but the ineffability of the everyday (which is part, perhaps, of what we mean by God).

Buddhism evidently involves a great deal of what could be called deconstruction. (This may not be exactly the same as the deconstruction of

Derrida and other postmodernists, but like that deconstruction it involves more than the academic processes of critique, something more self-engaging, including the unearthing of hidden motives and self-contradictions.) Parallels also suggest themselves between meditation and phenomenological "bracketing" in which judgments about the reality of what we experience are suspended in order to investigate more fully what is taking place at a phenomenal, experiential level. But this, of course, is an academic process aiming at clarification, rather than a search for spiritual enlightenment.

In Buddhism the desiring self, and the desired (or hated) object, are "deconstructed" or "bracketed," dissolved into evanescent bundles of karmic causation, by painstaking argument. But meditation takes this process further, into the immediate experience of the meditator, who is invited to look upon these evanescent bundles as they come and go, noting anything that draws her into a self-engaging "story" regarding them—like "this is nice" or "that is uncomfortable" or "this mediation is going well"—briefly noting that story and where and how it is happening, and then letting it go, so that in the end only the unnameable actuality of the flow is experienced.

That unnameable actuality does in practice have names, of course, like nirvana (the "blowing out" of the fire of the ego and its desires), *satori* (enlightenment), and *sunyata* (emptiness). It could be conjectured that it represents Chalmers' Edenic experience described in chapter 3, the direct acquaintance of things as they really are "in their true intrinsic glory," without the mediation of stories. Christian meditation teacher Mary Jo Meadow, in the course of meditation instruction, has affirmed that the experience of the world arrived at through long insight meditation practice corresponds with the world described by modern physics much more closely than does our everyday commonsense way of experiencing the world.

We identified Edenic experience with God's experience of the world, which is one with God's generating of the world as God's action and sustaining it with God's love. It is experience of the world "from the inside," experience of what it is to be this or that. Above it was noted that, while it is possible through insight meditation to see the world, with Buddhist austerity, as the "empty" dependent co-arising of events, it is also possible to see it as God's action and the inner knowing of the divine Mind. In enlightenment we could say that (in language verging between the Christian and the Buddhist) we come to know and love with the wisdom and compassion of (divine) Mind.

We may be speaking here of a focal experience on which the penumbra of religious stories and metaphysics converge. But, of course, those stories and metaphysics remain divergent and fragmented. Is there any way of bringing the fragments together in speech about the focus, or does the focus only emerge after the confused babble of religious tongues have fallen silent?

1↔4: METAPHORICAL INTERILLUMINATION

Besides the systematic deconstruction involved in meditation there is another way of arriving at Eden, or restoring a sense of what it is like to experience the world outside the conceptual structures wherein we normally "read" it. This is the use of metaphor, which Aquinas relegated to a lesser realm than that of analogy, but which arguably needs to be seen as complementary to analogy.

Aquinas' distinction between metaphor and analogy needs to be enlarged. In metaphor a word retains its original meaning, which stands in tension with the thing to which it is transferred, whereas in analogy the word so to speak allows its meaning to be transformed by its new context, because it is not just the word that is transferred, but rather, its whole range of alternatives is transferred across to the range of alternatives that apply to the thing described. And it is transferred by something—like causality in the case of Aquinas' health example, above—that preserves the structure of alternatives in the transfer.

Another example may make this clearer. When we speak of a red light ray we are using an analogy, because we could also speak analogically of a green or a white light ray, or any other color. The whole category of alternative possible colors is transferred to the light rays, and the transfer is made secure by the fact that light rays cause color experiences, so that the language of color has a structure that corresponds to, and can map onto, the structure of light rays. If, on the other hand, we speak metaphorically of say "sharp pinpricks of light," it is unclear what the alternatives are, because there is no pre-existing relation between pins and light. Would knitting needles of light, or hammers of light, be different in the same way as needles or hammers are different from pinpricks? Or would the opposite of pinpricks of light be something more like "swathing veils of light"? Whereas an analogy transfers a whole category of possible predicates to the description of the thing, in metaphor a word is applied to something it makes no literal sense to apply it to, and which therefore represents what Ryle famously called a "deliberate category mistake."[7] The puzzle is, how does such a "mistake" create a new meaning, rather than sheer nonsense? For example, when the poet Marvell describes the creative process as creating new worlds, "annihilating all that's made/ to a green thought in a green shade," the result might

7. In Ryle, "Categories."

simply be nonsense; how can a thought be green or any other color, or even colorless? The whole category of color words is inapplicable to thoughts. And yet the metaphor "works"—a new meaning is generated. How?

Literary critic I. A. Richards ascribed the power of metaphor to the "interaction" between what he called the "tenor" (the object described, in the above case light) and the "vehicle" (the word, like "pinpricks," used to describe it).[8] Philosopher Max Black took up this idea, arguing against both the "substitution" view that metaphor involves merely the substitution of one term for another, and the "comparison" view that metaphors are compressed similes or statements of likeness.[9] Black argued that these latter views render the reduction of metaphorical to literal statement an easy matter. "Interaction," on the other hand, opens up the possibility that metaphor may capture something beyond the reach of literal recasting; something utilized by science to describe, in its metaphorically based models, realities that literal language cannot reach. It is this power of metaphor that Paul Ricoeur has seized upon to argue that metaphor has cognitive value; that is, it enables us to experience and know things we otherwise could not. Likewise, I have argued that metaphor facilitates "interillumination," the "dialogue between two objects" described above in chapter 2.[10]

Black uses Wittgenstein's notion of "seeing as" to help us understand metaphorical interaction. When we call a man a wolf we encourage people to see him as a wolf. That is, we highlight his wolf-like features, or those features of his that correspond to the wolf set of "related commonplaces"—viciousness, greed, and so forth—and suppress those features of the man and of wolfishness that do not correspond. This is what I call interillumination. The concept of wolf, applied to a man in preference to the concept of man, sets going a new way of analyzing that man, a new set of correspondences that pick out a different set of features. Hence, we can argue about metaphorical truths, asking for example, "Is he really such a wolf? He seems very gentle to me."—"Ah! But he's a wolf in sheep's clothing!" The wolf metaphor may enable me to see things in the man that the man concept does not: it may interilluminate with new aspects of the pattern.

Now there is a sense in which metaphors "break the rules"; though some metaphors simply, like similes, compare unlikes, others, like Marvell's "green thought," constitute category mistakes. The illumination that metaphors generate always presupposes a dark background of unlikeness

8. Richards, *Philosophy of Rhetoric*, chs. 5 and 6.

9. Black, *Models and Metaphors*, ch. 3.

10. See Thompson, *Holy Ground*, 139–50, on which much of the present discussion is based.

or categorical distance. The man is not literally a wolf; if he were, no meta-phor would be involved. So Ricoeur speaks of a "tension" between likeness and unlikeness involved in metaphor. Yet something deliciously particular sparks across the conceptual gap. Because "thought" does not fit "green" in terms of our normal categories, our imaginations are set looking for a green something in a green shade that does so fit; a thought-like greenishness to which all that is made can be said to be annihilated. Associations of green growth and summer shade link up with forgotten corners of our memories of relaxed, quietly proliferating thought on summer afternoons.

Poetry, of course, is characterized not only by the use of metaphor, but also a distinctive use of sound. The material aspects of words—rhyme, meter, rhythm, alliteration, assonance, and so forth—matter for the mean-ing, in a way in which they do not in prose. This is because the sound of the words itself is used to interilluminate with what is described, bringing out yet more features of the reality evoked in the imagination. An army marching will be described in marching rhythms, while lazy green thoughts on lazy summer afternoons will be described in lazier rhythms. The sound of the verse, along with the metaphors, conspire not just to denote things but to evoke Edenic experience, the precise quality and texture of actuality itself. Speaking of the use of sound quality in Welsh and other poetry, Wil-liams notes how "odd" it is that

> our language can discover anything simply by playing games with itself. But . . . we cannot assume that our speech is either a leisure activity with no connection to its environment, or a handy means of cataloguing ready-made objects; it is something shaped by our body's participation in the "action" of the world. . . . Listening hard to what we say prompts new levels of under-standing. . . . We recognize that our "normal" conscious minds are habituated to screening out aspects of what is before us. . . . With extreme poetic, metaphorical, ritualised and formalised speech, we converse with ourselves, and with our unexamined perceptions, our half-conscious associations of sounds and sense alike, and are ready to be surprised.[11]

The non-habitual, unscreened Edenic experience and imagination that arises from this kind of word-use is central to the second naivety. Poetry has the power to enable us to move from the original naivety to the second: from the particularity associated with the first, where words are regarded as standing literally for realities, to a new particularity that is arguably deeper than the first. When we take the biblical story, for example, as standing for

11. Williams, *Edge of Words*, 135.

events that happened just as a described, a distance is created between us and those events. They stand apart from us in space, happening "somewhere else," and in time, happening "in those days." But when the story is read just as story, it can interilluminate directly with our story here and now. In the Orthodox liturgy, as in the Jewish Passover, the events are regarded as happening "today" as if we ourselves were present. In Ignatian meditation, likewise, we imagine the story as if we ourselves were part of it, with Jesus and the other participants present to us now, and then return to ourselves to move forward in our relationship with Christ in the light of what has just happened to us.

Finally, I would argue that interreligious dialogue can enable interillumination. First note that, beside the first naivety described above, the naivety of the believer who has long been familiar with and trusted the literal truth of the stories of her faith, there is a second kind. This is the naivety—perhaps the strongest case of hermeneutical naivety—of the unbeliever or believer in another faith, who reads the stories of a tradition she does not know, with the naivety of fresh eyes. She knows little or nothing of the contexts that give the story meaning for the believer, but she may be able nevertheless to illuminate aspects of the story the believer misses, and make suggestions that deepen the believer's own insights into the story. Metaphors that have lain dormant and unnoticed in one faith may be "untamed" by being seen as strange and unfamiliar by the other-faith believer. For example, a Christian reading or hearing the story of the Buddha's temptations may immediately think in terms of Jesus' temptations, and have suggestions to make that would not occur to a Buddhist, but may be accepted by him or her as insightful. And *vice versa*. (More on this under "Tents, Clouds, and Voices" in the conclusion.)

2↔4: ANALOGY AND METAPHOR IN RELIGION

At this point more needs to be said about metaphor in relation to metaphysics and analogy. Does analogy represent, as Aquinas thought, a surer way than metaphor of reaching theological truth? Or does metaphor represent a way of focusing Edenic experience, while analogy represents only pale abstraction? Or do we need both? Is it somehow characteristic of religion to make metaphysics out of metaphor and/or to allow metaphysical analogies to come alive through metaphor?

The difference between metaphor and analogy arises from the different place of each in our wider conceptual scheme. An analogy—and the scientific models that are based on analogy—takes a category of terms with it to map out an unfamiliar or as yet undescribed area of reality, whereas the metaphor stands or falls alone. The analogy represents a kind of capture of the unfamiliar, bringing it within the orbit of a well understood category of descriptions. For example, to describe an electric current as "strong" captures electric current for all "flow" terms, like "weak" and "fast" and "broad," all of which have their analogies in measurable features in electric currents (volts measuring the strength or power of the current, watts the volume, and so forth). The metaphor, on the other hand, orbits around both the old and the new realms, holding the two in tension. So "wolf" orbits around the animal and the man equally, effecting interillumination but no definitive capture of humans by wolfish categories of understanding.

Now this difference has two consequences. Because an analogy carries a set of related terms with it, each term has a coherent set of alternatives, suggesting, as noted, a structure of relations that we can vary and then measure the consequences. In the case of scientific models this structure of relations can be made mathematically precise and measurable; enabling us to experiment in a way in which is impossible in the case of metaphor. And analogies link up with the rest of our conceptual scheme in ways in which metaphors do not; which is why we can argue things and demonstrate truths using analogies, and so build up a scientific or metaphysical system, whereas metaphors and art generally cannot state truths, only show forth experienced or imagined phenomena. Metaphors suggest tantalizing, perhaps revolutionary, alternatives to our ways of seeing, which we cannot pursue in any experimental way, or assimilate in any total metaphysical understanding of things. On the other hand, metaphors have a power to change our lives, our wisdom, our tacit grasp of reality, which models do not.

Now I suggest that these contrasts between analogies and images give them a complementary role as far as reality is concerned. Analogies in science and metaphysics bring to light patterns ever more remote from our own, gathering the unfamiliar into the orbit of the familiar and calculable. They suggest what questions to ask of, and what experiments to perform on, realities with which we would not otherwise be able to interact, in order to perceive. Once we understand the electricity in a wire as analogous to a flow of energy (an analogy that can be made mathematically precise), we can think of experiments to perform to explore further its behavior and test out whether and with what modifications the model holds true. But suppose instead we use the river as a metaphor for life. The metaphor like the analogy invites questions, like where does life begin and end? and do we ever step into it twice? and is there anything permanent about it? But now there are no experiments we could perform to determine the answer. Rather than gathering the remote into the familiar, the image seems to project the familiar quality of our life into the strange and unfathomable.

For in the metaphor the abstracting process of analogy is reversed. The scientific analogy reveals the underlying structure of causal relations at work in an object; this enables us to disregard the fascination of the object's sensuous appearance, and to manipulate the object and make it work according to our own designs. But while concepts arise from the interillumination of patterns, in metaphor concepts themselves interilluminate in a special way that returns our attention to the original patterns. In Marvell's metaphor, for example, the concepts "green" and "thought" are brought together in such a way that the abstract structures of relations that they codify alter or even annihilate, bringing us face to face again with the sensuous and emotional associations, which are precisely those aspects of concrete actuality that science and metaphysics disregard.

Scientific and metaphysical analogies, then, enhance our power by suggesting technological developments and systematic worldviews that enable us to envision—and in the case of science, manipulate—the world to our own advantage. But there is a sense in which they systematically blind us. They restrict our vision of the particular by encouraging us to see it only as an instance of a general type, or only as an object to be used, or only as an instance of some more bold and sweeping truth. The world viewed by science and metaphysics in isolation from poetry and myth is an abstract world, lacking in those vibrant particular qualities like color and flavor and feeling and beauty, which for us give it life. Here metaphor restores the balance We learn about things not only by working on them with tools but also by playing games with them. We need the conceptual play of metaphor to wring concepts and distil from them the vividness of phenomena once again, in the power and wonder of their own unique impact and associations for us. It is through metaphor that we rediscover what life is like: what it is "in Eden" and in the mind of God.

Whereas analogies and models help us to cope with the unfamiliar, images stop us coping with, and hence ignoring, the familiar, and start us looking at its strangeness with fresh wonder. Science and metaphysics can offer a world that is "all there" so to speak before our gaze; but we meet it only as gazers, being ourselves outside the picture, lacking the qualities and values that might motivate us to act. Metaphor and art restore what it is like to be me here in this picture now, and to live with horror and delight in its overwhelming ever-changing texture. Metaphor and art enable the world to become not just a picture I look at, but something to which I am called to do justice; a pattern of life that lives in me, even as through and amidst it I live my life. And that is why—though I have not stressed it thus far—the second naivety is the place of interaction, transformation, and liberation.

Elsewhere I have described two ways in which metaphor (or "image") and analogy (or "model") may fuse together in the religious.

> We can make sense of the fusion of model and image in religious symbol in two ways: as the personalizing of ontological belief, or as the ontological rooting of poetic vision.
>
> In the first case metaphysics is rendered accessible to the imagination and made the focus of worship and contemplation, so that the metaphysical belief may bear fruit not only in the abstract, but also in the lives of ordinary people. . . . Here we start with a model of the cosmos; a model expanded to the point where the formulae are so deep and all-embracing as to lie beyond our ken, and the experiment to test the model broadens to be nothing less than a whole committed life.
>
> In the second alternative, a poetic insight is seen as the clue to the whole of reality. The attempt is made to effect not just the momentary renewal of the vision of the everyday, but a systematic conversion of the whole of experience to that insight. Not satisfied with taking the poem as a momentary annihilation of categories that later reassert themselves, the religious believer insists on taking the poem as the reality, and the prevailing categories, where these cannot encompass the poem, as so much illusion. Having taken this step, the believer has no choice but to construct a new account of reality on the basis of the poem. Thus Christianity proceeded from the myths, poems and hymns which the early Church sang as love songs to Christ, towards a revolutionary incarnational ontology which opts for Christ as the one reality by which to live. So Jesus Christ is at once an historical particular and a metaphysical being: a living symbol.[12]

The religions combine myth and metaphysics, and analogy and apophaticism. They both present us with the divine and dissolve it into nothing, and they return us to actuality by means of both meditation and metaphor. They draw together the objective vision set before us by analogy, and the subjective feeling distilled by metaphor. We now need to turn to see how these diverse factors, described in this chapter, may work together as stages in a process capable of bringing us to balance, truth, and liberation. Finally, we need to see how at all stages the process commits us to, and involves us in, engaging with reality through dialogue.

12. Thompson, *Holy Ground*, 170–71.

The conclusion to this chapter necessitates drawing together the threads, not only of the chapter, but of the argument of the rest of the book. So it will also serve as a conclusion to the book.

Conclusion:
Transfiguring Dialogue

CHAPTER 5 DEVELOPED AN account of the four elements of encounter, which together form—broadly speaking—a process of interfaith dialogue through which theology can come to be written. Chapter 4 had developed an account of the intrafaith dialogue involved in different ways of reading and dialoguing with secular texts so as to develop a theology. (As always, "theology" is to be understood in the broadest sense of the whole intellectual tradition of expounding any faith.) The question for us now is how the more complex process explained in the previous chapter relates to these earlier accounts. I offer Table 4 as an approximate template for how it may do so, to be expanded as this conclusion progresses. The italic type summarizes the table at the start of chapter 9, and the rest expands this in the light of chapters 4 and 5. As with Table 2, the "phases" described can be interpreted both as historical periods, and stages in a unified process of theological development.

Table 4: Dialogue, Theology and Hermeneutics

Thesis	1	2	3	4
Theology: Writing	Proclamation	Analysis	Apologetics	Incorporation
Theology: Reading	Imagination	Context	Deconstruction	Interaction
Content	Stories and ritual	Doctrinal and ethical systems	Arguments and critiques	Praxis and virtues
Mood	Imperative	Indicative	Interrogative	Subjunctive and optative
Concentrated development	Narrative theology	Scholastic theology	Atheology and radical apophasis	Liberation theology
Hermeneutical phase	1st naivety	Analogy	Critique	2nd naivety
Main content	Literal story	Metaphysical construction	Apophatic deconstruction	Story/reality interaction

1. In the first naivety, the texts are read straightforwardly as literally true stories, and stories and rituals make up the main content of the religion. In the reading of theology imagination predominates, as it always does in story-reading, but the imaginative aspect is generally not self-aware, but generates rather a fervent attachment to literal meaning. The creation of theology is dominated by the task of faithful proclamation and propagation of the story of faith. The mood is that of imperative command to change of life. The concentrated development of this strand at the expense of the others leads to narrative theology, with all its strengths and weaknesses.

2. The second phase is that of metaphysical construction based on the stories and analogies drawn from them. Faiths become worldviews with universal ethical implications. The stories are read within a broader context that enables critique and analysis, and thereby the development of doctrinal and ethical systems, expressed primarily in the descriptive indicative mood. These systematic theologies can over-develop into scholastic ends-in-themselves.

3. In the third phase critique, apophatic theology, and deconstruction predominate. The other is allowed to criticize and deconstruct faith's arguments in an apologetic attempt to whittle the faith down into something that can be demonstrated, or at least made easier to believe. Questions dominate the formation of theology, and this can generate a very skeptical kind of faith, or else a more mystical theology of negation.

4. In the second naivety there is a return to the stories and other face-value elements of the texts, but now the imagination is more aware of itself as such, and there is more emphasis on the relation of story to the creation of virtue in life, and more possibility of interaction and interillumination with those who live by other stories. Theology then grows by incorporation of alien perspectives, with the emphasis on the generation of new subjunctive possibilities and optative hopes for the transformation of life and world. Liberation theology represents the concentrated development of this aspect.

In this conclusion I shall argue that chapter 9's account does indeed serve to deepen and enrich the earlier accounts along the lines just sketched. That in turn enables us to see the complex interactions charted in that chapter as part of a coherent process of theological dialogue and discovery. Moreover, this theological process enables us to affirm the strands of postmodern theology described and critiqued in this book, but also to see them not as rivals but as belonging together in the process. Finally, the factors in some kinds of theology that mitigate against transformative dialogue between different faiths are overcome when they are seen as part of this process, which is essentially a matter of transformative encounter, both with one another and with what in most traditions is called God.

To take this deeper I shall use the story of Jesus' transfiguration, which can stand as a kind of parable of the theological process as a transfiguring encounter with reality.

THE (SEEMINGLY) INNOCENT LIGHT OF STORY

> Six days later, Jesus took with him Peter and James and John, and led them up a high mountain apart, by themselves. And he was transfigured before them, and his clothes became dazzling white, such as no one on earth could bleach them. And there appeared to them Elijah with Moses, who were talking with Jesus. (Mark 9:2–4)

The text here shines with the innocence of story. The narrative takes the classic form of theophany, or an appearance of God in glory, which is often set on a mountain top, evokes awe bordering on fear, and is accompanied by the voice of God (though here this appears later, at v. 7). In the transfiguration story, which appears at the heart of the three Synoptic Gospels, as in the baptism of Christ and some of the resurrection narratives, a genre often used of the appearance of YHWH to the Hebrew leaders and prophets is applied to Jesus. As if to bring home the point, Moses and Elijah appear on the mountain, representing the Law and the Prophets, the two major sections of the Hebrew Bible that Jesus and the writer of this story would have known. Both had encountered theophanies and other revelations on mountains. On Mount Horeb (Exod 3) Moses heard the voice of God speaking from the fiery "transfigured" bush. On Mount Sinai (Exod 19ff.; but described as Horeb—possibly another name for the same place—in Deuteronomy, e.g., 4:10) he saw the tabernacle, the model of the later Jerusalem temple; he heard God's utterance of the commandments amidst peals of thunder; on coming down from the mountain his own face became radiant (Exod 34:29); and at the end of his life, on Mount Nebo (Deut 34), he was given to see the whole of the promised land that his people, though not he himself, would enter. On Mount Carmel (1 Kgs 18:16ff.) Elijah called down fire from God on his sacrifice, triumphantly proving the superiority of YHWH to Baal; but then on Mount Horeb (1 Kgs 19), dejected, he did not hear God in thunder, earthquake, wind, or fire, but rather in the "still small voice" or "sound of sheer silence." In both cases the second mountain as it were qualifies the first by sounding a gentler, or even sadder note. Now on the unnamed mountain of transfiguration (traditionally identified with Mount Tabor in northern Israel) both triumph and qualification, including sorrow, come close together.

There is a bedrock of narrative here: the "naively" homely touch, typical of Mark, describing Jesus' garments as white "as no fuller on earth could bleach them." Narrative theology is right to encourage us to enter into such sensuous details in the narrative, and also to contemplate the marvelously complex and far from naive interweaving of stories—as just mentioned—evoked by the presence of Moses and Elijah. This sets up a series of interilluminations between stories as in a group of mirrors creating an indefinite array of reflections, which takes us straight away into the realm of metaphor, typology, and the second naivety. The writer of this story was clearly far from naive, used to reflecting on and imagining around the stories in his sacred texts.

That interweaving and the details of the story at this stage and the later stages discussed below take us beyond any naive storytelling. The transformation of Jesus' face and garments, for example, suggests either a reference to pagan theophanies (in which often those who appear to be merely human suddenly shine out, showing them to be gods in disguise), or to Hebraic theophany, but dramatically transposed, in that *Jesus himself* is made to take the place of the one in glory, who is normally YHWH. The story immediately demands an adventure into metaphysics, to decide whether Jesus here is here primarily the beloved Son of God, as the voice will soon proclaim, or as with the pagan stories, God in disguise, betrayed as such by his light. Such an adventure is, as noted in the discussion of Auerbach in chapter 6, invited by the apparent sparseness and underlying complexity typical of the biblical texts themselves. When these are stories, they are far from naive and non-metaphysical, though the "solid" Greek metaphysics the church has mainly used may not always be the best way to unpack them.

As the biblical narrative invites metaphysical questions, so it is always calling itself into question, in the way we shall soon see with the transfiguration story. It invites its own deconstruction: there is in postmodernism no greater cynicism, defiance, and despair voiced than in Ecclesiastes and Job, while the prophets use the Law to challenge the systems based on it. The many varieties of faith and doubt expressed in the Bible can, as we have seen, be woven into at least one, and possibly more, metanarrative of faith, namely the Jewish and the Christian metanarratives. But we have also seen how such attempt to harmonize biblical diversity is only one possible approach, and perhaps not the one that always does most justice to the text.

I have argued that is also legitimate to allow intrafaith diversity to invite us to a wider interfaith process, allowing the Jewish and Christian metanarratives as two among many possible stories to be spun, but not allowing either a monopoly. Rather we might allow the scriptural stories to weave together with the stories and metaphysical accounts set forth by faiths generally regarded as "other," in a manner that might involve both affirmations of and challenges to these traditional metanarratives. In the case of the transfiguration text it might prove worthwhile, for example, to set pagan and Hindu theophanies alongside that of Christ to see what interilluminative likenesses-in-unlikeness emerge; or adding to our hall of mirrors figures like Mohammed and the Buddha, letting them stand on the mountain with Christ conversing with him and the others in a discourse which (Luke tells us, in 9:31, but not Mark or Matthew) is about Jesus' coming death, but might range over other topics too.

Summarizing, the textual stories:

- by their own nature invite metaphysical interpretation: 1↔2;

- contain their own deconstruction: 1↔3;

- welcome a naive reading, but are subtler than they seem, moving us through speculation and critique to a second naivety: 1↔4.

In all, we certainly need to read parts of the Bible as a story, but as a polyvalent, imaginative mode of story that welcomes all the questions, including the metaphysical ones; a story that is always in dialogue with itself and with other stories and with us, and opens readily to those of other faiths too.

TENTS, CLOUDS, AND VOICES: ONTOTHEOLOGY UNBOUND

> Then Peter said to Jesus, "Rabbi, it is good for us to be here; let us make three dwellings, one for you, one for Moses, and one for Elijah." He did not know what to say, for they were terrified. Then a cloud overshadowed them, and from the cloud there came a voice, "This is my Son, the Beloved; listen to him!" (5-7)

The story continues with Peter's affirmation that the experience is beautiful (*kalos*)—though we are also told that, far from reveling in a "peak experience," he is confused and terrified—and his wish to build tents to contain Jesus and his companions, perhaps recalling the tent in which Moses continued to meet with God in the wilderness. Then light turns to darkness as the cloud overshadows them. Clouds are common features of theophany, serving to protect the recipients from the overwhelming and potentially annihilating effect of God's glory. The overshadowing (*episkiazousa*) is also familiar; it is the term used in relation to the power of God overshadowing Mary in her conception of Jesus (Luke 1:35). And the visual concealment seems to enable an auditory theophany, in the voice acclaiming Jesus as God's Son; this reiterates the voice at Jesus' baptism except that it is addressed, not to Jesus, but to the potential hearers.

Peter's suggestion of building tents, taken literally, is strange and impractical, but expresses a natural response to all uplifting but mysterious ("numinous") experience: a desire to cling on to it, to "tame" it, and to contain it in religious forms, so that it can be constantly available. Marion seizes upon Peter's suggestion as an analogy for the attempt to contain in metaphysical categories the overwhelming excess of experiences like that represented by the transfiguration.[13] Of course, Peter's suggestion is futile; the "tents" of our concepts can never contain the encounter with God. Marion argues that negative theology springs not from a negativity in our experience, but from an excess in it that defies all conceptualization. The

---

13. Marion in conversation, cited Caputo, *God the Gift*, 68-69.

light the disciples encounter in Christ on the mountain is something that cannot be contained in the "tents" of normal thought.

This confirms what chapter 8 argued about valid and invalid ontotheology, and its relation to apophatic theology. Ontotheology as an attempt to contain and reify experience is rightly resisted by narrative, liberation, and negative theologians alike. Confusion in the face of the saturated experience of actuality, and the apophatic "cloud of unknowing," need to be accepted. Nevertheless, there is ontotheological work—work on the relation of God to being, or life—to be done. After the darkness comes the hearing of the voice, with its proclamation of Christ as Son. That claim, along with the transfiguration itself, demands a retelling of the story so far. Christ has henceforth to be seen not only as the teacher from Nazareth, but the one who walks and talks with Moses and Elijah, and whom God calls his beloved Son. That retelling cannot avoid ontological questions of "who" Jesus is and "what" has happened to him. We need metaphysics for this, but a metaphysics that acknowledges its metaphorical roots and the need for negativity, irresolvable questions, and the invitation to contemplate mystery.

Jesus is here a metaphorical Son of God rather than an ontological God the Son; the term "Son" retains its associations with messianic kings and human sons, and has yet to become abstract metaphysical "begottenness." Metaphysics represents a bold attempt to rethink and systematize the world on the basis of deep-rooted metaphors like "light," "creation," and "Son." In the process crude physical and anthropomorphic features of the original stories are subjected to apophatic critique until they become appropriate to a transcendent God worthy of worship.

On the other hand, we may find our metaphysical systems prove inadequate to the stories and metaphors that inspired them, so that we need to return to the story and find a new metaphysics for it. Such moves form a necessary part of our attempt to do justice to God. But we will now read the stories in the new light of a second naivety that ignores neither metaphysical construction nor critique and deconstruction, but allows the stories to illuminate our lives as metaphors shining against a metaphysical background that is both light and dark.

Summarizing, metaphysical theology:

- interprets, refines, and returns to story: 2↔1;
- co-arises with negative theology: 2↔3;
- acknowledges and returns to its roots in metaphor: 2↔4.

Finally, this process clearly invites interreligious dialogue. Two ways have been noted in chapter 9. Firstly, metaphors and stories from different faiths may "naively" seem to interilluminate. Metaphysical exploration may then be used to develop both metaphors or stories to see if the process of refining and abstracting them enables a new way of thinking about reality, or ethics, that encompasses both. The two religions may then be seen as ontologically and ethically converging at this point, a matter that would be very significant without implying any general ultimate identity of the two religions. This is approximately the approach of Clooney, Fredericks, and other comparative theologians.

Or secondly, and less symmetrically, one might attempt to see the stories and images of one religion in terms of the metaphysics of the other, as for example in the writings of John Cobb and Aelred Graham.[14] The stories and metaphors of one faith might thus be transferred, as the metaphorical "vehicle" to the metaphysical "tenor" of the other religion. We might examine whether it makes sense to describe Christ as a Bodhisattva or to use the word *bodhicitta* (enlightenment mind) to describe grace.[15] One might try reading the story of creation in terms, not of the Aristotelian metaphysics of causality, but the Buddhist metaphysics of co-arising and emptiness.[16] Or working the other way, one might—as is often done—describe the three bodies of the Buddha in terms of the Trinity.

In terms of metaphysics and critique, of course, such a process is a scandal, riding roughshod over the context in which these terms normally derive their meaning. Yet is it not possible that the metaphorical power of religious ideas can sometimes be tamed by the metaphysical systems in which we habitually make sense of them, such that the context of the other faith is needed to "untame" the power of the metaphors behind them? May the transfer of a concept from its home context to one in an alien religion not sometimes create a spark of interillumination, such that, for example, we see aspects of Christ as Bodhisattva, or the three bodies as Trinity, that we did not see when we saw Christ solely in terms of the Chalcedonian formula, or the three bodies only as referring to historical and metaphysical realties as described within Buddhism? On the other hand, it may require new metaphysical and critical work to test out whether these new ways of seeing Christ and the Buddha represent genuine insights, or whether they are *simply* naive.

Once the distinction between the story and the metaphysics is grasped, plus the metaphorical grounding of all metaphysics (such that the

14. Cobb, *Mahayana Theology*; Graham, *Zen Catholicism*.

15. As for example in Thompson, *Buddhist Christianity*, 150ff., 133–34, and 53ff. respectively.

16. Cf. Thompson, "Creation, Dependent Arising."

metaphysics offers a way of interpreting the story, and the story a way of expressing and concretizing the metaphysics, neither being inevitably glued to the other), then there is no reason in principle why such moves should not be attempted. However, a metaphysical convergence will not mean that, in terms of the living of the faith, one does not need to return to the stories and practices of one of the faiths, albeit grasped with a fresh naivety assisted by the interfaith venture.

DESERTION AND DESCENT: DECONSTRUCTION

> Suddenly when they looked around, they saw no one with them any more, but only Jesus. As they were coming down the mountain, he ordered them to tell no one about what they had seen, until after the Son of Man had risen from the dead. So they kept the matter to themselves, questioning what this rising from the dead could mean. (8–10)

The vision dissolves. Jesus is only Jesus, *monos* with them, in a manner that conveys a sense of loss, and perhaps a foreshadowing of Jesus' desertion and solitude in Gethsemane and the cross. (In Luke these foreshadowings are clearer; there Moses and Elijah "spoke of his 'departure' which he was to accomplish at Jerusalem" (9:31).) The command to silence is in line with the messianic secret that is so much a feature of Mark, but also does justice to the ineffable experience on the mountain.

At this point the transfiguration story is (as so often with biblical narratives) deconstructing itself, or at least showing the need for all transfiguring visions to be dissolved, in the Tibetan Buddhist sense, so that we come back to earth not having contained the experiences in temples of the mind, located "on the mountain" somewhere else than were we normally live, but bringing the encounter with us, its indicative translated into the other modes. Perhaps an interrogative ("what *was* that all about?" or as here, "what can it mean to rise from the dead?") leading to a subjunctive ("maybe life could be different," "maybe resurrection is possible") and "an optative ("if only life could be more like that!"). Dissolving and deconstruction are nothing, of course, without a story, or a vision, or a metaphysical system to work on, and it is these things that once dissolved or deconstructed can lead, not to the void of cynicism and nihilism, but to a second naivety in which they live, purified of their inevitable ideological elements, as metaphors for a transfigured world.

Deconstruction in theology therefore:

- requires stories to deconstruct, in a process not entirely negative: 3↔1;
- can be regarded as the apophatic dimension called forth by metaphysics: 3↔2;
- returns us to see the story in a new, metaphorical light: 3↔4.

And in interfaith terms, as argued in chapter 5, one of the main services religions can perform for one another is to critique one another humbly, with a readiness to be critiqued in the same manner, to expose the blind spots and logical gaps the other cannot see, and to ask the questions that the other cannot ask herself; not of course with a view to destroying or proving oneself better but of arriving together at the second naivety.

Of course, the ideological power invested in all religions is likely mightily to resist this, which makes it the hardest part of the process to accomplish without provoking anger and resentment. It will become easier, of course, if the religions can find in their own tradition the equivalent of this negative interfaith process: the dark night and negative theology in Christianity and their equivalent in Judaism and parts of Islam; dissolving of the deity and the dialectics of emptiness in parts of Buddhism, and meditative detachment in Buddhism, Hinduism, and other oriental faiths.

Deconstruction raises the metaquestion of why we believe what we believe, but as noted in chapter 5, the answer to this question need not be negative, and after our apparent reasons for believing something are destroyed, we may be left with a more positive importance. What it is like to hold that belief may come to the fore, with the possibilities it holds for me of leading the good life. The placing of the transfiguration story not at the end of the Gospels as a goal (though some speculate that it was originally a resurrection story) but in its midst, where it emphasizes the obvious futility of containing the experience forever in temples on the mountain, and the necessity to come down back to a life as confusing as what went before: all this encourages a welcoming of something akin to deconstruction, though building temples where people can have reliable holy experiences has always been better for the church's business.

DIALOGUE AND HEALING:
METAPHOR AND LIBERATION

When they came to the disciples, they saw a great crowd around them, and some scribes arguing with them. When the whole crowd saw him, they were immediately overcome with awe, and

they ran forward to greet him. He asked them, 'What are you
arguing about with them?" Someone from the crowd answered
him, 'Teacher, I brought you my son; he has a spirit that makes
him unable to speak . . . .' (14–17)

(I have omitted verses 11–13, the discourse on the coming of Elijah. This is
probably a separate "saying" inserted into the narrative here because of the
mention of Elijah in the transfiguration narrative. It is not to be found in
Luke's parallel text, only Matthew's. In any case, it is the passage that follows,
quoted above, that is most relevant for our purposes.)

Here we return to the familiar Gospel hubbub of action: the crowd,
arguments involving the religious authorities, and sickness to be healed. Everything carries on as if nothing had just happened on the mountain, except
that the crowd "were immediately overcome with awe" (*exethambethe*). Awe,
astonishment, and fear are common responses in Mark to Jesus' miracles,
sometimes his teachings, and finally his resurrection. But here no miracle
has been witnessed by the crowd, and that invites us to conjecture that
something about Jesus remained perceptibly and awesomely "transfigured."
Perhaps, as when Moses came down from the mountain (Exod 34), his face
was still glowing, or perhaps a more subtle change is sensed by the people.
Significantly, whereas awe can often make people draw back, here it impels
them to rush forward to Jesus, with demands for healing. In any event, his
liberating work of challenging the authorities and healing the sick seems
to have been strengthened, somehow, by the experience on the mountain.

In our allegorical terms, the "naive" continuation of the story leaves
the illumination, the metaphysics, and the apophatic cloud behind, but they
have helped clarify the direction of the story and the path leading through
death to liberation. Authentic liberation theology, as argued in chapter 7, allows religions to interilluminate with their distinct understandings of what
liberation is, rather than applying a prior concept that derives from one religion or from secularism. It allow metaphors from the religions to untame
and liberate one another and generate a second naivety.

So the second naivety:

- draws on the same stories as the first, but is less confined to one tradition: 4↔1;

- moves ontology and ethics into a more active, engaged mode: 4↔2;

- affirms critique, which strengthens it: 4↔3.

I have of course been relating to the transfiguration narrative with a
second naivety of my own. I have looked closely at the narrative as it appears

in the biblical text, but not treated it naively as no more than a story. I have adopted a critical approach that treats the story as a construction, and hence analyzable and deconstructible. But I have also—with a kind of naivety— allowed the passage to speak allegorically and sometimes metaphysically, as having something to say about the process of theology itself.

THE INTERRELIGIOUS CITY

These four sections have used the transfiguration story to bring together themes from throughout the book to suggest:

- different kinds of postmodern theology can and must be brought together into a single process;
- this process is nothing other than engagement with a real God;
- but it requires that we work through explicit and implicit interfaith dialogue.

I recognize that this will prove, for all sorts of reasons, a difficult process to establish. It will take a very long time, and there will always be other ways of approaching one's religion and theology, some of them antithetical to what I am suggesting. My vision is naively utopian, though I hope my naivety is of the second kind. In this last section of the book I wish to come clean and set forth a naive, and personal vision, in the optative mode.

My first, youthful encounter with Buddhism was a book-focused critical appreciation of its metaphysics and ethics. A mid-life experience of walking amidst the Buddhist temples and the multiple Buddhas of Thailand, each almost identical but with subtle variations in face or gesture, served as a much needed corrective. Here Buddhism was expressed not in books and doctrines but by anonymous artists, creating a space full of the illumination of art and architecture with other art, with the life and gestures of the people, the chant of the monks, and the Buddhist *dhharma*, creating a whole form of life that hung together. As I climbed the increasingly and eventually alarmingly steep sides of Wat Arun in Bangkok, I felt myself living in literal space what I normally experienced as my inner, spiritual journey.

All religions do this. The architecture of Islam forms a luminous whole in the same way with the calligraphic, strictly non-representational art, the call to prayer, and the lines of prostrating worshippers. Christianity has several distinct forms of life: Orthodoxy and its art and architecture are different from Romanesque and Gothic and Quaker, but all have the same inner coherence of art and idea and life. The "secular city" fails to achieve this, its life-spaces being by comparison drab and confused, because secularism in-volves—arguably by definition—the separation of religion, politics, art, and science into separate spheres, each cherished in its own terms. There has been great modern art, but there being no secular cathedrals, it is located either in the shopping malls—those quasi-temples dedicated to the cult of commodities—or in the hushed, dedicated galleries where many offer the nearest thing they can to worship. And the reason for this is that the defini-tive quality of religion is its holding together of story, imagery, metaphysics, and life. That unity can, of course, be oppressive, but the shattering of the unity is merely oppressive in a different way, and, if we are to be liberated, it is a new, interactive kind of unity-in-difference that we need.

To return to opening sentence of this book, the really big question we face is whether being multicultural (and multi-religious) forces us to be secular. Because no one religion in a multicultural society can claim the privilege of forming the basis of the kind of unity just described, do we have to settle for a separation of religion from the other spheres of life? Though a surprising degree of nostalgia fills the public mind on occasions where we see the Church of England fulfilling its old role of master of ceremonies for the Christian state, no mass conversion to Anglicanism is going to result. But in the introduction I hinted that my preferred analogy for the future of the religions was as "suburbs of a great city, ill-defined as to boundar-ies, though clear where their center is, constantly interchanging traffic and people, some of whom live near a center, others on the borders, while no-body can identify the center of the city itself." In the future city we may hope to see the analogical or perhaps even literal equivalent of such suburbs, in the heart of which people will find the old interilluminative wholes of life, faith, metaphysics, and art, while elsewhere they may find new, more ex-ploratory areas that combine some of these ways into new wholes. Such a dialogical unity-in-distinctness formed out of many cultures and religions would be a more richly intersubjective way to live than that offered by secu-larism, which consigns religions to private, colorful but impoverished and sometimes deserted ghettos, to leave an affluent but overcrowded and greyly neutral public space. That City of God, shining with the divine, interillumi-native rainbow light reflected from the many faiths (including the secular faith), is the utopian hope towards which this book has tried to point.

Bibliography

Adams, Marylin McCord. "What's Wrong with the Ontotheological Error?" *Journal of Analytic Theology* 2 (2014). Online: http://journalofanalytictheology.com/jat/index.php/jat/article/view/jat.2014-1.120013000318a/222.

Althaus-Reid, Marcella, et al., eds. *Another Possible World.* London: SCM 2007.

Altizer, Thomas. *The Genesis of God: A Theological Genealogy.* Louisville, KY: Westminster John Knox, 1993.

————. *The Gospel of Christian Atheism.* London: Collins, 1966.

Auerbach, Erich. *Mimesis: the Representation of Reality in Western Literature.* Translated by W. R. Trask. Princeton: Princeton University Press, 1968.

Barth, Karl. *Church Dogmatics.* Edited and translated by Geoffrey Bromiley and Thomas F. Torrance. 4 vols. Edinburgh: T. & T. Clark, 1956–75.

Beaudoin, Tom. *Virtual Faith: The Irreverent Spiritual Quest of Generation X.* New York: Jossey-Bass, 1998.

Belcher, Kimberly Hope. *Efficacious Engagement: Sacramental Participation in the Trinitarian Mystery.* Collegeville, MN: Liturgical, 2011.

Bell, Daniel M. *Liberation Theology after the End of History: The Refusal to Cease Suffering.* London: Routledge, 2001.

Berman, Bob, and Robert Lanza. *Biocentrism: How Life and Consciousness are the Keys to Understanding the True Nature of the Universe.* Dallas, TX: BenBella, 2010.

Bhaskar, Roy. *The Possibility of Naturalism: A Philosophical Critique of the Contemporary Human Sciences.* London: Routledge, 1998.

————. *A Realist Theory of Science.* London: Verso, 1975.

Black, Max. *Models and Metaphors.* Ithaca, NY: Cornell University Press, 1962.

Bohm, David. *Wholeness and the Implicate Order.* New York: Routledge, 1983.

Booker, Christopher. *The Seven Basic Plots: Why We Tell Stories,* London: Continuum, 2005.

Buber, Martin. *I and Thou.* London: Bloomsbury, 2013.

Bulhof, Ilse, and Laurens ten Kate, eds. *Flight of the Gods: Philosophical Perspectives on Negative Theology.* New York: Fordham University Press, 2000.

Burrell, David. "Response to Davies, Ahmed and Valkenberg." *Modern Theology* 30.1 (2014) 153–58.

Caputo, John, and Michael Scanlon, eds. *God, the Gift, and Postmodernism.* Indianapolis: Indiana University Press, 1999.

Cavanaugh, William. *Being Consumed: Economics and Christian Desire.* Grand Rapids: Eerdmans, 2008.

Chalmers, David. *The Character of Consciousness.* Oxford: Oxford University Press, 2010.

————. *The Conscious Mind: In Search of a Fundamental Theory*. Oxford: Oxford University Press, 1996.

Clooney, Francis. *Comparative Theology: Deep Learning across Religious Borders*. Malden, MA: Wiley-Blackwell, 2010.

————. "Current Theology: Comparative Theology: A Review of Recent Books (1989–1995)." *Theological Studies* 56 (1995) 521–50.

————. *Theology after Vedanta: An Experiment in Comparative Theology*. Albany, NY: State University of New York Press, 1993.

Cobb, John. "Dialogue without Common Ground." In *Weltoffenheit des Christlichenm Glaubens: Fritz Buri zu Ehren*, edited by I. Abbt and A. Jäger, 145–54. Tübingen: Kaltzmann, 1987.

Collins English Dictionary. Complete and Unabridged Edition. London: HarperCollins, 2003.

Cornell, Drucilla, et al., eds. *Deconstruction and the Possibility of Justice*. New York: Routledge, 1992.

Cornille, Catherine. *The Im-possibility of Interreligious Dialogue*. Chicago: Independent, 2008.

Cox, Harvey. *The Secular City*. London: Macmillan, 1966.

Cupitt, Don. *The Revelation of Being*. London: SCM, 1998.

————. *Theology's Strange Return*. London: SCM, 2010.

Davies, John. *The Mind of God: Science and the Search for Ultimate Meaning*. Harmondsworth, UK: Penguin, 1992.

D'Costa, Gavin, and Ross Thompson, eds. *Buddhist-Christian Dual Belonging: Affirmations, Challenges, Explorations*. Aldershot, UK: Ashgate, 2016.

————, ed. *Christian Uniqueness Reconsidered*. London: SCM, 1990.

————. *The Meeting of Religions and the Trinity*. London: Bloomsbury, 2000.

Deleuze, Gilles. *The Fold: Leibniz and the Baroque*. Translated by T. Conley. Minneapolis: University of Minnesota Press, 1992.

Demson, David. *Hans Frei and Karl Barth: Different Ways of Reading Scripture*. Eugene, OR: Wipf and Stock, 2012.

Denys the pseudo-Areopagite. *Mystical Theology*. In *Essential Writings of Christian Mysticism*, edited by Bernard McGinn, 284–89. New York: Modern Library, 2006.

Derrida, Jacques. *Of Grammatology*. Translated by G.C. Spivak. Baltimore: John Hopkins University Press, 1973.

————. *Writing and Difference*. London: Routledge, 2001.

Doyle, Michael W. "Kant, Liberal Legacies, and Foreign Affairs." *Philosophy and Public Affairs* 12.3 (1983) 205–35.

————. "Kant, Liberal Legacies, and Foreign Affairs, Part 2." *Philosophy and Public Affairs* 12.4 (1983) 323–53.

Ford, David. *Christian Wisdom: Desiring God and Learning in Love*. Cambridge: Cambridge University Press, 2007.

————. *Self and Salvation: Being Transformed*. Cambridge: Cambridge University Press, 2009.

Ford, David, and Frances Clemson, eds. *Interreligious Reading after Vatican 2: Scriptural Reasoning, Comparative Theology and Receptive Ecumenism*. *Modern Theology* 29.4 (2013).

Fredericks, James. *Buddhists and Christians: Through Comparative Theology to Solidarity*. Maryknoll NY: Orbis, 2004.

Frege, Gottlob. "Sense and Reference." In *Translations from the Philosophical Writings of Gottlob Frege*, edited by P. Geach and M. Black, 56–78. Oxford: Blackwell, 1960.

Frei, Hans. *The Eclipse of Biblical Narrative: A Study in Eighteenth- and Nineteenth-Century Hermeneutics.* New Haven: Yale University Press, 1974.

Fukuyama, Francis. *The End of History and the Last Man.* New York: Free, 1992.

Fuller, Peter. *Theoria: Art and the Absence of Grace.* London: Chatto and Windus, 1988.

Fynn (Sydney Hopkins). *Mister God, This is Anna.* London: Collins, 1978.

Gerkin, Charles. *The Living Human Document: Revisioning Pastoral Counselling in a Hermeneutical Mode.* Oxford: Abingdon, 1959.

Gethin, Rubert. "The Buddhist Faith of Non-Buddhists: From Dual Belonging to Dual Attachment." In *Buddhist-Christian Dual Belonging: Affirmations, Challenges, Explorations,* edited by Gavin D'Costa and Ross Thompson, 179–95. Aldershot, UK: Ashgate, 2016.

Goldberg, Michael. "God, Action and Narrative: Which Narrative? Which Action, Which God?" In *Why Narrative? Readings in Narrative Theology,* edited by Stanley Hauerwas and L. Gregory Jones, 348–65. Grand Rapids: Eerdmans, 1989.

Graham, Dom Aelred. *Zen Catholicism.* New York: Harcourt, Brace and World, 1963.

Griffiths, Paul. *An Apology for Apologetics: A Study in the Logic of Interreligious Dialogue.* Maryknoll NY: Orbis, 1991.

Gutiérrez Gustavo. *The Power of the Poor in History.* London: SCM, 1983.

———. *A Theology of Liberation: History, Politics and Salvation.* Translated by C. Inda and J. Eagleson. Rev. ed. London: SCM, 2001.

Gyatso, Tenzin, the Dalai Lama. *Kindness, Clarity and Insight.* New York: Snow Lion, 1984.

Harré, Rom. *The Principles of Scientific Thinking.* London: Macmillan, 1970.

Hauerwas, Stanley. *With the Grain of the Universe: The Church's Witness and Natural Theology.* Grand Rapids: Brazos, 2001.

———. *Working with Words: On Learning to Speak Christian.* Eugene, OR: Cascade, 2011.

Hauerwas, Stanley and L. Gregory Jones, eds. *Why Narrative? Readings in Narrative Theology.* Grand Rapids: Eerdmans, 1989.

Hayek, Friedrich. *The Fatal Conceit: The Errors of Socialism.* Chicago: University of Chicago Press, 1991.

———. "The Pretence of Knowledge." In *Nobel Lectures in Economic Sciences, 1969–1980,* edited by A. Lindbeck, 179–88. Singapore: World Scientific, 1992.

Heelas, Paul, et al., eds. *Detraditionalisation.* Oxford: Blackwell, 1996.

———, et al. eds. *The Spiritual Revolution: Why Religion Is Giving Way to Spirituality.* Oxford: Blackwell, 2004.

Heim, Mark. *Salvations: Truth and Difference in Religions.* Maryknoll, NY: Orbis, 1995.

Hick, John. *God and the Universe of Faiths.* Oxford: OneWorld, 1973.

———. "The Possibility of Religious Pluralism: A Reply to Gavin D'Costa." *Religious Studies* 33 (1997) 161–66.

Hick, John, and Paul Knitter, eds. *The Myth of Christian Uniqueness.* Maryknoll, NY: Orbis, 1987.

Higton, Mike. "Scriptural Reasoning and the Discipline of Christian Doctrine." *Modern Theology* 29.4 (2013) 120–37.

Hinkelammert, Franz J. *Cultura de la Esperanza y Sociedad sin Exclusión,* San José: DEI, 1995.

Jameson, Fredric. *Postmodernism, or, The Cultural Logic of Late Capitalism.* New York: Verso, 1991.

Jansons, Linards. "What Is the Second Naïveté? Engaging with Paul Ricoeur, Post-Critical Theology, and Progressive Christianity." Online: www.academia.edu/14690650/What_is_the_Second_Naivet%C3%A9_Engaging_with_Paul_Ricoeur_Post-Critical_Theology_and_Progressive_Christianity, 2014.

Jantzen, Grace. *God's World, God's Body.* Lexington, KY: Westminster John Knox, 1984.

Jenson, Robert. *Systematic Theology, Vol. I: The Triune God.* Oxford: Oxford University Press, 1997.

John Scotus Eriugena. *Periphyseon (the Division of Nature).* Translated by I. Sheldon-Williams and J. J. O'Meara. Montreal: Bellarmin, 1987.

Julian of Norwich. *Revelations of Divine Love.* London: Burns and Oates, 1952.

Kavanagh, Aidan. *On Liturgical Theology.* Collegeville, MN: Liturgical, 1981.

Kee, Alistair. *Marx and the Failure of Liberation Theology.* London: SCM, 1990.

Keenan, John. *The Meaning of Christ: A Mahayana Theology.* Maryknoll NY: Orbis, 1989.

Knitter, Paul. "Catholics and Other Religions: Bridging the Gap between Dialogue and Theology." *Louvain Studies* 24 (1999) 319–54.

Kuhn, Thomas. *The Road since Structure: Philosophical Essays, 1970–1993.* Chicago: University of Chicago Press, 2000. Online: https://en.wikipedia.org/wiki/Commensurability_(philosophy_of_science.

———. *The Structure of Scientific Revolutions.* 2nd ed. Chicago: University of Chicago Press, 1970.

Küster, Volker. *The Many Faces of Jesus Christ: Intercultural Christology.* Maryknoll, NY: Orbis, 2001.

Lakoff, George, and Mark Johnson. *Philosophy in the Flesh.* New York: Basic, 1999.

Lash, Nicholas. "Ideology, Metaphor and Analogy." In *Why Narrative? Readings in Narrative Theology,* edited by Stanley Hauerwas and L. Gregory Jones, 113–37. Grand Rapids: Eerdmans, 1989.

Lindbeck George. *The Nature of Doctrine: Religion and Theology in a Postliberal Age.* Philadelphia: Westminster John Knox, 1984.

Locke John. *An Essay Concerning Human Understanding.* Oxford: Oxford University Press, 1975.

Lonergan, Bernard. *Method in Theology.* London: DLT, 1972.

Lossky, Vladimir. *The Vision of God.* London: Faith, 1963.

McCabe, Herbert. *The New Creation.* London: Bloomsbury, 2010.

McCulloch, Diarmaid. *A History of Christianity.* London: Penguin, 2010.

McGinn, Bernard, ed. *The Essential Writings of Christian Mysticism.* New York: Modern Library, 2006.

Marion, Jean-Luc. *God without Being.* Translated by T. A. Carlson. Chicago: University of Chicago Press, 1995.

———. "Is the Ontological Argument Ontological? The Argument according to Anselm and its Metaphysical Interpretation according to Kant." In *Flight of the Gods: Philosophical Perspectives on Negative Theology,* edited by Ilse Bulhof and Laurens ten Kate, 78–99. New York: Fordham University Press, 2000.

Marx, Karl. *Capital: A Critique of Political Economy.* Translated by S. Moore and E. Aveling. London: Lawrence and Wishart, 1954.

Massumi, Brian. *A User's Guide to Capitalism and Schizophrenia*. Cambridge: MIT, 1992.

Maximus the Confessor. *On the Cosmic Mystery of Jesus Christ*. Translated by P. M. Blowers and R L. Wilken. New York: St. Vladimir's Seminary, 2003.

May, Gerhard. *Creatio ex Nihilo: The Doctrine of "Creation out of Nothing" in Early Christian Thought*. Edinburgh: T. & T. Clark, 1994.

Merleau-Ponty, Maurice. *The Phenomenology of Perception*. Translated by R. C. McLeary. London: Routledge and Kegan Paul, 1962.

Milbank, John. "The End of Dialogue." In *Christian Uniqueness Reconsidered*, edited by Gavin D'Costa, 174–91. London: SCM, 1990.

———. *Theology and Social Theory*, 2nd ed. Oxford: Wiley-Blackwell, 2006.

Miles, Jack. *God, a Biography*. London: Vintage, 1996.

Moyaert, Marianne. "Recent Developments in the Theology of Interreligious Dialogue: From Soteriological Openness to Hermeneutical Openness." *Modern Theology* 28.1 (2012) 25–52.

Murphy, Francesca A. *God is Not a Story: Realism Revisited*. Oxford: Oxford University Press, 2007.

Nagel, Thomas. *The View from Nowhere*. Oxford: Oxford University Press, 1989.

Netland, Harold. *Dissonant Voices: Religious Pluralism and the Question of Truth*. Grand Rapids: Eerdmans, 1991.

Norman, Edward, *Christianity and the World Order*. Oxford: Oxford University Press, 1977.

Ouspensky, Leonid. *Theology of the Icon, Volume 1*. Crestwood, NY: St. Vladimir's Seminary, 1992.

Owen, Wilfrid. "Parable of the Old Man and the Young." In *Collected Poems*, 42. New York: Directions, 1965.

Pattison, Stephen. *Saving Face: Enfacement, Shame, Theology*. London: Routledge, 2013.

Panikkar, Raimundo. *The Intra-Religious Dialogue*. Rev. ed. Maryknoll, NY: Orbis, 1999.

———. "The Jordan, the Tiber and the Ganges." In *The Myth of Christian Uniqueness*, edited by John Hick and Paul Knitter, 89–116. Maryknoll, NY: Orbis, 1987.

———. *The Trinity and the Religious Experience of Man*. London: DLT, 1973.

———. *The Trinity and World Religions: Icon–Person–Mystery*. Madras: Christian Literature Society, 1970.

———. *The Unknown Christ of Hinduism*. Maryknoll, NY: Orbis, 1981.

Petrella, Ivan. *Beyond Liberation Theology: A Polemic*. London: SCM, 2008.

Pieris, Aloysius. *An Asian Theology of Liberation*. Edinburgh: T. & T. Clark, 1988.

Polanyi, Michael. *Personal Knowledge: Towards a Post-Critical Philosophy*. Chicago: University of Chicago Press, 1973.

———. *The Tacit Dimension*. London: Routledge, 1966.

Polkinghorne, John. *Reason and Reality: The Relationship between Science and Theology*. London: SPCK, 1991.

Popper, Karl. *Conjectures and Refutations: The Growth of Scientific Knowledge*. London: Routledge, 2002.

Quine, W. V. O. *Word and Object*. Cambridge: MIT, 1960.

Race, Alan. *Christians and Religious Pluralism: Patterns in the Christian Theology of Religions*. London: SCM, 1983.

Rahner, Karl, et. al. *Karl Rahner in Dialogue: Conversations and Interviews, 1965–1982*. New York: Crossroad, 1986.

Rawls, John. *A Theory of Justice*. Rev. ed. Cambridge: Harvard University Press, 1999.

Rescher, Nicholas. *The Strife of Systems*. Pittsburgh: Pittsburgh University Press, 1985.

Richards, I. A. *The Philosophy of Rhetoric*. Oxford: Oxford University Press, 1936.

Ricoeur, Paul. *The Rule of Metaphor: Multi-disciplinary Studies of the Creation of Meaning in Language*. London: Routledge, 1978.

————. *The Symbolism of Evil*. Translated by E. Buchanan. Boston: Beacon, 1969.

Rivera, Mayra. "Glory: The First Passion of Theology?" In *Polydoxy: Theology of Multiplicity and Relation*, edited by Catherine Keller and Laurel Schneider, 167–85. London: Routledge, 2011.

Rorty, Richard. *Philosophy and the Mirror of Nature*. Princeton: Princeton University Press, 1979.

Rowland, Christopher, ed. *The Cambridge Companion to Liberation Theology*. Cambridge: Cambridge University Press, 1999.

Ryle, Gilbert. "Categories." *Proceedings of the Aristotelian Society*, New Series 38 (1937–38) 189–206.

————. *The Concept of Mind*. Harmondsworth, UK: Penguin, 2000.

Sacks, Jonathan. *Not in God's Name: Confronting Religious Violence*. London: Hodder and Stoughton, 2015.

Saussure, Ferdinand de. *A Course in General Linguistics*. Translated by R. Harris. London: Duckworth, 1995.

Schmemann, Alexander. *Introduction to Liturgical Theology*. Crestwood, NY: St. Vladimir's Seminary, 1966.

Schmidt-Leukel, Perry. *Buddhism and Christianity in Dialogue*. London: SCM, 2005.

Sellars, Wilfrid. *Empiricism and the Philosophy of Mind*. Cambridge: Harvard University Press, 1997.

Smith, Wilfred Cantwell. *The Meaning and End of Religion*. Minneapolis: Augsburg Fortress, 1991.

Strawson, P. F. *Individuals: An Essay in Descriptive Metaphysics*. London: Methuen, 1959.

Sung, Jung Mo. *Desire, Market and Religion: Reclaiming Liberation Theology*. London: SCM, 2007.

Tarski, Alfred. "The Semantic Conception of Truth and the Foundations of Semantics." *Philosophy and Phenomenological Research* 4 (1944) 341–76.

St. Thomas Aquinas. *Summa Theologiae: A Concise Translation*. Translated by Timothy McDermott. London: Methuen, 1989.

Thompson, Judith, et al. *Theological Reflection*. SCM Studyguides. London: SCM, 2008.

Thompson, Ross. *Buddhist Christianity: A Passionate Openness*. Winchester, UK: Hunt, 2010.

————. *Christian Spirituality*. SCM Studyguides. London: SCM, 2008.

————. "Creation, Dependent Arising and Dual Belonging." In *Buddhist-Christian Dual Belonging: Affirmations, Challenges, Explorations*, edited by Gavin D'Costa and Ross Thompson, 49–67. Aldershot, UK: Ashgate, 2016.

————. *Holy Ground: The Spirituality of Matter*. London: SPCK, 1990.

————. "Postmodernism and the 'Trinity': How to be Postmodern and post-Barthian Too." *New Blackfriars* 83.974 (2002) 173–88.

————. *Spirituality in Season: Growing through the Christian Year*. Norwich, UK: Canterbury, 2008.

————. "What Kind of Relativism?" *New Blackfriars* 70.826 (1989) 189–99.

———. *Wounded Wisdom: A Buddhist and Christian Response to Evil, Hurt and Harm.* Winchester, UK: Hunt, 2011.

Thuan, Trinh Xuan. *The Quantum and the Lotus: A Journey to the Frontiers where Science and Buddhism Meet.* New York: Three Rivers, 2004.

Torrance, Thomas F. *Theological and Natural Science.* Reprint. Eugene, OR: Wipf and Stock, 2002.

Tsakiridou, C. A. *Icons in Time, Person in Eternity: Orthodox Theology and the Aesthetics of the Christian Image.* Burlington, VT: Ashgate, 2013.

Turner, Denys. "Christians, Muslims, and the Name of God: Who Owns It, and How Would We Know?" In *Do We Worship the Same God? Jews, Christians, and Muslims in Dialogue,* edited by Miroslav Volf, 18–36. Grand Rapids: Eerdmans, 2012.

———. "Marxism, Liberation Theology and the Way of Negation." In *The Cambridge Companion to Liberation Theology,* edited by Christopher Rowland. Cambridge: Cambridge University Press: 1999.

Vanstone, William. *Love's Endeavour, Love's Expense: The Response of Being to the Love of God.* London: DLT, 2007.

Volf, Miroslav, ed. *Do We Worship the Same God? Jews, Christians and Muslims in Dialogue.* Grand Rapids: Eerdmans, 2012.

Ward, Keith. *Pascal's Fire: Scientific Faith and Religious Understanding.* Oxford: Oneworld, 2006.

West, Angela. *Deadly Innocence: Feminism and the Mythology of Sin.* London: Continuum, 1996.

Williams, H. A. *The True Wilderness.* London: Constable, 1965.

Williams, Rowan. *The Edge of Words: God and the Habits of Language.* London: Bloomsbury, 2014.

Wirzba, Norman. "Christian Theoria Physike: On Learning to See Creation." *Modern Theology* 32.2 (2016) 211–30.

Wittgenstein, Ludwig. *Philosophical Investigations.* Translated by G. E. M. Anscombe. Oxford: Blackwell. 1967.

Wright, N. T. *The New Testament and the People of God.* Reprint. London: SPCK, 2013.

Index

ine optimization (SEO) tricks. That's because there
n't any. Back in the day, probably five years ago, you
ld niche down to a topic—say, losing belly fat—then
 a domain like howtolosebellyfat.com Because that
ic was in the title of your web address, Google's crawl-
would index you for that search term. *They must really
w how to lose belly fat. It says so right here!*

ere were other aspects that Google rewarded sites for,
, like how many links went to a page and how many
es keywords showed up in articles. Those things are
l factors, but not as much. People figured out how to
ne the system. They'd get a whole bunch of links to
int to the website or have useless articles filled with
words, and for a little while, Google rewarded that.

d then the Google Slap happened. They got tired of
ple being artificially ranked higher and changed all
their requirements. Overnight, pages that had been
wing up as top results got dropped completely out of
rch results, nowhere to be found.

ere are probably still ways to game the system, but I
nestly stopped trying to keep up. What I do know for
re is that there are plenty of people succeeding without
y games at all. They've built legit sites and channels
at people want to come back to. They've got legit links
inting to them because of their high-value content.

When I create content, I know that 95 percent of my audience may never buy a thing right away. But 5 percent of
them will pay me very well. I know it's hard not to think
about sales when you're not making money yet, but it'll
come. For now, focus on getting in front of everyone
inside your market. You can make an offer of help when
the timing is right.

BE HELPFUL, BE YOURSELF

Now that we know we don't have to cold-call, and we
know not to blast a sales pitch all over the place, let's look
at our options for getting attention. To do this, we need
to think about our market again. If you've been working through these steps as we talked about them, you
should have already found a good, broad market. Then
you niched it down and validated that there are people
interested in it and buying things (or clicking links). So we
know there are people out there, ready to pay attention to
someone. Now we need to figure out what they're looking
for and where they are showing up to look for it.

Are they looking for video tutorials on YouTube or podcast discussions on iTunes? Are they going straight to
Google for articles or asking their friends on Twitter? Are
they skimming images on Pinterest or searching hashtags
on Instagram? If you're reading this book ten years from
now, the platforms will no doubt have changed, but the

principle stays the same. Where are your people hanging out, and how do they want to consume information? Identify where they are, and meet them there with what they're looking for that is helpful.

Possibly the most important part of this is meeting them with helpful content. To be helpful, we've already talked about not giving them a sales pitch. We also can't show up as someone else. It's hard to build a bond with someone who isn't being authentic. You have to ask yourself what you're comfortable doing. Obviously, all new things feel a little uncomfortable. That's not what I mean. I mean don't start with a podcast just because I have one if you're a born writer and your market loves to read. Remember, you're coming into this market with your perspective and personality. You've got to be true to who you are to make that work!

Remember, you don't have to be an expert to be helpful. People used to come up to us during a photography shoot or if they saw that we were carrying a camera and ask what kind of equipment we were using. We'd gone from "how are you possibly going to do photography" to photography being the thing everyone asks us about. It was almost appealing that we weren't experts who knew everything there was to know. That made us trustworthy and reliable—we had been where they were, and we had shortcuts that could help them do well much faster than we had.

There are three categories of conten audio, video, and text. My strengths which is why this book was such a l stayed with my strengths until I w myself. Just because you're not go things doesn't mean you can't get tl with what comes naturally to you. If y venture or adding something to an ex want to focus on the content and prc alyzing camera fright or banging you keyboard.

Now, let's quickly validate again. If yo Tube and you know you want to make do your keyword exercise again there. and see what comes up. Again, we're st the "how" of any of this content. That chapter 8. Right now, we just need an of things will get the attention of you you'll feel most confident when you me YouTube autofill so it brings up sugges you quickly spot five video topics? Are you could talk about? Of course they a *thing*. You've got this.

NO GAMES, NO GIMMICKS

You might have noticed I haven't give

And when a Google Slap happens, they aren't penalized at all. In fact, they rank even higher when all the crap sites around them get filtered away.

These cycles of gaming, penalties, and rewards happen on every single platform. Marketers figure out a way to climb to the top using tricks and "tactics," and then the platform gets wise and issues an eBay Slap or a Facebook Slap and everyone comes crashing down—only to figure out the next loopholes and do it all over again.

My advice? Don't play those games. Stay aboveboard with high value to your market. It might seem like it takes longer to build at first, but when everything shakes out over time, you're going to be fine and your business will rise to the top.

⚡

**TAKE ACTION EXERCISE:
FIND YOUR PEOPLE**

Get clear on these three questions before trying to dig any deeper:

1. What kind of information does your market want?

2. Where are they looking for it?

3. Are you an audio, video, or text person?

Next, we'll work on the "how" of creating attention-grabbing content by building on this foundation.

CREATE THE BOND
BEFORE THE PAYOFF

From the first time I sold something online to someone outside of my home state, I was hooked. There was something so eye-opening about that moment. Your brain can't categorize it with garage sales or providing a local service. You're connected to something much bigger now. All bets are off. The limits have officially been removed.

At first, back when I got started with all of this, most people wrote off working online as a scam. Any so-called opportunity could just be another get-rich-quick thing. It looked too good to be true. Today, we know that people can make money online, but we also know that lots of people make money online by telling other people how to make money online. It still looks too good to be true—like Amway all over again.

I didn't want to fall into either of those categories, but I was so excited about what we had accomplished that I wanted to let the world know. This literally changed our lives, and now I wanted to share it with others.

Before I jumped in, I took a step back. In fact, to this day, every time I feel like a new move or a pivot is coming, I take some time to look around at where I'm at. I ask myself, "What have I recently done that other people would find valuable?" Just then, I was in the middle of running a successful photography business that I'd started from scratch. We didn't know anything about cameras and hadn't taken so much as a night class—just jumped in with books and a ton of trial and error.

"If I could speed up that learning curve for someone else," I wondered, "would they pay me for it?"

I had the market chosen—newborn and family photographers, just like me—so I started to test whether I could get their attention. I decided to post on YouTube and share our story. I talked about being a construction worker tired of working sixty-plus hours a week. I shared how my wife and I started the photography business to free up our time and set our own schedule. Then I ended the video by simply asking for people to comment if they had an interest in starting a photography business, because I was thinking about creating some training in the future. If they left a comment, I would give them free access to that training (that I hadn't yet made).

About a hundred people commented on that video over the next three weeks. Apparently, I had their attention. Now I had to create a bond.

(Side note: It's funny, because back then I had no idea what I was doing. But I did know that I wanted to get the attention of people that were like us—people that had an interest in photography but didn't have proper training or a degree. Always keep in mind who your market is and what it wants. Targeting the right people is critical to being successful in any business.)

RELATIONSHIPS COME FIRST

Relationship building, or creating a bond, is the stage where we spend time providing value for the people we are attracting. They're listening and paying attention—asking for something from them too soon can push them away.

The best way to build the relationship is through list building. I'd already done that with my photography clients, collecting email addresses and sending them a message whenever we ran a special for the studio. For online businesses, your list might look like YouTube subscribers, followers on social, or email list subscribers. You want them to be notified whenever you have new content so that you can keep offering value to them over and over again. Think of your list as a list of your friends that you are communicating with on a regular basis.

I created a landing page, and my lead magnet was pretty simple. Just like I'd ended the video, I wrote, "Enter your name and email address, and if I come out with some training, I'll give it to you for free."

For the next three to five months, all I did was build a relationship with my subscribers. I'd create a new video about something like the basics of lighting or setting up a home studio. All I was doing was walking back through everything we had done over that last few years. Every video published for free on YouTube, and every video had the same email or subscriber opt-in offer. I'd also put the video on a blog that I set up, and I'd email my small list whenever new content went up.

After about six months, I'd built my list to about 1,000 people, and I started to get some feedback. People had questions. They were getting stuck. I'd respond in the comments or with another video that answered whatever problem they were having. We wound up having conversations and engaging like friends might.

At this point, I'd still never made a training course before. But I decided to take all of the content that I'd made over that six-month block and distill it down. I locked myself in my office for a weekend and mapped everything out as though I were teaching a course. Instead of giving it to people as a course, though, I had those recordings transcribed and turned into an e-book. I figured if I got enough downloads on the e-book, there'd probably be enough demand for a course, too.

Out of a thousand people on my list, I got over five hundred downloads. I'd built a relationship that meant I was ready to ask for a sale.

WHAT IS...*A LANDING PAGE?*

Don't overthink a landing page. It's just a single webpage where people can enter their names and email addresses to gain access to whatever you have to offer. Usually, it's connected to a lead magnet, which is exactly what it sounds like—something that will attract people so that they decide to opt-in as someone who is interested. Giveaways make a great lead magnet, for example. *Enter to win* usually comes with opting into a list. The magnet gets the attention, and then once people are on the list you can build the bond.

OFFER VALUE WITHOUT A RETURN

If you've just met someone for the first time, you're probably adding value to that relationship. You won't call them up the next day and ask for a favor. Even when you've known someone for a while, a relationship still has to go both ways. We've all got that one guy who always needs something when he talks to you. Uncle Jimmy always wants help weeding the garden or cleaning out the garage. You love the guy, but it doesn't take long before you don't pick up the phone when you see Uncle Jimmy's name on the caller ID.

Don't be that guy.

When you follow up with people on a regular basis, it can't be to just ask for something. Follow up with your subscribers with the main goal of delivering value on a regular basis and letting them get to know you. I like to give people results in advance, before ever asking for anything. The other huge mistake I see businesses doing is hiding behind their companies. The more you can have a real person representing your business and brand, the more people will connect with you. You won't be just another business—you're you, and you're the one people will eventually want to buy from or learn from.

Email lists are just one way to connect with our audience. There are other ways, too. With retargeting options on

YouTube, Facebook, and Instagram, we can stay in front of our followers in all sorts of creative ways, with even more to come in the future, I'm sure. Wherever people are hanging out, ad platforms will be created. The *how* of it doesn't really matter—what's important is that you're staying in front of people and giving them the opportunity to connect with you.

The content that you're creating should offer value to your market, like the how-to videos I made, but they should also connect your readers, listeners, or viewers to your story. My very first video was about how I'd been in their position just a couple of years before, and sharing my story or learning process is still a big part of how I interact with people. Bring your story into the mix—why are you so passionate, why do you think they need this content, what made you start creating something for this market? You don't have to have a down in the dumps, rags to riches story in order to connect with people. It could simply be that you enjoy that thing and didn't see anyone else sharing from exactly your perspective. Here's why I love sharing my guitar experience. Here's why I wanted to show you my findings about bass fishing. Here's why I wanted to go on this yoga or plant-based diet or healthy eating journey with you. Share your story and tell them why you're showing up for them.

TIME OUT

If you're already in business as you're reading this, it's a good idea to revisit your existing market as well as whatever you're adding, and pivot toward that. What do your people really want and need? Can you convey that messaging to them, or is there someone else who can? Connecting with your market and building a relationship with it is an important piece. Focusing on that relationship can help your business grow so much more than generic follow-ups and ad campaigns.

HELP THEM GET WINS

Marketers often think about building trust on their end, but building a relationship can go both ways. While you're sharing your own story, you are also helping people move along in their own journey. If you're showing someone how to win a bass fishing tournament, you won't just throw everything out that they need to know at once. Maybe you'll teach them something that they can do on the weekend that will prove to themselves they can do it. Bit by bit, you'll help them take steps along the way that will get them there.

A lot of times, they don't know what needs to happen to accomplish their goals. You're going to be the one to help them with that. If you don't already know what they need to do, you can experiment yourself and let them know: "I'm going to be experimenting with this process. If you want to learn along with me, you'll want to stick with me.

I'll report back every week." As you help them have little wins and victories or bring them along as you learn, your bond with them will strengthen.

This is what one of my listeners did. His name is Jesse, and he was learning how to distill alcohol. He didn't have an established distillery, but he started a YouTube channel early on and invited people to learn along with him. Meanwhile, there are little glasses and tubes and tools you need in order to properly distill alcohol, and he was able to promote those alongside the content he was creating.

When your audience comes to you, they have a finish line in mind. In Jesse's case, they want to know how to distill alcohol, too, or others might want to win that bass tournament or grow those plants. If you help people in your market win, will they really be done? Of course not. They'll find another goal, or they'll have different struggles or questions as they keep going. Having a goal is just picking a big win that you can get them to so that you can figure out their starting point and the steps that you can move them through. With those steps identified, it becomes much easier to figure out what kind of content to create and send.

Start with the keywords that you've used to niche down your market and validate content. If you haven't done it yet, go back over the last two chapters to refresh. Go to the platform that your market is hanging out at and run some searches. I always go to YouTube, no matter the platform I'm working in. The top five things that come up are what you should be writing about. It's what your people are struggling with and looking for, which means it's their starting point. It seems too easy, I know, but it doesn't have to be difficult to be effective.

(Side note: I want you to think of you or your business as a guide that helps people get from point A to point B and then on to point C. The journey never stops. You might start by talking to a beginner and then become an intermediate and an expert, and then you will always have content to help through whatever level. It's important to choose a level to help first, almost like another niching down step.)

TWO-WAY INTERACTIONS

With your topics in hand, you can start to prepare the content. If you're still struggling with feeling qualified, it helps to think of yourself as a reporter or a guide. A reporter doesn't have to be the expert. They do research, compile the information, and report back with what they've found. By doing that work for people, you'll demonstrate that you can actually help them.

The best content doesn't come from an expert to the

masses but from one friend to another. People like to feel like you're talking to them. Every time I write, I treat it like I'm writing to a friend. It can help to picture the person who is in your market and starting with the need that you're meeting with that piece. Get so dialed into who they are and where they are in life that it becomes your avatar. Whenever you create content, it's for the number of followers you have or the whole subscriber list. But treat every single piece of content like it's for that one person—that avatar. It will apply to your whole market better, and to each individual person, it will feel like you're talking right to them.

WHAT IS...*AN AVATAR?*

An avatar is simply a super clear picture of your target market, as though they were a single, specific person. When you write to your avatar as a friend, I don't mean saying, "Hey, friend!" and then going on with your normal marketing message. Instead, think about how you'd reach out to a good friend with some new information. I don't think I'd write to my friend Jim by starting out with, "Hey, Jim!" That happens with more distant interactions. I'm more likely to just say "You've got to check this out!"

This also applies to fancy newsletters. Stop that. My friends don't send me emails with a bunch of HTML and pictures. Only big brands do that when they're trying to sell to me. Lose the header image and product photos and just talk to your people. (Bonus tip: Text-only emails are more likely to make it past spam filters.) The more direct and personal your message and presentation is, the more people will relate to you. Eventually, a connection and the trust element will form.

CONSISTENCY AND FOLLOW-UPS

Maybe the most important part about building a bond and relationship with your audience members is following up with them. In sales, they typically reverse this whole process—you make a cold pitch early on and then try to build a relationship as you follow up hoping for a response to that ask. The follow-up here is just about adding to the relationship you're building.

On Wednesdays, my emails are usually a short notice that new content is up. On Fridays, they are longer. I talk about my week—at the time of writing this section of the book, I shared a story about my oldest daughter and me talking over lunch about luck and opportunities, which I turned into a business lesson. Wealth doesn't just happen, but past work opens up opportunities. They can expect to hear from me like this every single week with consistency, and every week they're getting to know me more and more. I'm a family guy who values my time with my kids.

Here's the email I sent so you can get an idea of how it looks.

> Yesterday, I was having lunch with my oldest daughter (Alexis) and we were having a conversation about LUCK and Opportunity.
>
> I was explaining that when I was 23, I thought people just

got lucky or they walked into good fortune, but now at the young age of 46...I think way differently :-)

It took me busting my butt and learning as I went to realize this lesson.

Putting myself out there and constantly TAKING ACTION!

That's how I GOT LUCKY!

Most successful people don't just wake up and get lucky one day.

They work at it every day and learn from every experience.

I get people that say...I launched a product and it failed.

You need to think long term and know that you grew from that experience.

That's a SUCCESSFUL MINDSET!

I'm reminded of this in my *Inner Circle* every time we meet, because they see the BIG picture and are willing to TRY New things.

These guys and girls are Successful, but still willing to learn every day.

It's also helpful to have others push you a little beyond your comfort zone.

I know that helps me a ton.

So, the next time you think someone GOT LUCKY, look and see how they got there.

I'll be willing to bet that their LUCK came from past experiences and NEVER GIVING UP!

This week I interviewed a girl that started a little BLOG a few years back and now is supporting her family from her efforts.

She gets over 500k visitors every month and has so much leverage now to launch anything she wants.

If you were to look at her blog and her life, you would think it was all handed to her.

She got LUCKY!

NOPE, she busted her butt and still works hard every day.

Scary, but Exciting Note: Bloggers like her are your new competition

What I mean is content creators (bloggers) can launch

products easily and send a ton of traffic that will allow them to rank FAST!

WHY?

She has assets like....

Traffic from her blog: 500k people per month

Email list: 50k subscribers

FB Page and Group: 45k people

All she has to do is pick a product that her market wants and source it.

Then, she lets her people/list know about it on Amazon and BOOM #1 seller.

But, it starts with choosing a Solid Market/Niche.

If you're still STUCK and need help choosing a market... check out this training here.

You have to know the right market and products they want first, that's the secret sauce.

I hope this story helps you see business differently, so you can build something AMAZING!

One step at a time :-)

OK, let's dive into this week's content.

Podcast Episodes

Monday: *TAS 584: Weird NICHE Gets 500k Monthly Visitors and Making 6-Figure Income*

Wednesday: *TAS 585: (TRAINING) The 5 Step Content Trifecta Strategy for More Traffic and SALES*

Friday: *TAS 586: Ask Scott #183—Can I Use MY Email List To Launch Competitive Products on Amazon?*

Lots of great stuff and more to come.

Have an awesome weekend.

Take care and Take Action!

Scott

As you can see by that email, I was sharing a story about me personally and also giving people the confidence and push to keep going.

Another huge advantage is if you've sent out emails to your list and someone replies, you can answer them directly but also address their question in a follow-up response. If you get replies on a Facebook or YouTube post, engage with them and follow up in upcoming content. Not only do comments and conversations build a relationship with your people, but that also gives you intelligence into your market. You'll start creating content around what they really want and need—and it gives you a little bit of validation, a win that can keep you moving even when you might not be making money yet.

Your follow-up can be really simple: "Jim had a question on YouTube about X, Y, and Z, so I figured I'd jump in with a quick video with the answer." That's it. It will meet needs, give you direction for new content, and demonstrate that you're an authority on the topic. People are asking you questions, and you've got answers.

Follow-ups are about consistently connecting with your people. Randomly posting YouTube videos isn't as effective as showing up every Wednesday and Friday without fail. You can use a theme like Whiteboard Wednesday or Motivation Monday, or you can create your own entirely.

You can leave space open for questions. You can track a learning process. You can go without a theme and just walk them through a topic, answering questions as they come up. No matter what, sending something, even when it's not perfect, is always better than sending nothing. The most important thing is to stay connected on a regular basis. Consistency is the secret formula.

PLAN YOUR CONTENT

The value of your content is the center of everything that you do. When you create excellent content, then Google changes and Facebook Slaps don't really affect you—especially with a solid email list that you're in touch with. The same people who tell you email lists and blogs are dead will also complain about algorithm changes. But here's the thing: at this point, I've moved past worrying about how many people see my Facebook posts. I don't have to worry about it. Making good content for a good market and following up with them to build a relationship is really all you need.

No matter what type of content you want to start with— audio, video, or text—make sure you use multiple platforms. If you are dependent on one channel, whether that's Amazon or eBay, Google or iTunes, it's putting all your eggs in one basket. If something happens to that channel or you get suspended after a complaint, you're out of business until it's fixed. Get a website. That's a piece of real estate that you'll always have. As you build over time, you'll get traffic there as well as whatever external channels you use. You can direct people to your channel and then to the website, which should include a blog.

WHAT IS...*A VIDEO PLAYLIST?*

On YouTube, you can create a playlist of multiple videos. Every time you create a video, add it to a playlist of similar videos, and it will automatically play for your viewer, one after another. YouTube loves it when we do this, because that keeps people on the channel longer. We love it because when YouTube loves us, our channels build.

So let's say you shoot a video about the right bass fishing lures for a murky pond. Once you've uploaded that video to YouTube, add it to a playlist of any other videos related to that topic—how to catch more bass in ponds. After that, send your video to a transcription service like Temi.com or Rev.com, and create a blog post with the video embedded and the transcript under it. Or edit the transcript into a post all on its own. Lastly, share the post to Facebook (or, better yet, upload the same video directly), and send out an email to let everyone know it's live.

If you do that fifty-two times a year, you'll have fifty-two articles and fifty-two videos that all have links pointing back and forth to each other.

When that turns into traffic, your original platform—iTunes, YouTube, Amazon, etc.—will see the outside traffic coming in and reward you for that. When we start running ads and monetizing in chapter 9, you'll see how valuable those multiple streams really can be.

TIME OUT

The podcast listener of mine who was learning how to distill alcohol recently shared his own Take Action Moment with me. After listening to me talk so much about the power of finding a niche market, publishing content on a regular basis, and creating that trust factor... he decided to commit to putting it into action. His goal was to publish one new video per week for fifty-two weeks. He chose YouTube as his platform and set a goal of 500 subscribers by the end of the experiment.

Remember what I said earlier—you need to play, just start, and see what you learn. That was his attitude. He wanted to learn about distilling alcohol, so he decided to document the process and progress over twelve months. After the year was up, he wrote me an email telling me how he showed up every week, recorded new videos, and posted them on YouTube. The results blew me away. He had 15,000 subscribers and was making just over $1,000 per month from ads, affiliate sales, and Patronage, which is a donation site. People are actually paying him monthly to keep posting new videos. *Crazy, right?*

What's even crazier is I just checked since I last chatted with him, and he's over 20,000 subscribers with momentum growing fast.

Now he has built a loyal subscriber base on YouTube, and when he posts a new video, he gets 3,000 to 5,000 views within days. With that kind of viewership, he can launch his own products if he chooses to, and he has learned a ton through this process. No matter what he does with his distillery, he can take these skillsets and apply them to any business venture.

I'm so proud of him for going for it. This is a great example of what the take action effect looks like in practice: you learn by doing, not by thinking about doing. Now there's no telling where this will take him in the future.

MAKE A MAP

Content plans help us strategically connect our content with our audience. When we know what we're making, it's easier to get ahead of production and stay consistent. To build a plan, go back to the keyword research that we did a couple of chapters ago. You can run your searches on YouTube or Google, or you can use Google's free keyword tool that it gives to all of its advertisers. Using that keyword tool can tell you the search volumes for keywords, which gives you plenty of ideas for content.

I still prefer to use YouTube. Look at the views on top videos for your topic. Look at how much engagement there is. Look at the types of comments there are, which can give you even more ideas of what people are looking for, what you might be able to create, or how you can address that content even better. Do this for the top ten topics in your market. You can find those by searching—how to catch more bass—or by looking at the most popular videos on a popular channel.

Next, think about how you'd answer the question your market is asking. If you're working on "how to catch more bass," what would you say to someone who walked up to you and asked that question? You'd need to have the right pole, the right lures, the right tools—each of those are a topic, plus another overall "must-haves for every bass fisherman" post.

For each topic that you list out, make some bullet points. What would you talk about on the video or podcast or in the content? Don't overdo it here. You don't need everything into one post. People don't want to sit through a twenty- or thirty-minute video, and you don't want to make that much content at once either. But people will click through five different five- to ten-minute videos. I call it snackable content. Say just what you need to say, and let the rest of the information be a different piece of content.

That's it. Content planning really doesn't need to be complicated or difficult. It's good to plan out ahead so that one piece can lead into the other ("If you missed my last video, I'll drop it in the description below..."). On a basic level, you've just got to find those top topics and then create something around it—in fact, create as much content around it as you can.

DON'T HOLD BACK

The temptation to hold information back in order to sell it might be a thought, but I'm here to tell you it's not true. People will always want to purchase information in a neat, structured package. They want ninety-day sprints and five-module courses. Before you make those, you can give away literally all of that information in your content. I've heard it phrased as advice to "give away your best nugget."

People want structured information, but they want it from someone they trust and believe in. If you're really going to create a bond and relationship with people, you've got to give away your best stuff. Win them over by delivering results. They'll love you for it, and when it's time, they'll pay you for it, too.

TAKE ACTION EXERCISE: MAP IT OUT

It's time to make a map! Go through the steps above and plan out the next five to ten pieces of content. Don't forget that you'll share your content on social media and to your newsletter subscribers to move them to blog posts, and ultimately send them to your home-base website.

Here's an example:

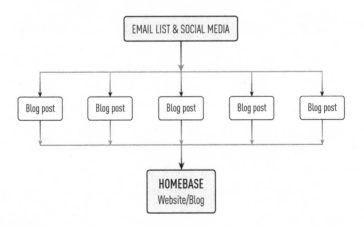

THE PATH TO EASY MONEY

After my e-book in photography got such a great response from my email list, I figured I was on to something. I'd spent enough time getting to know my market and exactly what they were looking for, and I built up a relationship with them so that they knew and trusted me, that I was finally comfortable offering something for sale. I didn't know exactly what I would make from it, but I was pretty confident that it was at least worth a shot.

Back to my office I went, this time to create course content.

The recurring theme for my audience members was that they wanted to do photography, but on the side. They didn't have a studio and didn't want to invest in it as a full-time thing yet. As I created the course, what started out as how to do the business started to shift in order to answer their concerns. That's when I decided to take pictures of my elaborate, hand-painted backdrops to turn them into digital files, and as I made them for the course I put them up on eBay for about thirty bucks each. People who bought the course would get the files as bonus material, and I'd teach them how to use them.

By the time the course was finished, it included lessons about the business model as well as ten CDs—because back then you couldn't just download them—plus a booklet with printed information. I had someone lined up to create the CDs and print the books locally, but not until orders had been placed. By the end of the course, people would know exactly how to create their own studio digitally without having to find a large space and invest in everything we'd purchased.

The whole time I was working on the course, by the way, I kept maintaining that relationship with my audience. I let them know what I was working on and what was included, but I also made sure they knew it was limited. You always want to build scarcity into the offer, but this was more than that. I couldn't offer support to unlimited people, so I set the cap at seventy-five.

Right around the same time, I invested two grand in a

course called *Product Launch Formula* by Jeff Walker, hoping I could make this work. I followed everything he'd taught me to a tee.

(Side note: Boy, this was a big investment at the time. I had a lot riding on this launch—I was hoping that investment would pay for itself right away. I was determined to make this work, or at least to learn through the process. Did I ever!)

The week before the launch, I posted three videos—Monday, Wednesday, Friday. Each one was content-driven and value-driven, just like everything else I had put up before. People could learn something from each of the videos, moving them a little bit closer to their goal of building their own photography business.

The fourth video, that next Monday, was the offer. This was my first offer to them, so I was a little bit nervous. (Okay, okay, I was scared.) I'd never done this before. I had a lot going on with the photography business, and setting this course up had been a ton of work. What if I put myself out there and no one wanted it?

The offer video was simple: "I've given you a ton of value that you can go out there and implement. Or if you want the whole thing packaged up in a bundle, I'll give you my training, the CDs, and everything in between. Only seventy-five people can get in on this program, though, so if you're interested, be ready." I felt like Apple building up to a new iPhone release, only I didn't feel at all like Apple. There was so much anticipation and scarcity in the offer/pitch. *Seriously, though. What if no one wants this?*

So Monday came and I posted the video in the afternoon, and told them that I'd open the cart on Tuesday at 3 p.m. Eastern time. First come, first served. This is something I learned inside PLF (*Product Launch Formula*) and I still do this to this day. Letting people know something is coming is huge, and they will be ready and waiting.

After I planned all this I realized, *whoops*, Tuesday was also my kids' elementary school bowling club day. I was actually the guy in charge of helping the principal of the school, and I never missed. I wasn't about to now, but I just told a thousand people to be ready at that exact time.

I told my wife, "I think I screwed up. I need your help."

You have to understand, this was back before automatic timers or anything like that. You had to manually open and close carts, which basically looked like changing the landing page links. It was all stored in an FTP backend area, so I had to show her how to switch the main page's source from the closed link to the one that was live and ready for sales.

"At 2:59," I told her, "I just need you to change the links of those files."

She was nervous—and so was I, if I'm being honest.

I knew she could do it, and at 2:59 I was sitting in the bowling alley, staring at my flip phone, waiting for an update. All the kids were having a blast as usual, but I was super anxious and nervous inside.

Crash. Good throw, sweetie!

At 3:05, my phone rang: "You're never going to believe it, Scott."

Oh, man. "Did it work? Did it open? Is there anybody there?"

She said, "Yeah. I think...I think there's $3,000 in our PayPal account. Hold on a minute..." She refreshed the page and said, "Actually, there's $5,000 in the account."

I couldn't believe it. You're kidding me.

She refreshed it again and said, "No, I'm not. There's $5,500 now."

Strike! Great job, Scotty. Nice shot!

I was still trying to be present, but my mind was officially blown. I'd only ever heard about this stuff from big "internet marketing" gurus and ridiculous sales pitches. Every time she would refresh, the number would go up by five hundred or a thousand. I'd done it. It was a lot of work, and there was more to come. But I'd made it through my first online launch and come out on the other side with the biggest three-day payday we'd ever seen. This moment changed my life forever and opened my mind even bigger. We made from that course what our photography business would make over the entire Q4. That was it. My eyes were open.

I didn't have to add photo sessions. I didn't have to work myself to the bone. I had to niche down in a market, get their attention, build a bond, and foster a relationship, and then the sales would come. That's the winning formula.

WHAT IS...*A PITCH?*

Any offer of a product or service is a pitch, not just full launches. It's funny, because I met Jeff Walker recently, and he told me to remove the word pitch from my vocabulary and use the word offer instead. While some offers/pitches are much softer than others, always avoid a harsh "go buy my stuff" type of message, and always make sure you have some kind of bond in place first. Technology is making it possible to spot these bonds with incredible efficiency, like separating out people who have watched certain percentages of a video so you can target them with an offer. When you're not running a launch, a great offer can be as simple as "Thanks for watching my videos! Some people asked me about this, so I've created a training around it. If you're interested, you can go here and check it out."

We use the same approach when selling physical products in e-commerce businesses, too. The idea is to build the relationship and then sprinkle offers into content or follow-ups.

SELLING WITHOUT FEAR

Even after the work of building a relationship with your market, it's still scary to sell. We're worried about making people mad (there will be some, and that's okay). We're worried that it won't work (maybe not for everyone, and that's okay, too). We're worried that we've wasted time or money. (I'll show you how to keep that risk low, so I promise you're okay!)

The one thing you can't do is avoid sales. It's going to

happen. Everything we've worked through so far has built up to this point, where you're figuring out how to get sales from your blog, ad revenue or sponsorships on your podcast, YouTube influencer sponsorships and ads, or a product or service launch. *It's going to happen.* But it's a long-term kind of thing. When you're focused on the long-term and building toward a vision and then consistently work toward it, there isn't much to fear. If you build it right, the sales really will come.

On the other hand, you can't force sales. You can't be driven by them. Sales come all on their own as a product of finding the right market, grabbing their attention, and building a bond of trust with them.

Whenever I step into any new venture or product, I follow these steps to a tee. Whenever I coach people or talk to the members of my Inner Circle, whenever I talk about this on my podcast, these are the steps we follow. They're proven and tested. There will always be a market, and markets will always have their niches. There will always be places for people to stand out and get attention. There will always be ways to build a relationship with people, and people will always want to buy from someone they can trust. That's why this process makes selling easy.

AVOID THE BAIT AND SWITCH

There will be people who get upset. I'm not going to lie to you. Some people want everything to be free. That's just going to happen. It's okay to let them go. As long as you're not doing a bait and switch on them, there's nothing you can do about it.

When people get upset about an offer, they're worried they've been tricked. They stop trusting you. Why? Because they've seen it all before. Someone gets them all excited and worked up, acting like the information is valuable, but then it turns out to be just about selling something. They feel used. To protect that relationship through the offer, you'll have to treat them well all the way through.

A bait and switch has two sides: the before and after.

Before the offer, if you already have things for sale—maybe an Amazon or eBay store, a Shopify site, whatever it is—make sure it's visible. Keep your links up. Mention your product now and then. ("I'm out here on a boat using my XL5000 fishing rod that I designed, because I was frustrated with the market...so we're going to talk about catching more fish.") If you don't have a product yet but are working on it, let them be part of that process. ("I'm always frustrated with the way yoga mats slide on the floor, so I'm working on developing one with ridges on the bottom. What do you think will work best?")

When they get interested in your content and start clicking around, it won't be a surprise that you sell things. They know it's there, and if they want to look harder they will. If not, then they are free to just enjoy your content.

After you've made an offer, don't stop providing value. Don't shut down for the people who didn't buy anything. Every time that I do a launch to a list, whether in the photography space or from my podcast, I'll go really aggressive with good content until it's time to make the offer. As long as the launch is live, I'll go aggressive with sales. Then when it's over, I go right back to them with amazing (free) value.

If a friend of mine tried to sell me something in person and then stopped talking to me when I said no, that's not really a friend at all. Yet it happens all the time. Just recently a woman wanted to have lunch with my wife and get to know her, only to flip the script and make the lunch all about her multilevel marketing business. When my wife wasn't interested, the woman disappeared. That's not friendship, and it will undermine all of the relationship building you've been working on.

DON'T STOP THE STORY

The work of cultivating relationships and building bonds doesn't really stop. Even when an offer is happening, it's still part of your story and theirs. Keep that as part of your content and the way you interact with your audience members. Let them be part of the process of building something. Be honest about what you're learning and where you're growing.

If you're endorsing a product, especially an affiliate product (we'll get to that in a minute), tell them why you like that product. Why have you used it? How was it valuable to you? Give them your honest opinion about it. Explain why they should check it out or how it could help them and why. If you're having a sale, explain why they should buy right now. Why did you create it, and why should they check it out? Why is it on sale?

Just like your personal story, your product story doesn't

have to be dramatic. You might want to celebrate your birthday with a sale. That's fine. That's a story. They will buy it or ignore it, but as long as your email led with valuable content, they won't be bothered by it enough to break the bond.

Add value alongside everything, including an offer. Anytime I write an email with an offer, it also includes lessons. It includes something valuable to readers whether or not they buy. When you preserve the relationship with your market and don't alienate them with "buy, buy, buy" messaging, you're actually keeping them in the sales cycle.

Only about 5 percent of your market is ready to buy at any given time—that leaves 95 percent out there waiting that won't be ready for as much as six or twelve months. When you show up in front of the whole group with consistency and deliver value even before they're ready to buy, you have a much better chance at reaching the group than the other businesses who ask for too much, too fast.

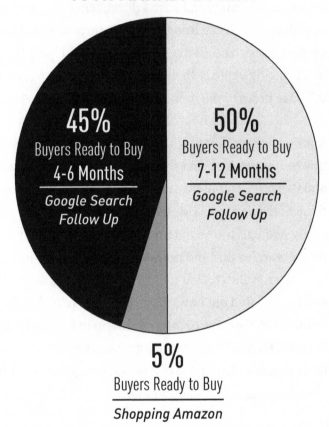

Most miss this "huge" detail
YOUR MARKET BUYERS

45%
Buyers Ready to Buy
4-6 Months

*Google Search
Follow Up*

50%
Buyers Ready to Buy
7-12 Months

*Google Search
Follow Up*

5%
Buyers Ready to Buy

Shopping Amazon

SLOWLY BUILD REVENUE BEFORE THE LAUNCH

If you're building content and spreading it across several platforms, then keeping in touch with your audience just like we talked about—after a year you'll have more than fifty pieces of content on multiple platforms, all driving interest and traffic. After about twelve to eighteen months, that can snowball. When you have traffic in the 50,000 range and have a decent email list built up, a product launch can bring in significant revenue. While interacting with people, seeing how you're helping them, and bringing value to their lives can be rewarding, most of us are here for the money, too—at least at first.

Another approach is to start with the products and work this backward. You find the product, list it on Amazon, and then create content around the product. I've seen it done both ways, and I've seen it work both ways. If you really need an immediate monetary reward, then you might want to find the product sooner. That's fine, as long as you validate that there's a market, look at what's selling, and find out how many sales they're making per month. We'll get more into validation in just a minute. For now, I want to show you a couple of ways you can also make revenue during that first twelve to eighteen months from creating and posting content.

ADS

As internet users, to us ads seem like a sleazy way to monetize attention. Those spammy sites that have ads popping up all over the place can be a complete turnoff to ads in general. That's definitely not all there is to an ad. Your site doesn't have to be littered with ads, and they don't have to be a primary focus. You can also look into research on where ads are best displayed and choose ad platforms that are reputable and reliable.

Google's AdSense platform allows you to display ads on your site and will pay you per click from visitors. When you get a little bit more traffic, you can branch out into bigger ad networks like Mediavine (after 25,000 unique visitors per month) and AdThrive (after 100,000 unique visitors per month).

Usually, the ad content will be tailored to the content you've created or directly to that person. That feature is called re-targeting, and it will use the bass fishing gear that they were searching for yesterday as the ad on your platform today. If your content is related to what your market is looking for, which is the ideal, you're more likely to get a click.

Ad revenue can start being generated very early on; even if you have just a hundred visitors a day, you can start to see money being earned. Even making five bucks a day at first can feel like progress, and you don't have to sell directly to your market to make this happen.

(Side note: As I write this book, we've been building a website out with content over the past eighteen months, and we just hit $2,749 in one month from ad revenue alone. The crazy thing is, we are seeing the traffic growing, which will most likely increase ad revenue even more.)

AFFILIATES

Being an affiliate is like being a partner. On Amazon, affiliates are called associates. When you sign up for an Amazon Associates program, you can promote Amazon links and then earn commission. Generally, commissions are between 4 and 8 percent, increasing the more you sell. You can scroll down to the bottom of any website and see if it has a partnership program or affiliate program—sometimes you can work out a partnership even when the site doesn't yet have an affiliate program set up. Some of these partnerships can be as much as 40 to 50 percent commissions. ClickBank is another great source of affiliate links, usually for digital products, with a much higher commission. There's also JV Zoo and Commission Junction. (It can also be cool to explore those platforms to see what your market is buying and what you might be able to sell to your audience.)

With an affiliate partnership, anytime you want to do a product review or talk about something you're using—fishing gear, yoga mats, guitar strings—you use your affiliate link in the blog post. When someone buys the product, you get a percentage. With Amazon, you also get credit for anything someone buys twenty-four hours after clicking your link. If someone goes Christmas shopping the day after they checked out your $19 fishing gear, you'd get a percentage of the $1,000 camera or other random items in their shopping cart. It's pretty cool.

You might also be able to partner with someone else (and bring in some added attention) with sponsored posts. If someone has a product they want to get in front of your audience, they will pay you to create a post or mention to your audience. Sometimes they will write the post themselves, or you may write one yourself. Either way, you can decide who you want to partner with and promote products.

BOOKS AND SERVICES

As you build content, you'll quickly realize how much your experience and knowledge is needed and wanted by the people in your market. All of the content that you're creating can be eventually compiled into an e-book or Kindle book. You don't have to be a major author to release a fifty-page guide and offer it for sale on Amazon. You can send people on your email list to buy your book on Amazon (instead of just emailing them an e-book) and can get ranked on Amazon to be found by that audience in that niche. At one point, we were making over $1,000 per month in Kindle book sales by taking our past content and creating a digital e-book. That also helps make you an authority in your market and can help you grab even more attention.

(Side note: If you do publish a Kindle book, I would recommend creating a special bonus or resource that can be linked to from the first few pages of the book. This will allow you to capture a name and email address to build your list from inside the book. Plus, the link can be seen in the preview of the book even if they don't buy it.)

Another way to generate revenue is to leverage your experience to do private coaching or lessons, online or locally. If you're a baseball coach and want to start a business selling products that help kids hit or pitch better, private coaching lessons can bring in revenue while you're working on your other goals. Even if you don't do it long-term, taking some time to coach in the beginning can develop your authority and bring some money in while everything else builds.

VALIDATE YOUR PRODUCT FIRST

The reason a lot of people don't start with a physical product is that it costs money. There are investments, and with investments come risks. Throughout this book, we've been building up a side hustle that can eventually go full-time. We're not risking an existing business or job based off of hope or dumb luck. This is a concentrated, strategic effort. When it comes to launching a product, we'll keep similar precautions. I'm not going to ask you to buy thousands of units of a product or to lose the farm in ad campaigns. Instead, you can carefully validate a product or venture before it goes live to make sure the market and potentially products are vetted.

With my first course, I validated my market over time, first with an ask, and then an opt-in, and then an e-book—all before I put the time in on creating a course. Even then, I didn't print seventy-five copies before launch day. I waited until the need was there. Asking your audience directly is a great way to validate if you've already got a list and good interaction with them. It's the best way to eliminate risk, because you know they want it.

I've gone as far as not even creating the product before it was purchased. When I started my podcast, I did about fifty episodes before I offered anything. Then we did a webinar, where I taught people as much as I could in sixty minutes. At the end of it, I told them I was thinking about creating a full training that would take them step by step, looking over my shoulder, doing the exact thing I'd just taught, but in much greater detail. "If twenty-five people raise their hand, I'm going to do it. It'll cost $497 if you join right now."

Within one minute of the link being available, all twenty-five spots sold—and I hadn't created a bit of content for the course yet. Since then I've presold course training every time. People vote much more accurately with their wallets than anything else. If I don't get enough people to make it worth the work to create the course, I'll refund the people who did raise their hand (and sometimes offer them an e-book or something shorter instead).

Another way to validate a product is to start with affiliate marketing for a similar product first to see whether your audience is interested. If it starts to sell, you can create and source your own physical version of that product. I've seen this done a number of times for both existing businesses and brand-new content creators.

Finally, if you're going to sell a physical product, you need to make sure the numbers are there. We can use the numbers that Amazon publishes to tell us whether that kind of product has buyers. Amazon uses a ranking number called the Best Seller Rank (BSR) and can tell you who is doing well in each category. There's also a tool called keepa.com, which will show you the BSR over time for any given product. Anything below 8,000 on that list usually means it's selling fairly well. Other tools like Jungle Scout will compile all of that research for you without you actually having to sort through it yourself. This is a must-have tool if you are validating product sales on Amazon.

WHAT IS...*PRODUCT VALIDATION?*

Exploration is a key part of the take action effect. Playing, discovering, and trying new things brings us wins that we didn't know we could reach. But before you dive in on an investment, whether that's time or money, make sure you've explored enough to know what you're getting into. We can't ever guarantee success, but we can limit our losses by going in cautiously. And on the other side, when we let the data determine our next steps, that's when we really start going places. Before you go after a product or offer, make sure you use the take action framework:

• What's the market? What's the niche?

• Are digital or physical products being sold there? Are there affiliate links or advertisements?

• Can you publish content to grab people's attention?

• How will you build a bond or relationship in that market?

There are more steps to product validation, but if you can't get through those steps, you don't need to go any further. These are the first few steps that will help determine the potential.

If you already have a business and you want to dominate your market, follow these steps as well. Most of the time, businesses are not reaching and serving their markets at the fullest potential. These principles can help you build out your business to create a true future-proof business with multiple assets.

PHYSICAL PRODUCT SALES

With an idea of the numbers your product might do, don't

buy more inventory than what's actually moving. My test runs are usually only about five hundred units. If they sell at a steady clip, we'll reorder and keep going. If not, we will drop the price and liquidate the product. As long as you're not putting your last $3,000 for the mortgage into test inventory (don't do that), careful validation takes a lot of the risk out of it.

Wholesaling products is a good way to get started with an already proven product. Major brands and companies often offer wholesale arrangements. This means you'll buy the product at a deep discount, sell it, and the difference is yours. You can sell on your own website, Amazon, eBay, or anywhere that your wholesale agreement allows.

The simplest way to do wholesale is to have a drop-shipping arrangement, either direct from the wholesale company or through the Fulfillment by Amazon (FBA) program. With drop shipping, you don't have to keep or ship the inventory at all. The company does all the heavy lifting for you. You sell the product and either send the wholesale company the orders to fulfill or use a third-party fulfillment, such as Amazon.

WHITE LABELING AND PRIVATE LABELING

When you go to the supermarket to get cereal, you'll be able to choose from a couple of different brands of the same basic cereal. There's always the name brand, like Kellogg's, and the store brand, like Publix or your local grocery store. Inside, the cereal is not necessarily any different at all. In fact, both might have been made by Kellogg's. White labeling takes a product that is similar or the same and lets you label it with your own branding.

When you take that product and adjust it slightly and then put your own branding on it, it's called private labeling. Maybe you want to create a garlic press that has a better handle and is easier to use. You can work with a manufacturer to make the adjustments and then brand it as yours with your company behind it.

FUELING THE MOMENTUM

If you're an e-commerce business and you have a product, you should be doing everything leading up to this point in the book. Selling a product isn't where we stop—it's only part of the cycle. You should be creating content, using affiliate links, putting ads on your website to monetize traffic, and staying in touch with your audience to keep that relationship strong.

If you're just starting out, lead with your market no matter what. Whether you start with a product or wait, it is up to you, but tending to your market should come first every time.

In a perfect world, here's how I'd get started from scratch, with a hypothetical $5,000 investment, and it's exactly what I do every time I start something new: First, I'd niche down a market—not just one level, but as far as it goes. I'd go from pets down to dogs to German shepherd puppies. Then I would find five topics and three to five products people are searching for with that keyword, and I'd start to think about the concept I wanted to create.

I'd think about the best product that would serve my market by looking at the first page of results on Amazon for top German shepherd puppy training products. On that first page, I'd look at each item and then scroll to the "frequently bought together" section. What other products are people buying when they buy this product? I'd narrow it down to three products that sell well together and then take $3,000 of my investment and get the first product manufactured. Let's say it was a puppy training leash.

While the product was being developed and manufactured, I'd start creating content. I'd put up a blog and start to bring leads in with a giveaway of at least $100 in value. With some attention starting to build, I'd email my new list the content that I'd been publishing using the keywords that helped me find the right product. I'd keep building toward 50,000 website visitors—which I would expect to have after about eight to twelve months—and then start to put ads on the blog. But in the meantime I would expect to have my first product sourced and ready to launch on Amazon in ninety days.

When my product came in, I'd list it on Amazon and start to let my audience know about its release. I'd announce a launch promotion and send my email list and blog traffic over to Amazon to buy. When all of that traffic hit Amazon and sales started to happen, Amazon's algorithm would notice and reward me by showing me to more people. We call this getting ranked in search for product keywords. Now I'd start to show up for people searching for puppy training leashes who would wind up finding my product.

Also, during this time I should start to see some traffic from the blog content I'd published so far and from the emails I'd been sending. By now I would probably have a YouTube channel started with content published there on a regular basis, too. The plan would be to continue the content publishing over the next several months, and by this time, my ads would be running, and I'd be making at least a thousand a month just from ads, not to mention the sales from Amazon, possibly YouTube revenue, maybe a Kindle book from the web content, and wherever else I'd monetized my channels.

That's it. That's the framework. That's what makes sales and generating revenue easy, and it's what I use on my businesses and with all of my coaching clients. If you embrace the take action mindset and stick with it even when you aren't getting immediate returns, your business will thrive. The key is having a plan and taking action consistently. If you base it all on something you love and are passionate about, you will show up on a daily basis, put in the work, and become truly future proof.

⚡

TAKE ACTION EXERCISE: SPOT THE WINS

I know it's still hard to be patient while you're building out your business and working toward freedom. For this exercise, create a list of some short-term monetary wins.

Look for affiliate opportunities and ad platforms—make a plan to start adding some revenue potential and get it in place ASAP.

Then make sure to count all of the other wins from your efforts, too. Remember, your business is full of high-value assets, and not all of them come with a paycheck right away! This might look like subscribers, great feedback, or simply doing something you love every day.

CONCLUSION

FUEL THE MOMENTUM

———

With the success of my product launch way back in the digital photography days, I might have given you the impression that my current podcast was my first. That I've got the golden touch and everything I do succeeds. Wouldn't that be nice?

Unfortunately, while the take action effect is powerful and does get results, the take action life is messy. When you let yourself be curious and spend time playing, sometimes your results are going to teach lessons more than generate income.

My first two podcasts (not one, but two) were duds. For the first one, I was forty years old and in the best shape of my life. I was also really into doing Insanity and Beach Body-type products, and a buddy of mine thought it would be great to talk about. We were both older and loved nutrition and fitness, so it sounded great. We recorded seven episodes, and then fizzled out. Neither one of us gave it enough love to keep it going, and we quit.

Later, I picked up the mic again to talk about business. But it wasn't specific to photography. It wasn't specific to e-commerce. It was just...business. Without niching down, I couldn't get any attention. There's just too much noise out there to be that broad.

Why *The Amazing Seller* podcast?

By this point, I had been living with that take action mindset for years through ups and downs all over the place, and my newest business model I was testing was selling physical products on Amazon using its FBA service.

Instead of waiting until I was an expert and then teaching, I used the podcast to bring people along on my journey. As you've probably picked up by now, I love teaching what I learn through experiences, and this was a new interest of mine. Plus, I knew that by sharing openly I would create attention in a market and build a relationship with people the more I shared and helped others. Are you seeing the common thread here? I pretty much follow the same principles in anything I do now.

I didn't know exactly how I was going to monetize—how to make money from this audience or topic. I didn't have a product in mind. But I knew that if I was able to get attention and bond with people, eventually something would appear that I could monetize. There's no way to know all of the steps before they happen, so sometimes you've just got to hit go—to take action and see what comes of it.

I'd been following Pat Flynn for a while, and his podcast was doing the exact same thing but from an affiliate marketing standpoint. He'd just lost his job and decided to try this online thing, and the podcast was him sharing his journey along the way. I had been in the online space for years at that point, but I knew I could share my journey as I explored this new angle on Amazon.

I decided to be totally transparent and share stuff for free, even though others were charging for this information. I would just share the play-by-play and see what happened.

With a topic I loved and a niche I could speak to, I had plenty of attention. The more people would email and ask me questions, the stronger my bond with this amazing audience became. The framework I'd been following for years was in place yet again, and all I had to do was figure what they needed and see if I could offer that for sale.

I decided to do a webinar, where I'd spend an hour breaking down how I launch products on Amazon. At the end,

I announced and let the audience know about a class I might do. I said, "If you're interested, great. If not, that's fine, too." I thought about a $297 price point, but my personal business coach, Jaime Masters, immediately asked me why I wasn't charging more. She asked me, "Don't you think it's worth at least $497?"

"Yeah, I think it's worth about $1,000. There are courses out there selling for four times that and not offering what I am," I told her.

"Don't start lower than $497."

It was the most I'd ever charged, and I was nervous to even try, but I agreed. When the day of the webinar came, about five hundred people attended. We had a great time, and at the end I held my breath and presented my first ever offer to them.

This is what I'm thinking about doing. This is what this course will look like. I haven't created a bit of it yet, but if twenty-five people sign up, I'll do it.

This was how I offered the sale and figured I'd get them to raise their hands with their credit cards.

Within ninety seconds, we had twenty-eight spots filled. We couldn't turn the thing off fast enough. (Crazily enough, three people from that group are part of my $25,000 Inner Circle and have all built seven-figure businesses themselves.)

Since then, I've sold out multiple live events and have added live conferences for online business builders. They're all selling out and creating results—and it all came from hitting record on my third podcast while I experimented yet again with this framework that has changed my life. If I listened to that inner voice, I would have stopped without ever seeing this incredible impact on my life or my listeners' lives.

RESULTS AREN'T ALWAYS FUN

I know that was supposed to prove that I don't have the golden touch, but I'm telling you, these successes aren't unique to me. I'm just a regular guy who happens to be a little bit further down the road than you are right now. If you want to follow me down this path, you are more than welcome to. I'll take you where I've been and show you the holes in the things we all try and help you fit this mindset and framework into your own life.

But I do have to warn you, you have to be ready to take actions that don't always have great results.

When my wife and I were selling garden bridges on eBay,

I learned very quickly that when something starts working and you haven't differentiated yourself in it, other people will come in and compete with you. More accurately, they'll price you out. The bridges that we were selling for $130 got all the way down to $50 before long. Instead of saying it was a good run and calling it quits, I figured out how to stand out.

We'd buy up the bridges as normal, and then I'd take them out of the box and stain them one of three different colors and then box them back up and list them with options. No one else was doing that, and our price jumped back up almost to where it had been. When I decided to move on from bridges, it wasn't because I had "failed," but because I was doing work again, and it defeated the purpose. Digital products that didn't have to be fulfilled made much more sense for the life I was building.

This next crazy incident could have made me quit, but it didn't.

Later, when I started New Photo Biz, my YouTube channel, to talk about building the photography business, I had a blast. I built up a library of videos and gathered four or five thousand subscribers. Some of the videos had over 20,000 views. I spent a year and a half as the New Photo Biz guy, and that's where I launched my first product, fully branded.

On the heels of my successful product launch with a fantastic brand and thriving channel, everything was great... until I got a call from the owner of a company called PhotoBiz. Their business wasn't to help you launch a new photo biz, but it was a website hosting platform where they would build a site for your photo biz. And she'd already contacted her attorney.

She informed me that I was in violation of a trademark and was to take down all of my assets and resources or she would sue me. So much for living large. I panicked. All of that money I'd earned was going to have to go into this lawsuit. All of the work I'd done was wasted. Everything I'd put out there had to come down. It was completely devastating.

It was a result. What could I learn from it? How could I fix it?

I picked myself up and decided to take action. I called the owner up and explained the situation to her. The domain was available, so I assumed I was safe. I was happy to accommodate and change stuff, but I had traffic coming in from the content I published. Did she really want to deal with that much traffic looking for me but finding her? What could we do to be friends and not enemies?

She was on board. She decided to have me sign an agreement that from then on I would create things under a new name, but let me keep everything for a year and have it point to a new domain and channel. That gave me time to move my audience over. I was still upset about the whole situation, but at least I hadn't lost everything overnight. I learned then to always keep an email list, because it's the one thing that you can keep if everything else is taken. (I also learned to check my brand names better. The second one not only was vetted through the old business owner and LegalZoom, but it fit what I was doing better, too—New Portrait Biz became our new name.)

I could write a whole other book telling you stories of things that I tried that came short of success. Heck, I almost died when I decided to make another entrance to our portrait studio using a gas-powered saw in a basement. (I finished the entry by using an electric chisel for eighteen hours. It was worth the numb hands, but maybe not worth carbon monoxide poisoning.)

I'm grateful for all that I've learned along the way, but I'd also love for you to skip some of the pain and hard lessons I had to learn. I can't go back and shake twenty-two-year-old Scott's shoulders to get him to change his mindset, but maybe I can help you shake yours up a little. I wouldn't want to get to where I am today in any other way, but maybe you can get there faster.

YOU ARE FUTURE PROOF

Now that you're done with this book, the work is about to begin. Before our time is done here, I want you to really think about your life—where it is and where you want to be. I want you to get clear in your why. I want you to look back at the Take Action Moments in your own life and realize how much of a difference they made. We don't give ourselves enough credit for what we're capable of when we're bogged down in the day-to-day, especially when we're feeling worn down and defeated.

I want to see you aware of your own strength—your own genius. You have a passion and a perspective that the world is looking for, and when you get their attention and cultivate that relationship there's no limit to what you can do.

There is no feeling in the world like the limits being lifted off of your shoulders. You can do anything you want to do. I can see it from here. And when you decide later that you don't want to do that thing anymore because you're bored or because it didn't turn out like you wanted it to or because you got passionate about something else—you'll be able to follow these steps and do it all again in something else.

I want you to take what you've learned here and turn it into a plan, whether you just need to get started over the next few months or you're going to map out a product launch over a year. You already know what to do: establish a brand around a market in something you're interested in, attract that market by creating really great content for them, follow up and build a bond with them, and stick with it for twelve to eighteen months. That's it. Don't get distracted. Don't think there's an easier way. Don't chase shiny things when you haven't finished polishing what you've got. Keep at it. Stay focused. Listen to your audience and become their high-value reporter. You want to become the go-to resource in your market.

With a repeatable framework and a resilient mindset, nothing in the future can take you down. You're building a future-proof self. And by taking care of your business assets by building it right—keeping that bond with your audience and never relying on just one platform—you're building a future-proof business. You'll be able to pivot and grow in any direction you want to. You'll be able to start from scratch as many times as you want to. You'll be able to take this framework and plug it into any situation and make it work.

The secret isn't in the steps, though they are proven. The secret isn't in the business, because you can do anything you want. The future-proof piece is you and your willingness to keep moving forward, to keep taking action no matter what life throws at you. And that's an effect I can't wait to see.

It's up to you. TAKE ACTION and create the life you want—the life you deserve.

I'm rooting for you!

APPENDIX

NINETY-DAY ROADMAP TO SUCCESS

——

By now you know that you can start taking action at any point on your journey. You don't have to figure everything out at once, though. The only way to learn this process is to do it. Don't worry about wasting time or trying to get everything perfect right away. If something doesn't validate the way you want it to or work out the way you'd hoped, find the lesson in it and start over—and this time, you'll know the process better. You'll have built up those skills to be able to do it again.

Use this ninety-day sprint to get moving and keep moving. Follow it all the way through, or use it as a launching pad to send you off in the direction that works for you and your market. While you can modify this to work from any stage, it works best for someone just starting out. Check the Quick Action step if you have an existing business or if you're feeling overwhelmed by the steps here.

DISCOVERY: 1–3 WEEKS

- **Days 1-3: Identify—What market are you interested in or passionate about?**
    - Spend some time with your vision board and mind maps to figure out what you've enjoyed in the past, what you know about now, and what you'd like to spend time exploring.
- **Days 4-7: Niche—Narrow your market down to something specific.**
    - You don't just like to fish, you like to bass fish in ponds. You don't just garden, you grow indoor succulents. Keep narrowing down until you have something specific you can start with.
- **Days 8-14: Validate—How are physical and digital products selling in that space?**
    - Look around. Don't exclude any platforms from this stage. The goal here is to see whether there's any income-generating potential in this space. Look for top sellers, websites, ads, affiliate links, and types of products.
- **Days 15-21: Locate—Which platforms are people using; where is your market hanging out?**
    - Again, even if you think you won't ever record

a video in your life, don't limit your exploration here. How are people showing up in that market? Are they primarily on YouTube or Instagram? Is there a big market on Amazon? Think about what your market needs and how they're looking for solutions.

Important: If at any point you realize your initially identified market can't be validated, start over. You want to get this right!

PLANNING: 2–4 WEEKS

- **Days 22–30: Replicate—Who is *crushing it* in this market? Which influencers can you learn from?**
  - Take some time here to look at the best of the best. You won't copy them directly, but you have a lot to learn from them. Follow them, get on their newsletters, and take notes.
- **Days 31–35: Personalize—What channel or medium would be easiest for you to be authentic and consistent?**
  - Now it's time to think about your strengths. It's hard to commit to something you're miserable doing, and you didn't set out to be miserable! Do you enjoy speaking? Are you comfortable on camera? Do you write? Be honest with yourself— what will you enjoy working as a side hustle and eventually as your full-time gig?

- **Days 36–50: Prioritize—Discover top content in your niche and decide what to publish first.**
  - Go back and look at the top players in your niche again, even outside of your medium. Figure out their top content to identify the top topics you need to tackle first. Turn these topics into a map that you'll follow to begin building up your content library.

CREATION: 3–5 WEEKS

- **Days 51–60: Offer—What lead magnet can you create for email list building?**
  - Could you create a contest or giveaway that people would enter to win a prize? Would a mini e-book be helpful? A step-by-step PDF guide? What about a printable checklist? Think about something that you can offer them in exchange for getting on your newsletter. Remember, you don't ever have to hold back—be generous with information, and your audience will love you for it.
- **Days 61–80: Build—Create a website/blog as a home base to send people to from your platform(s).**
  - Now it's time to put it all together. Your home base is how you ensure your business lasts no matter what the algorithms and platforms decide to do. Even if you've decided to start with Amazon, still

use your website as a platform for content and ads and to gather your audience for your newsletter.

- **Days 81–90: Commit—Create a PLAN and commit to being consistent.**
  - ○ This is where the rubber meets the road. Consistency makes this work—even when there are setbacks, even when something doesn't work. Make a plan for what you're going to do and when you're going to work on it. Then stick with it! A year from now, you're going to be amazed at what you've accomplished.

QUICK ACTION STEP

———

Maybe this sounds like too much to you. Maybe you already have a business or an identified market and don't feel like you need to start from scratch. Here's what you can do:

- Every week, for fifty-two weeks, make one new piece of content.
- You can talk about your discovery process as you learn or try something new; you can talk about the day-to-day of your business; you can break down things your customers need to know...the important thing is to consistently make new content every week.
- If you don't feel like you have something to say, review products. Use an affiliate link for them whenever you can.

- You don't have to worry about scripting, and don't worry about taking a bunch of time.
- If you're not comfortable on video, do the same thing on your blog. If you do record a video, you can leverage that content by putting it on both YouTube and turning it into a blog article.
- After fifty-two weeks, you'll have a content library building up new traffic—and I guarantee at least one of those will stick.
- Watch for the biggest traffic generators that might give you a clue about new ways to niche down.

RESOURCES

———

I've created a special area for you (my book readers) that includes in-depth interviews of some people I've shared in this book, my P.A.C.E training series that outlines the four core pillars of building a successful business, checklists, sprint maps, and online workshops.

You can find all of the resources you need to get started at TakeActionEffect.com/Bonus.

Here are some of the audio interviews that are included in the BONUS area:

- Alex—travel market
- David—drone market
- Cassidy—succulent market
- Louie—bass fishing market
- Kevin—leaving corporate America

* * *

Share your Take Action Moments on social media as inspiration for others!

Take a minute to share a picture of yourself holding a copy of *The Take Action Effect*. Tell us your biggest take-away from the book using #mytakeactionmoment as your hashtag.

ACKNOWLEDGMENTS

I have to start by thanking my wife, Lisa, who has been a huge part of my success and always been the one to give me courage and strength whenever I doubted myself. Also, for being the best mom to our three kids, Alexis, Scotty, and Kayla. You are such a special person, with a kind heart, and I love you so MUCH! You are my ROCK!

I want to thank my KIDS for giving me a strong WHY in life and showing me the lessons I've learned in fatherhood. I love you guys more than words can describe, and I am so proud of each and every one of you.

Dad, I wouldn't be the man I am today if it wasn't for your lessons and mentorship through the years. It wasn't easy growing up at times, but watching you push ahead, even when times were tough, showed me how to be strong and loyal to family. I love you, and always remember, you are my hero. I love you!

I want to thank my mother, Joan, who is no longer with us here on earth but I know is with me every day. The lessons I learned about being open and honest no matter the circumstances I'll never forget. You've made me a better man and father. I miss and love you so much. I know you would be so proud.

Jimmy Krill, my brother from another mother. I never had a brother growing up, but you were one to me. Thanks for always being there when I needed you and also pushing me to believe in myself. You encouraged me to write this book and title it *The Take Action Effect* because of my life story. I appreciate you and I love you, man!

There are a few other people I want to thank that have been a huge part of my life and helped me TAKE ACTION and believe in myself through the years.

I am so thankful I met you, Chris Shaffer and Joel and Angel Bower. You are not only business partners but truly part of my family. You guys have been a huge part of my life over the past few years and have given me the push at times to truly believe in myself to reach new heights. I love you guys!

Pat Flynn, thanks for inspiring me to follow the non-guru path and stay true to myself. Your friendship over the past couple of years has meant the world to me, and I really appreciate you. I love you, man!

Jaime Masters, you are a rock star. You were my first ever business coach, and you've changed my life forever. You pushed me to believe in myself and see the path to my future. You are truly a special person, and I appreciate you so much.

There are so many others that have been a part of my journey, and I want to thank anyone and everyone that has inspired me and taught me life's lessons.

ABOUT THE AUTHOR

SCOTT VOELKER is a husband, father, and serial entrepreneur who has spent the last 20 years building lifestyle businesses that have allowed him the flexibility and freedom to enjoy more time with his family. He's also helped thousands of people all over the world with his podcast *The Amazing Seller,* and is one of the leading influencers in the field of e-commerce, helping other entrepreneurs build their own six- and seven-figure brands. To connect with Scott, visit his website. www.theamazingseller.com

CPSIA information can be obtained
at www.ICGtesting.com
Printed in the USA
BVHW071750071019
560430BV00006B/91/P